A BOY FROM GEORGIA

A BOY FROM GEORGIA

COMING OF AGE IN THE SEGREGATED SOUTH

HAMILTON JORDAN

EDITED BY **KATHLEEN JORDAN**

ADDITIONAL EDITING AND RESEARCH BY **HAMILTON JORDAN JR.**

FOREWORD BY **PRESIDENT JIMMY CARTER**

THE UNIVERSITY OF GEORGIA PRESS ▪ ATHENS AND LONDON

This publication is made possible in part through a grant from the Bradley Hale Fund for Southern Studies

Excerpts from chapters 10 and 14 first appeared in Hamilton Jordan's 2000 memoir *No Such Thing as a Bad Day*, originally published by Longstreet Press Inc.

Paperback edition,
Published by the University of Georgia Press
Athens, Georgia 30602
www.ugapress.org
© 2015 by Gah-Lee, LLC
All rights reserved
Designed by Melissa Bugbee Buchanan
Set in Trade Gothic and Sabon

Most University of Georgia Press titles are
available from popular e-book vendors.

Printed digitally

Library of Congress Cataloging-in-Publication Data
Jordan, Hamilton.
    A boy from Georgia : coming of age in the segregated South / Hamilton Jordan ; edited by Kathleen Jordan. — First edition.
        pages cm
    Includes index.
    ISBN 978-0-8203-4889-6 (hardcover : alk. paper) —
ISBN 978-0-8203-4890-2 (e-book)
    1. Jordan, Hamilton—Childhood and youth. 2. Politicians—Georgia—Biography. 3. Jordan, Hamilton—Family. 4. Albany (Ga.)—Social life and customs—20th century. 5. United States—Race relations—History—20th century—Anecdotes. 6. Albany (Ga.)—Biography. I. Jordan, Kathleen, editor. II. Title.
    F291.3.J67 2015
    975.8'953043092—dc23
    [B]

                            2015013484

British Library Cataloging-in-Publication Data available

Paperback ISBN 978-0-8203-5294-7

"You belong to it, too.
You came along at the same time.
You can't get away from it.
You're a part of it whether you want to be or not."

THOMAS WOLFE, WRITING ABOUT HIS "LOST GENERATION"

CONTENTS

FOREWORD

I have often said that no other human being has affected my career more profoundly nor more beneficially than Hamilton Jordan.

In 1966, Hamilton introduced himself to me after I made a speech as a state senator and was considering a campaign for governor of Georgia. Though he was young—still in college—it was apparent after a brief conversation that he had a wonderful mind, able to condense complex topics into clear, simple points. A week or so later, I called Hamilton on the phone and asked him to organize students for my gubernatorial campaign. He turned me down at first, saying he already had a job for the summer spraying mosquitoes. But he reluctantly changed his mind when I remarked that I'd just as soon give up the governor's race if killing insects was more important to him than my being governor.

Well, we lost that race. But he capitalized on our mistakes, and in 1970, he added his careful planning and his guidance to my success-ful race for governor. As my executive secretary, he was in effect the "number two" man in the government of Georgia. The breadth of his knowledge and his sound judgment as a very young man were exem-plary. He was an extraordinary leader.

It was a troubled time, and Hamilton and I found common ground in our interest in Georgia and U.S. history and shared a similar journey to understanding human and civil rights—though he was twenty years my junior. Our moral character and compassion for others had been formed by observations of growing up in the South when it was high time for a change.

In Hamilton I saw an ease of communication with others—a humor and a charisma that attracted bright, young people to my campaigns and later to serve in my gubernatorial administration. Hamilton had the ability to make people want to do the right thing and to sacrifice their own egos and agendas for a greater good.

We began a form of communication where in addition to frequent conversations he would produce correspondence in thoughtful memos on a variety of subjects both political and about policy. He could distill a cross section of opinions and research into an objective, brief document that expressed the pros and cons of a decision.

Hamilton devised a strategy that became famous, to solve one of the most intricate political riddles on Earth—how do you get a relatively unknown Georgia peanut farmer elected president of the United States of America?

We did what Hamilton proposed, and we went to the White House together. Although he initially rejected any formal title as chief of staff, he was naturally recognized by others as their leader.

Hamilton was a driving force behind the Panama Canal Treaties, the Middle East peace process, the safe return of the hostages from Iran, and every other good thing that we attempted or accomplished while in Washington. His political skills were legendary—and so was his character. His charisma and sense of humor kept us afloat during the darkest times.

This book is not about the years he spent working for me but rather about the years that led him to me. Written in Hamilton's clear prose and nurtured into publication by his children after Hamilton's death in 2008, this memoir traces his evolution from childhood to the time just before we met. Much is known about Hamilton as the architect of my presidential campaign and chief of staff. This book shows the foundation of his ability and the journey of his development into the bright, committed young man who changed my life forever.

President Jimmy Carter

INTRODUCTION

While being southern was a vital part of my dad's identity, I was ashamed of it growing up. I'd fantasize about the life I'd read of in Eloise books—prancing around the Plaza Hotel, drinking tea and wearing peacoats, watching the snowfall in Central Park. New York seemed magical to me, as if every day there was a scene from a Christmas movie.

I remember lying and telling people on my church basketball team that I was born in the North, and that my family moved me here against my will—how tragic. It wasn't that I was unhappy in Atlanta. I was very happy. I had a loving family and great friends and wanted for nothing. But my relationship with my heritage—that felt complicated. Being tied to a region known for its conservative values and closed-mindedness? Racism and religious polarity? No, thank you. That didn't suit me. I'd tell my dad, "I'm from the South, but I'm not southern."

"Kat, you were born in Florida. You are the most southern person in this family."

"No, Florida doesn't count. Because of Florida's proximity to Cuba, I am the most *Hispanic* person in this family."

It wasn't until my dad died after an arduous, downright exhausting two years of combating peritoneal mesothelioma—his sixth cancer—that I had the chance, as a nineteen-year-old, to begin to consider my identity as a southern woman. And it was all because of this manuscript.

My dad had been working on this book for a few years, and it was not finished when he died. He left my brothers, my mom, and me with this manuscript, to which we have made as few edits as possible in an effort to preserve the integrity of the work. At the time of his death, he did not know that we would go on to finish this book; we didn't either. It would make him happy to know that you're reading it.

Some people may know my dad's name because in 1976, in the aftermath of Watergate, he helped to elect a good and honest man president. He learned firsthand the painful lessons of post-Watergate Washington, initially celebrated by the press as a conquering hero on the covers of *Time* and *Newsweek* and then turned into a caricature of himself before President Carter and his administration were defeated in a landslide in 1980.

There were dozens of books written about those four years in the White House, one of which was my dad's. *Crisis* detailed the final year of the Carter presidency and the four hundred–plus days of complex negotiations that led to the release of American hostages in Iran. This book, however, is not about the Carter presidency.

Others may know my dad from his decades battling cancer, recounted in his memoir *No Such Thing as a Bad Day*, which described his personal struggle with three varieties of cancer. It also provided an outline he would use to encourage aggressive treatments and, most important, an optimistic outlook for victims of the modern cancer epidemic. Although his battles with cancer continued all through his adult life until his death, this book is not about that disease.

This is a Georgia boy's story of growing up in the segregated South in the 1950s and 1960s—a society only a half step removed from slavery. In the small town of Albany, Georgia, Hamilton tells a candid coming-of-age story, exposing some of the most joyful and the most ugly moments of his youth. He saw and lived on both sides of the civil rights movement. He lived through the anxieties caused by Sputnik and the Cold War, which played out in dramatic—and sometimes comically exaggerated—detail in his small hometown. He also played a lot of football with his buddies, chased a few girls, and discovered an exciting new kind of music called "rock 'n' roll." And he stumbled across a little-known peanut farmer who was smart enough to put some stock in a young, cocky kid with very big dreams.

This book, a rich sliver of his legacy, does well to round out a tradition of my dad's lifetime: drafting blueprints to guide people to light. From his famous eighty-page document that led a Georgia peanut farmer to national office—and is still cited as one of the most intelligently crafted campaign memos in American history—to his memoir about his struggles with cancer that touched the lives of tens of thousands of people, to this deeply personal account of growing up in the segregated

South, Hamilton left in his wake a trail of lessons. This book has given my brothers and me the rare and strange privilege of learning about our father in the past tense—and through an entirely new lens. I fear children often do not have the desire to know their parents as anything other than parents before it's too late. Before, he was my father and my hero—the most important man in my life. Now, he's even more.

Working on this book has been a labor of love, and it's guided me to a very solid sense of pride about where I come from. I'm proud to be from the South, and so are my brothers. I know my dad wouldn't approve of the fact that we got tattoos in his honor, but I'd like to think he'd smile knowing they're in the shape of the great state of Georgia.

I'm proud of this book, and I hope you enjoy it.

Kathleen Jordan

A BOY FROM GEORGIA

Part I

■ ■ ■

AN ALBANY CHILDHOOD

Chapter One
■ ■ ■

LEXINGTON WAYS

The creak of the large oak door, then slow, muffled steps across the floor woke me in the pitch-black dark of the early morning hours. A match skipped across a rough surface, bringing on a small flame. My eyes squinted in the darkness, curious to know the source of this noise but at the same time unsure whether or not I wanted to wake up.

As my eyes adjusted, the tiny glow of the match flickered on the walls and tall ceilings, and light started to fill the room, revealing the outline of a person crouched before the fireplace. As the light intensified and my sleepy eyes opened wide, I saw a familiar figure holding the tiny match up under a piece of scraggly kindling wood, pine knots soaked in kerosene, which lit easily to start a real fire.

He took four or five pieces to form a crude square in the blackened fireplace grill. Then he reached back into the large copper bucket, felt around, and picked out several small pieces of coal, carefully placing them on top of the wooden pyre. Making a rustling noise, he crumpled a couple of pages from an old issue of the *Atlanta Constitution*, twisting them into long, tight paper sticks and setting them carefully under the metal rack cradling the fire. He touched the burning kindling to the newspapers, and soon the flames were jumping up higher and higher, licking the large pieces of wood, which started to burn, pop, and crackle.

The small fire grew quickly; soon, wood and coal were burning, and the whole room was toasty warm. Great bursts of light danced across the walls and high ceilings of the bedroom. Taking the ornate copper-handled poker from the stand on the hearth next to the coal bucket, he nursed the fire, rearranging the coals and wood, occasionally leaning over to place another larger piece of wood carefully on top.

The figure bringing warmth and light to my room was a black man known by everyone as Old Black George—and even he referred to himself in that way. Why Old *Black* George? The name distinguished him from a white farmer who lived down the road, a man my grandfather Hamp called "white trash." So Old Black George it was.

The first several times George woke me with his early morning fire making, I was frightened and would sit up in my bed and cry loudly. Worried that my crying would wake my cousins, who were my temporary roommates on these trips to our grandparents' home, George would tiptoe over quickly in his socks—creaks in the floorboards marking each step—and squat down by the head of my bed to pull the covers back up around my neck, tucking me in.

He would gently pat my shoulder, and I'd feel his warm breath against my ear as he whispered softly, "Don't worry yourself one little bit, Mister Hamilton, it's just me, Old Black George. I ain't gonna let nothing get you! Go to sleep, Mister Hamilton. Go to sleep."

It was strange that he called himself Old Black George, and me Mister Hamilton. I was only three or four at the time, around 1948. This is my earliest memory.

George was thirty, maybe forty years old when I first knew him. There were black folks on my grandfather's farm who were brown and others about the color of a cup of coffee with milk in it. But George was as black as the ebony keys on the grand piano in the living room.

And "black" wasn't the only name they were called. Some called them "colored." Some called them what I would later hear referred to as the "n word," a word that my grandmother Mur said was a dirty, filthy word. Mur even said that if she ever heard me say that word, she would wash my mouth out with soap. She must have forgotten to tell that to everyone else in the South because I heard the word "nigger" a lot growing up whenever I visited my grandparents in Lexington and in my South Georgia hometown of Albany.

As for being called "Mister Hamilton," I was just a kid. No one in Albany or anywhere else had ever called me "Mister Hamilton." But my older brother, Lawton, explained that these were just "Lexington ways," the ways people did things in the dusty little town where Mur and Hamp lived. I got the message that it was best for me to keep my head down and not to ask too many questions about the way things were done.

■ ■ ■

A small farm town, Lexington was only eighteen miles from Athens and our beloved University of Georgia, where my grandfather got his law degree and all of his children went on to earn their degrees.

Helen and Hamilton McWhorter were my mother's parents. My father's father died before I was born, so Hamp was the only grandfather I ever knew. His real name was Hamilton, but everybody called him "Hamp," which seemed a suitably affectionate nickname for this warm, lovable man. We called my maternal grandmother "Mur"—the first sound that Lawton babbled over and over and over when she held him, her first grandchild, as a newborn. The name stuck, and from that moment on, they were "Mur and Hamp" to the rest of our family.

Driving into Lexington from Athens, we could identify Mur and Hamp's home as the big house on the right, sitting back several hundred feet from the road. A broad walkway of packed white sand led from the road to the house, the walkway outlined by large pecan trees with graceful limbs extending over a gently sloping green lawn. The sprawling, two-story wood house, painted white, had green shutters on the windows and a porch in the front that wrapped around the sides with beautiful, well-loved rocking chairs. As grandchildren began to visit, a swing set was installed on the lawn, then a rope swing with a seat hanging from a giant oak's branch. On the side of the yard, you could still see the bare outline of a neglected clay tennis court, which had been built and maintained during the time that my uncles were growing up there.

I associate the very best things about my early life with Lexington: family, cousins sleeping in the same large bedroom upstairs, playing in the barn, and—most of all—the wonderful meals that brought us all together. Hamp—naturally playful, fun-loving, and full of jokes and tricks—turned into a kid when his grandchildren arrived. It occurred to me at an early age that perhaps Mur's only purpose in life was to stuff us with yummy food and worry and fret over any sniffle or the slightest scratch. She was the ultimate mother to us all.

Hamp was a lawyer by training and later a judge, but I remember my mother and others saying simply that Hamp was "in politics." Of average height and medium build, Hamp had a head full of white hair and a small potbelly. My grandfather always had a cigar with a little gold band (Hav-A-Tampa) in his mouth. He never lit the thing but just chewed on it constantly, pausing occasionally to spit the soft, gooey mush out into one of the copper spittoons that occupied a special place next to his large chairs in the living rooms and bedrooms. The master bedroom in the back of the house also served as a meeting place where Hamp and his friends could laugh, gossip, and have a drink or two from the bottle of Jack Daniel's locked in a cabinet near his bed.

Hamp was a perpetually friendly and lovable man; he was eternally draped with his grandchildren—hanging off his arms, hugging his leg, or sitting in his lap. Yet, as long as I knew her, Mur remained thin as a rail and sickly. More than once, I heard family members describe her behind her back as a "walking miracle." As I got older, I understood. Mur had two different kinds of cancer early in her life. She was one of the first women in the country to have a "radical mastectomy" for her breast cancer, and when she was diagnosed with colon cancer, Mur had a colostomy.

We knew none of this growing up—only that our dear Mur was frail and moved very slowly. She must not have weighed much more than eighty pounds. Every other night, she announced that this was her "bathroom night"—some mysterious, unexplained ritual that began right after dinner and lasted well into the night. Mur kissed us goodnight before going into the bedroom. We never saw her again until early the next morning, when she would once again be standing at the bottom of the steps, calling us down for breakfast.

Mur and Hamp had separate bedrooms on opposite sides of the first floor, probably because Hamp was constantly hosting meetings in the large master bedroom, occupying his favorite red leather chair right next to a writing table and phone. But I also wondered if it might be because Hamp did not like the strange smell that filled Mur's bedroom coming from the "medicinal cigarettes" she smoked to help with her pain. Twenty years later, I learned that strange, putrid smell in Mur's bedroom was probably marijuana. And that wasn't the only secret that lingered in the air of her Lexington home.

■ ■ ■

I usually went back to sleep before George had put his finishing touches on the fire and slipped out of the room. But his early morning visits were much appreciated by the cousins when we finally had to leave our snuggly warm beds and step out into the cool morning air. Even Georgia got cold at Christmastime.

The call to get up came when we first heard the constant ringing of a bell, interrupted by Mur's high-pitched voice, calling up from the bottom of the circular stairs. She would shake her little silver-plated bell back and forth and plead with all of us, "Time to get up . . . don't let your breakfast get cold, children! Time to get up!"

Rattling off the names of each grandchild, oldest first and working her way down, Mur mixed enticements, certain to speed us up, with her pleas in her shrill voice:

"Lawton, Lawton Jordan . . . you get up, ya hear? There's a plate full of crisp bacon down here, piping hot, just like you like it! You're the oldest . . . be the leader! Get up, and get moving!"

"Albert, Albert Jones . . . Annie's cooked pancakes for you . . . come on down here!"

"Little Hamilton, Little Hamilton, there are cheese grits waiting for you! Cheese grits are no good cold, sweetheart, better hurry!"

"Sydney, Sydney Jones! How did my princess sleep? Annie's got you a plate full of pancakes with fresh strawberries and maple syrup."

The items on the menu inspired us to jump out of bed into the still chilly morning air. We attacked our clothes, draped neatly over several chairs, forming a half-circle around the fireplace. Stripping off our cotton pajamas, all of us dressed right in front of the fire, constantly turning around as we did, searching for a balance between the too warm fire and the too chilly room.

Long as I could remember, I looked forward to seeing my cousin Sydney, a pretty girl about my age with long black hair, slip her nighty-night over her head. I usually tried to sneak a peek, but as I got older, she must have caught me staring, because Sydney began turning her back to me when she dressed, which still allowed me the chance to see her bottom covered by the white, tight-fitting cotton underwear. Then one Christmas holiday, when we were around eight years old, it just happened—the "cousins' bedroom" became the "boys' bedroom." No more Cousin Sydney sleeping (and dressing) with the boys.

With visions of pancakes, cheese grits, and crisp bacon waiting for us on our plates, we raced down the circular wooden stairs, two steps at a time, gripping the banister to keep our balance, landing hard on the main floor. Cousin Albert often abandoned the banister and tried to pass on the right, which meant he got to be the first to push open the double swinging doors to the large dining area.

A dark wooden table dominated the room, long and rounded and loaded with plates of steaming hot food. By adding sections of the table when all her children, grandchildren, and other family were in Lexington for Christmas, Thanksgiving, and summer holidays, our grandmother could squeeze about thirty tall, wooden-back leather chairs around the table.

Meals were big events at Hamp and Mur's house. Hamp sat at one end of the long table and Mur at the other. Uncle Hamilton was my mother's oldest brother and a confirmed bachelor who lived with his parents and managed the farm. He sat next to Hamp on his right, and then me—because I was named for both my grandfather and my uncle. My grandfather explained, "We three Hamiltons have to stick together." That made me feel very special.

The rule was that no one touched any food or even a piece of silverware until everyone was seated. Hamp would raise his hands to quiet everyone down and quickly rush through his traditional blessing. Sometimes he said it so fast it sounded like just one long word, "Lord-make-us-thankful-for-this-food-and-for-all-the-provisions-of-thy-bounty," except for the loud "A-mennn," which Hamp dragged out, sometimes as long as the blessing itself.

Annie, a black lady who had worked in my grandparents' home for decades, prepared these delicious Lexington breakfasts. She, of course, did not join us as we ate. There was little talk to be heard from the children as they devoured the wonderful food, hoping there would be "seconds." Uncle Hamilton might report the birth of a calf overnight, a problem with a tractor, or the news that one of the "hands"—a term used to refer to the black men and women who worked on the farm and in the house—was sick and needed to take the day off.

Mur might use breakfast as an occasion to inquire about the day's schedule of activities, ask Hamp if he had any guests coming for dinner (people were constantly dropping in to see him), and assign some chores to the hands, usually related to some special meal she was planning.

Home refrigerators had not yet made it to Lexington, so Mur might ask George to go down to the freezer locker in the middle of town, where you could store meats for a monthly fee, and get a side of beef for dinner, or she might have asked Henry, George's younger brother, to catch a few chickens so that Annie could cook her specialty—and our all-time favorite—fried chicken.

Old-timers around Lexington, white and black, agreed that they had never seen anyone anywhere who could do what Henry did with a chicken. He would walk behind the tall green hedge in the backyard— this separated the big house from the row of modest white wooden houses where the black families who worked for Mur and Hamp lived— to the chicken coop next to the red barn. Quietly standing there, Henry eyeballed his prey: several dozen plump chickens wandering around the yard, hunting and pecking for kernels of corn.

Chickens possess more speed than intuition and cannot be counted among God's smarter creations. But even they seemed to sense that something was up whenever Henry arrived, leaning up against the coop, not saying anything, just looking . . . looking . . . looking. Unless you kept your eye right on Henry, you would never even notice, but you might look around and find that Henry had quietly moved several paces closer to the chickens . . . then closer . . . and closer.

Suddenly, he dashed toward his target, his long arms outstretched, grabbing repeatedly for the poor chicken, which had broken into a literal run for its life. Sometimes it would take him two or three tries until he would wrap his thumb and forefinger around the chicken's neck before the bird turned and pecked at him with its sharp beak. But Henry always got his chicken.

Henry carefully held the squealing bird, wings and feet flapping, at full arm's length from his body. Muscles rippled under the dark skin of his arm as he walked forty to fifty yards to the towering old oak tree, where a rope—stained pink and red—hung from a low, fat limb. By the time he reached the oak, the bird had run out of energy; exhausted wings and feet surrendered and dangled from the bird's body. Quick as a flash, Henry swung the bird up over his head, round and round in a circle a couple of times, and then suddenly reversed direction. There'd follow a brief, shrill screech from the bird and then a sickening "pop"—its neck snapped in two. The chicken usually went completely silent and limp then. If there was no popping sound or the bird continued to squeal or squirm, Henry had to swing it round and round, trying to pop it again.

Two times almost always did it.

When it was done, Henry laid the limp chicken on the weathered-gray cutting table near the big oak, took the shiny silver hand ax that was hanging by a leather strap from a rusty nail on the side of the cutting table, and, with one swift stroke, chopped the chicken's head off, splattering blood on the table and anyone nearby. (On more than one occasion, I can remember Mur talking to Henry just like he was one of her grandchildren: "Now go put on some clean overalls before you come back in this house!") Henry tied the chicken's feet to the end of the rope hanging from a limb of the oak and "drained" the bird, blood first running and then slowly dripping out onto the ground while Henry went to get another.

When I was ten—old enough to play behind the hedge and visit the barn on my own—I walked double-time by that limb with the rope hanging down, red on the end. I remember sometimes rubbing my neck in an effort to imagine what it must feel like to have your whole head just chopped right off. But none of this ever stopped me from eating Annie's fried chicken or asking Mur for seconds. I now wonder if that hanging rope ever conjured up something darker for Henry.

While Mur darted in and out of the kitchen, making suggestions and sometimes giving orders, Annie clearly reigned supreme as the Queen of the Kitchen. A large black woman with a pleasant smile, she always had a kerchief wrapped around her head and wore long, colorful cotton dresses that grazed the floor. Not surprisingly, Annie favored her own family with the key jobs in the kitchen of preparing and serving the food. Her daughter Cat was our playmate, and Annie raised Cat to help out in the kitchen and sample her mother's good works. She was my age and already serving an apprenticeship to work inside. Cat was all happy and fun-loving playing with us in the yard but seemed so serious and quiet indoors as she stood back from the table, waiting for requests to refill glasses of iced tea or bring out a plate of fresh hot biscuits.

Sometimes at breakfast, but always at the end of the dinner meal, my grandmother rang her little silver bell loudly to summon Annie from the kitchen. Annie appeared slowly, face shiny and dripping with sweat from hours working over the hot wood-burning stove, wiping her hands on the white apron she wore to protect her floor-length dress. Annie's apron displayed colorful evidence of the meal just served, and she beamed as we heaped compliments on her: "That's the best fried chicken I've ever eaten!" or "That corn bread, Annie, I don't know how you do it, but it just melted in my mouth!" and on and on. Annie just nodded her head and mumbled over and over again, "Thank you, ma'am . . . thank you, sir . . . thank y'all!" As we got older, the cousins would occasionally bestow our greatest compliment on Annie, rising together for a standing ovation, which embarrassed Annie so much that she quickly ducked back through the swinging wooden doors into the sanctuary of her kitchen.

Once or twice a week during the hot summer months, George set up the ice cream churn on the back porch and surprised us with his different concoctions. Peach was my favorite; the chunks of icy, fresh peaches looked like bits of sunshine against the rich vanilla ice cream. After devouring heaping bowls of ice cream and being formally excused from the table by Mur, the cousins dashed through Annie's kitchen — ten to fifteen degrees warmer than the rest of the house — past the large iron wood-burning stove and out to the back porch.

Annie knew what we wanted and instructed George, "Get these chillen that bow." He'd then retrieve the long bow from the churn, which had been used to mix and turn the ingredients into delicious ice cream. Laying the long bow across the big serving plate with ice cream still stuck to it, Annie distributed utensils, and in an instant, six or eight little hands, spoons flying, made quick work of the bow. I am not sure why, but all the cousins agreed that ice cream from that bow tasted even better than the ice cream served in the fancy bowls in the dining room.

George and Annie, hands on her hips, just stood back smiling.

When the grandchildren got too loud and rowdy at the dinner table ("rambunctious," Mur said), Hamp pulled a crisp dollar bill from the silver money clip in his back pocket, waved it over his head, and declared that a game of "tombstone" had begun. This brought about an immediate silence as his grandchildren marched quietly into the living room and sat cross-legged on the floor around Hamp's big, brown leather chair in the corner.

The rules were simple: all grandchildren buttoned their lips immediately, some pretending to lock their lips and throw away the key, and, like tombstones, we all sat totally quiet, not saying a word or making even the slightest sound. Hamp was the judge and jury. His rulings were the law and appeals were not even considered. Any talking or noise meant instant elimination from the game. Once eliminated, you could make faces and try to get others to talk, but if you made any noise yourself, you would be sent to the big swing on the front porch where you had to sit by yourself until the game was over. Sometimes the games lasted as long as an hour. Cousin Sydney held the record, once winning a game that endured over two hours. Even Hamp was glad when that game was over.

The world seemed like such a simple, peaceful place when we visited Hamp and Mur in Lexington—big meals, copious family time, watching the light fade while we talked for hours on the porch, rocking back and forth. A child in my position might think, *How could life get any better?* But things had been falling apart all around us for years, and they weren't about to stop.

Army Brat

The RKO news film, playing in movie theaters all over the country, showed white-uniformed sailors, many on fire, jumping from the burning decks of the USS *Arizona*, the USS *West Virginia*, and the USS *Oklahoma*—each battleship lilting forward or aft or to the side before ultimately sinking into Pearl Harbor. The harrowing images gave powerful visual meaning to FDR's statement to Congress: "Yesterday, December 7, 1941—a date which will live in infamy—the United States of America was suddenly and deliberately attacked by naval and air forces of the Empire of Japan."

Less than forty-eight hours after the surprise Japanese attack, my daddy—like so many other young Americans—waited in line at his local U.S. Army recruitment office to volunteer for military service. Thirty years old and married at the time, my daddy was pleasantly surprised to be offered a commission as a second lieutenant in the Quartermaster Corps, only because he had played trumpet in his high school ROTC band. Later in life, when we were old enough to ask the question, "What did you do in the war, Daddy?" and actually get the truth, my father snapped to "attention," attempted a crisp salute, and explained, "Instead of packing a gun, I was in charge of a company that packed toilet paper. Ask the guys in the infantry if you don't believe me—it's hard to shoot straight if you can't wipe your ass!"

My daddy's important role in the war took my parents first to Shreveport, Louisiana, where my older brother, Lawton, was born; then on to Ogden, Utah; and finally to Charlotte, North Carolina, where I was born on September 21, 1944. This was his last military posting.

At the time of my birth, the invasion at Normandy was over, and the Allied forces had driven the Nazis from France. In a little more than six months, Adolf Hitler—after a last-minute marriage to his mistress Eva Braun—committed suicide with his bride in his Berlin bunker. Benito Mussolini attempted to escape disguised as a German officer near Lake Como, and he was caught, shot, and hung with his mistress upside down in the city square. Onlookers spat on his body, pelting it with rocks, rotten fruit, and trash.

While the war in Europe had been won and was winding down, the fierce conflict against Japan in the Pacific had not. When I was less than a year old, the United States dropped atomic bombs at Hiroshima and Nagasaki, ending the war with Japan and changing forever the nature of armed conflict among the major powers.

Ham-toon

After the war ended and my father was discharged from the army, our family moved to New Orleans in 1946 so my father could learn the insurance business from his uncle, Richard Lawton, for whom he was named. While I was playing on the nearby beaches as a toddler, Daddy gave me a nickname that stuck and was carefully recorded in black-and-white photos. In one is a stout little toddler, head full of black hair, standing in the shallow water with his chubby hand firmly in his daddy's grasp. The next picture shows a young Daddy pouring a bucket full of salt water on the child's small head. Apparently, this had become a ritual. Mama and Daddy reported I would close my eyes briefly when the water ran down my face, smile, cackle out loud, spit the salt water out, and just stand there while Daddy did it over and over again.

Mama confessed that she was a little worried that I seemed a bit slow to talk, but she clearly remembered my first complete sentence, standing on the beach, trying to get Daddy to fill and pour just one more bucket. "Pour cold wa-wa on Ham-toon's head," I begged, "Ham-toon" being about as close as I could come to saying my big three-syllable name.

From that day on, Daddy called me Ham-toon. Somewhere along the way—around the sixth or seventh grade—he stopped using it publicly to avoid embarrassing me in front of my friends, but the name continued at home. Even after I had grown and we were alone, Daddy still called me Ham-toon, usually followed by a big hug. Tears often welled up in Daddy's eyes, and he would turn away from me or leave the room. After I had my own children, I understood the emotion of remembering simpler, more innocent times.

Chapter Two

■ ■ ■

AW-BEN-NY

After the war, Mama and Daddy moved to Albany, Georgia, because they thought it was a good place to raise a family and for Daddy to start his new life insurance business.

Our new hometown "Aw-ben-ny," as the locals pronounced it, was tucked away in the corner of southwest Georgia. With a population of only twenty-five thousand people—more than half of its citizens black—Albany was still easily the only city in the area. Founded in 1836 and located on a navigable river, Albany was in the middle of the flat, fertile land that people called the "breadbasket of the Confederacy." You could drive fifty miles in any direction from home and see the same thing—flat land; rich, dark soil; and blacks working in the fields and orchards to plant or harvest peaches, pecans, peanuts, and cotton. Always cotton. Named for Albany, New York, since that city was also sited on a river (albeit one somewhat larger), my Albany straddled the muddy Flint River, which flowed right through the middle of town.

As I learned countless times during school trips to the local Carnegie Library, the late 1800s and early 1900s saw lots of active traffic and trade on the Flint. Hordes of boats would move cotton down the river to be processed at one of the many cotton mills that sprung up around Albany after the Civil War, built and owned by Yankee families who had moved south during that dark period for white southerners, an era that historians called Reconstruction.

In his second inaugural address, Abraham Lincoln indicated his desire to welcome the South back into the Federal Union like the lost prodigal son in the Bible. "With malice toward none, with charity for all," he had said. However, after his assassination, Republican radicals in the Congress chose to make the postwar period one of vengeance and retribution that left emotional and economic scars that remained for more than a century. By the time we moved to Albany, nearby trains and trucks and highways facilitated the transportation of cotton and other crops. I could count on one hand the times that I saw *real* boats on the lazy, muddy Flint River, and they were only small fishing boats in the spring or summer, usually steered by older black men. Cane poles dangled lines with live bait—squirming worms or crickets—dropped down in the muddy water while fishermen tried to catch the lounging fat catfish, scavenging the bottoms of the river. It was often said, "You would never eat 'em if you thought too much about what they are." But cooked up properly, fried in a thick batter and served with a plate of sizzling hush puppies doused with thick red Heinz catsup, the bottom-feeding catfish were considered good eating—a South Georgia delicacy we called "redneck caviar."

■ ■ ■

Hamp always said the only difference between Georgia and Alabama or Mississippi was Atlanta—considered a real city. Otherwise, all three states were rural, heavily dependent on white farmers for both their politics and their economies, and totally dependent on blacks for planting, tending, and harvesting their crops—for very low pay.

There were a lot of reasons why South Georgia land was so fertile and productive, and one of the oft-quoted facts was that an ocean had covered the area in prehistoric times. Indeed, one need only to cross the muddy Flint River—which ran south and divided the town of Albany from what we called East Albany—to see big white sand dunes that stretched for miles in a line running east and west. It was just like the sand you would expect to find on a beach, but here it was in southwest Georgia, at least 150 miles from the Gulf of Mexico. Walking among these sugar-white dunes, it was easy indeed to imagine that this was a beach in some prehistoric age.

Albany was described by one of its citizens as "the biggest acting small city anywhere." Growing up, I often heard folks brag that Albany had just about everything that Atlanta had—Atlanta just had more of it.

Sprinkled throughout this southwest corner of Georgia were small towns of two or three, five, or even ten thousand people, and all of these towns relied directly or indirectly on farming. Some towns, like Valdosta, for example, were known for their tobacco and warehouses.

Another, Bainbridge, was famous for its turpentine and pulp mills; Cairo for its delicious syrup; Dawson and Plains for their peanuts; and everybody everywhere grew the white fluffy stuff we called King Cotton.

Folks flocked to Albany from these smaller towns. Albany had everything: a big hotel, two fancy restaurants, several department stores, two military bases, and Radium Springs: a large natural warm spring. Some called it the biggest freshwater spring in the South, a claim toned down later in the 1950s after chambers of commerce in Arkansas and Tarpon Springs, Florida, challenged the title with some justification.

On Saturdays, folks from throughout "SoWeGa" — the moniker given the region by the local newspaper, the *Albany Herald* — came to Aw-ben-ny to shop and spend their money. The men usually wore their overalls or khaki work pants and white T-shirts. Some just sat on the front hoods of their pickup trucks or dusty Chevys or Fords, taking a bite of their Bull Durham chewing tobacco or puffing on a Camel or Lucky Strike cigarette, and talked politics or sports (mostly high school football). While they hung around their trucks and automobiles, their wives and daughters did their shopping, often dressed up in their "Sunday-go-to-meeting" clothes.

Some of the farmers from out of town settled on the green wooden benches that encircled the old courthouse; others wandered off to drink a beer or get a half pint of booze, which they could tuck away in their overalls. When the weather was warm, a few cars with cane fishing poles sticking out of rear windows parked around the Dougherty County courthouse. These men would walk the couple of blocks down to the Flint to buy fresh worms from a thriving business run by young, shirtless black boys in blue jean cutoffs.

Albany was the big fish in the small pond of southwest Georgia. We were proud of that distinction and often felt the need to put the word "biggest" or "greatest" or "best" in front of anything related to our town. For that reason, I grew up thinking that my hometown was more special than it probably was. But I would not have had it any other way.

The call letters of the most popular radio station were WGPC, generally regarded as standing for World's Greatest Pecan Center, and if one doubted that claim, she or he had only to drive from Albany in any direction to see pecan orchards everywhere on both sides of the road. Inside each orchard were seemingly endless straight rows of mature pecan trees, and in October and November, there were thousands and

tens of thousands of nuts on the green branches, broad limbs, some that
dipped to the ground. Swarms of black women wearing long dresses
and white turbans wrapped around their heads (just like "our" Annie
at Mur and Hamp's), bent at the waist to pick up pecans off the ground
and tossed them, without looking, into their large, light-brown croaker
sacks.

Ragsdale

There was one special thing about Albany that I did not hear about
growing up—Albany's thriving red-light district, called Ragsdale. But
the good citizens of Albany did not let this great sin stain its reputation
as a good Christian—and overwhelmingly Baptist—community.

Ragsdale was operated "under the strict supervision of a medical
staff," one old-timer recalled, probably making conditions sound better
than they were. The Ragsdale houses were all built alike in a row and
sported neon signs—as if they needed that additional attention. All had
latticework surrounding the large front porches, and the women hung
out there in the late afternoons and early evenings with their finery on,
occasionally shouting out to passing cars. They could be heard but only
barely seen.

One neighbor did admit to driving through Ragsdale a few times on
a way to "somewhere else" and, with more than a little pride, claimed
that he was yelled at. But he was quick to add, "I never did anything
but look!"

"One weekday," he continued, "I was walking down the busiest block
of downtown Aw-ben-ny, looked around, and suddenly found myself
all alone, the only person on the street in the entire downtown. There
was zero traffic. I heard a commotion, looked up, and saw two fancy
Packard Phaeton convertibles—full of women—turn onto Pine Avenue
right in front of the courthouse. There must have been six or eight gals
in each car. Those women were draped all over those Packards, some
sitting on the top of the front seats, waving, some on the very back of
the car in the jump seat. These gals were made up nice, all dressed up
and mighty pretty. They were having themselves a sure-nuff good old
time!

"Now, at first I thought it was a parade or some promotion, so I
ducked into Crowe's Drug Store to find out what the heck was going

on. The druggist laughed at my question and said it was 'Ragsdale hour,' when the madams of the Ragsdale houses were allowed to bring their girls into town to shop for a brief period. Of course, all the proper women got off the street in a hurry for fear that someone would think that they were one of *them*. And most of the men disappeared from the street for fear one of the girls might recognize one of their clients and call out his name."

By the early 1950s, the mere existence of Ragsdale was on a collision course with Albany's progress and economic growth. As a direct result of the influence of Georgians Carl Vinson and Richard Russell—chairmen respectively of the House and Senate Armed Services Committees—the U.S. government built what became the largest marine corps supply center in the world right outside Albany. As our local congressman was always quick to point out, the marine facility, combined with the existing Turner Field Air Force Base, gave Albany the largest per capita concentration of military bases and jobs of any place in the United States. Through the Korean conflict and the fifty years of the Cold War, these military installations were a vital part of the Albany economy.

Meanwhile, Ragsdale continued to operate openly well into the early 1950s, until the leadership of the two military bases formally complained to the city leaders that too many of their soldiers were showing up at the military clinics with gonorrhea. It was reported that when closely questioned about their recent personal activities, many of these soldiers had mentioned Ragsdale. Having to choose between tolerating illicit sex versus losing both tax and business revenues represented by the military bases, the city leaders "did the right thing," and Ragsdale was effectively closed in the early 1950s. Several of the more popular of the Ragsdale girls stayed around; one got an apartment in a nice section, where she was ostracized socially by the neighbors, and ultimately she left town.

One girl, allegedly the most popular and best looking of the ladies, moved into the Gordon Hotel downtown and continued her "practice" there. According to local lore, she played a part in ending the marriage of one of the wealthiest and most powerful businessmen in Albany, and then she married him a few years later. Their union was the talk and scorn of the town at the time, but four or five years later, she was welcomed into the membership of the Albany Junior League, an exclusive, gossipy, but obviously forgiving society of "the finest Christian ladies" in town. It says a lot that a woman associated with scandal and perceived moral failings could eventually be accepted into the coterie of these selective and elitist southern women because she was white and now had money, while the community's upstanding black women were relegated to standing in the corner in uniform, pouring glasses of iced tea on command.

■ ■ ■

I never could figure out what the real population of Albany was when I was growing up. Some reports said that there were eighteen to twenty thousand citizens, while the Chamber of Commerce suggested that Albany was a "thriving city of about 25,000 people." These discrepancies never made sense to me. Later I was told that this figure was arrived at because the federal government could never find white census takers who could read and write and were willing to go door-to-door in "colored town," and—of course—there were no black census takers. The census numbers used for that part of town known as Harlem, where black people lived, were mere guesstimates.

A more reasonable explanation was offered by an old-timer who suggested that the number of whites in Albany was consistently exaggerated for fear that Albany would become known as a majority "colored town," hurting the city's image and reputation as the unofficial hub and capital of southwest Georgia.

Years later, with the advent of the Great Society, the distribution of federal grants to communities were based strictly on population and affirmed by census numbers. As it turns out, greed won out, and the city leaders of Albany decided they needed an accurate count. While cussing this "federal meddling" and "social engineering," the good folks of Albany decided to get as many federal dollars as possible, even while accepting it under mild protest.

Pine Avenue

Pine Avenue, ironically lined not with pine trees but with enormous palm trees, was the major street and dividing line running east and west through Albany. I can't recall a single black family living north of Pine Avenue during my childhood.

The modest public transportation provided by the city existed almost exclusively to transport black women and men from South Albany over to jobs on the white side of town, where they cooked, cleaned houses, and did yard work, returning home across town at the end of the day. I never rode a city bus in my life, nor did any of my friends or their parents. Other than an occasional trip into "colored town" to pick up a cleaning woman or a babysitter, white folks in Albany had no reason to venture across this unspoken, but important, social boundary.

Another person, reflecting on Albany in the 1950s and 1960s, offered these candid and typical insights into the race issue: "We were all still suffering in the 1940s from the Civil War. The bigoted Yankee politician was holding us all down, whites and blacks. Black folks had no decent schools or education—all they knew was farming and manual labor. This gave the rednecks someone to look down on: the nigger.

Later I read in magazines and newspapers and heard people say that the white South was preoccupied with segregation and in maintaining control over the black population, which in some areas approached 30 to 35 percent. Southwest Georgia was sometimes called "the Black Belt," and many counties and the entire area had at least a 50 percent black population.

I remember it differently.

■ ■ ■

There was nothing to be preoccupied about. Segregation was legal, accepted, and understood. It was the bedrock of the political and economic system as well as the social order. There was not a blatant or open or even a subtle challenge to segregation in the 1940s and early 1950s. Indeed, President Truman's order to integrate the military brought a sharp reaction. The racist Dixiecrat Party, led by Strom Thurmond in 1948, carried several southern states in that presidential election—but not Georgia.

It took many years for the legal challenges to the system resulting from the 1954 Supreme Court ruling in *Brown v. Board of Education* to touch the lives of most white southerners in even a remote way. Although the Court held that "separate but equal" public education was unconstitutional, theoretically ending school segregation, the implementation of this decision on any significant scale took years, and still today there is widespread inequality in public education. I graduated from a high school with a couple thousand students in 1962, and there was not a single black student in my school. Four years later, I graduated from the University of Georgia—fourteen years after *Brown v. Board of Education*—with 25,000 students, only two of whom were black. (One of those black students was Charlayne Hunter-Gault, who went on to become a highly respected television journalist. Another was Hamilton E. Holmes, a celebrated medical doctor and professor.)

I am ashamed to say that—with the few exceptions noted within these pages—while growing up in South Georgia, I was oblivious to the system of segregation and its odious implications; that oblivion carried on well into my teenage years. Yes, I noticed along the way many ironies and injustices of the system, but I accepted—like my ancestors and most of my contemporaries—the unfair system I lived in and, through my silence, condoned and consequently supported it.

In the process of writing this book and conducting personal research, I spent many hours looking through old copies of the *Albany Herald* from the 1950s and early 1960s. The *Herald* was owned and operated by James H. Gray, a Dartmouth-educated man from Massachusetts who got the license for the first television station in southwest Georgia, served as mayor of Albany for many years, was chairman of the state Democratic Party, candidate for governor, and a close friend of John F. Kennedy. Wealthy, politically connected, and owner of the major news outlets in Albany and southwest Georgia, Jimmy Gray was a leading proponent of segregation. I often thought that he felt a need to prove to his southern audience that he was at least as much of a true believer in racial segregation as they were. He wrote long and erudite editorials in the *Herald* criticizing the "race mixers" and Martin Luther King Jr.

My recent review of the *Herald*—which most Albanians read every day—provided insight into how these racial stereotypes and feelings were reinforced and inflamed. The most popular column in the newspapers, *Albany Today*, appeared on the front page and was a composite of news, tidbits, and club and civic announcements. It was shocking to me how many of the columns started with some bit of news that featured a derogatory story about a crime involving a black citizen. The exception was when some negative story about Albany black folks did not top this popular column.

I wondered as I read these columns how this obvious and ultimately successful attempt to stereotype a group of people had been both tolerated and so effective. It only added to my own sense of shame that not only did I fail to recognize it, but I didn't dream of challenging it. I simply accepted it.

907 Fourth Avenue

My family lived at 907 Fourth Avenue in Albany. That number—907—was stenciled on the curb in black letters against a painted white rectangle. Home for us was a one and one-half story wooden house built in the late 1940s on a double lot. It was a plain-looking structure with no obvious style or theme, and it was painted white and topped with a gray shingled roof. It was just a house with a front porch, four tiny bedrooms, and two bathrooms. Lawton and I slept in the bedrooms upstairs on either side of a shared bathroom. Mama and Daddy slept in the master bedroom downstairs connected to the hall, where there was another bedroom all fixed up and waiting for the new baby. Later, we added a playroom that ran along the side of the house, which became the main place for the family to gather, relax, and watch television.

It wasn't the biggest or most fancy house in the neighborhood, but it was our happy home for over twenty years.

We lived two blocks from Slappey Drive, the biggest street I had ever seen. People said you could get on Slappey Drive, head due north, and drive and drive and drive until you eventually ended up in Atlanta. It was hard for my young mind to understand how one road could be that straight and go that far. I often tried to picture how they made the road straight enough so that you would actually "hit" Atlanta. Suppose the calculations were off by a few or many miles? What would happen, I wondered, if you missed Atlanta and drove right on past it?

I remember riding down to the corner of Fourth and Slappey on the blue-and-white Schwinn bicycle I got on my seventh birthday. Lawton showed me how to get some of Mama's old playing cards she used for bridge with her girlfriends and—by using wooden clothes pins—snap them onto the spokes so that when the wheels turned, the cards rotated against the spokes, making a pop-pop-popping noise, close enough to the sound of a machine gun to be really cool.

Adorned with mirrors mounted on the handlebars, my new bicycle took me farther from my home than I'd ever been alone. I rode down to Slappey Drive to watch the giant Caterpillar road machinery shake and quiver as thick, barely-liquid concrete dripped slowly out of a large metal funnel into huge frames of yellow pine. Then, teams of black men, wearing only shorts or jeans and boots in heat that felt at times like 110 to 120 degrees, used long metal rakes first to distribute the concrete pouring out of the funnel into every corner of the wooden form and then large flat boards to level it. They then sprayed water onto the concrete to smooth it out, and they waited for it to "set up," then dry, and then become U.S. 19, which ran all the way from Florida to Michigan, where it ended at the Canadian border. And Albany and I were part of all of that.

Daddy

My father—Richard Lawton Jordan—was born and grew up in Macon, Georgia, a small city in the middle of the state, the oldest son of a bank president. I remember Daddy saying proudly, "Papa was the richest man in Macon."

My father loved to pull out the fat, brown-leather book with the words "Photograph Album" engraved on the front from the center drawer of the old mahogany wooden desk that once sat in his boyhood home. Daddy slowly thumbed through the pages of old and mostly faded black-and-white pictures mounted on the black paper. He always paused at one particularly faded picture of an old-timey car with no top adorned with garlands of roses and carnations. Two young boys in knickers sat in the front seat with a black driver, and a grim-looking man and woman sat in the backseat with a sweet little girl in a white dress.

"Our family had the first automobile in all of Macon," my daddy told us. His finger moved from face to face. "That's Mama and Daddy, Carrie Mae, Robert, Jimmy, and me. We drove that car in the Confederate Memorial Parade for several years and were usually the star of the show—until the Depression."

There were no driving laws or restrictions or even licenses back then, and Daddy's lifelong love affair with automobiles began in 1924 when he was twelve years old and got his own first car. Stuffed in the back of the album were loose pictures and a favorite large postcard featuring Daddy's boyhood home in Macon on Vine Avenue, a classic two-story antebellum house with huge white columns surrounding it on all sides.

"In one year, I went from being the son of the richest man in middle Georgia to losing my father, losing the home where we were all born and raised, and being forced to go door-to-door in the neighborhood where we had once lived, selling Maxwell House coffee to our neighbors. All so I could buy food for Mama and the family and pay rent on the tiny apartment we moved into."

My daddy said that he thought at the time he was a great salesman but later realized that their former neighbors were just being kind and trying to help his family in a small way, probably thinking, *There but for the grace of God goes our family.*

I used to think that my daddy was either forgetful or thought we were stupid, because he told these same stories about Macon and his boyhood over and over and over again. But my mama said that it was important that we listen to Daddy's story. "Remembering is a way for your daddy to grieve for his own daddy, who died so young."

I thought I understood.

Our New Baby Sister, Helen

When I was five years old, my sister was born at Phoebe Putney Memorial Hospital in Albany. My brother and I—with me on tippy toes—stared through the thick glass window as the nurse inside pointed to a chubby baby with a head full of black hair, wrapped tightly in a pink blanket with eyes shut tight, asleep in the nursery. I knew what it was like to have a big brother but could not imagine what a little sister would be like. She had gotten a lot of baby presents—most of them were baby clothes and girly things that I had zero interest in playing with. I was afraid she was not going to be much fun.

I was surprised when Mama told us in her hospital room that the new baby girl in her arms was going to be named for her mother.

"You mean she'll be Mur Jr.?" I asked.

Mama and Daddy got a good laugh out of that one, but she told me that the baby's name would be Helen.

I was playing in the front yard when Mama came home from the hospital in an ambulance—not because anything was wrong with her, but because new mothers stayed in the hospital for four or five days in those days, and then in bed for several weeks. They were instructed to walk as little as possible during that first month.

Mur came down from Lexington to spend some time helping Mama, but I overheard my mama warning that she was not going to argue with Mur again about having a wet nurse, a practice of having one of the black women from Lexington breast-feed the new baby so that a new mother could get some rest and avoid what Mur called "that unpleasantness." Given Mur's attitude, I guessed that Mama and her brothers and sister might have had wet nurses. I often wondered if either Lawton or I had had a wet nurse from Lexington. My parents and baby Helen slept in the bedrooms downstairs while Lawton and I stayed upstairs in the two tiny, pine-paneled bedrooms separated by a small hall that led to our small shared bathroom. Although we liked to say our house had two stories, one and one-half was closer to the truth because the front parts of my and Lawton's bedrooms actually slanted downward following the slope of the roof.

The normal fear of the dark that a lot of kids have was magnified in my case since my bed was right next to the door that led to the dark attic. Although Lawton's bedroom was right across the hall, barely ten feet away, he always locked his door at night, partly to have his privacy but also because he knew that it added to my fears. Lawton was not a bullying older brother, but he would occasionally tease or provoke me, as any older brother is wont to do. I doubt he realized how very scared I was.

There was another factor that made it all more complicated. The doctor who delivered me had announced to my parents that I was a fat, happy, and healthy baby, but I had bowed legs that "a good-sized pig could run through without touching." The doctor also announced that I had the flattest feet he had ever seen. After I was safely in my mother's arms for the first time, the physician pulled my daddy aside in the hall outside of Mama's room to suggest that a specialist examine my legs and feet once I started to walk. As a result, I had to wear therapeutic leg braces and orthotics every night of my childhood. They were cumbersome and made a lot of noise when I walked in them.

When the wind blew or if it rained heavily, all kinds of creaks and squeaks came out of that attic. There were a lot of nights when I would begin to cry and start to get out of bed. But even though her bedroom was downstairs and under Lawton's bedroom, Mama would hear my clunky orthotic shoes on the floor and quickly be at my bedside, soothing me with hugs and words and rubbing my legs and feet—which were always sore by the end of the day from wearing my corrective footwear—until I was asleep. Whenever I marveled how Mama heard me, Daddy would remark that he himself never heard a peep, but that my mama was blessed with "mother's ears," which God gave to all women to hear when their children called or cried. As I got older, when I had trouble going to sleep or if I woke up in the middle of the night, I would turn on a little light that Mama had given me and read a comic book—maybe *Batman* or *Captain Marvel*—until I fell asleep with the little light on. Growing up, I burned out a lot of batteries in that little nightlight. But I never did get used to sleeping next to that spooky, pitch-black attic.

■ ■ ■

On one side of our house lived the Masons—nice, respectable, and contented members of Albany's middle class—and their two daughters. Mrs. Mason was a teacher, and Mr. Mason was the manager of the A&P supermarket on the corner of Third and Slappey. Next door to us on the other side was a wealthy banker and his wife and son, the Brimberrys, and at the top of our street was the Weatherbee mansion, an enormous estate that took up almost an entire block and was surrounded by an imposing brick wall, tall as a grown man.

The Weatherbees were carpetbaggers—Yankees who migrated to the South during Reconstruction to take advantage of business opportunities emerging from the ruins of the Confederacy. But even though the Weatherbees had been in Albany for several generations, owned the Flint River Cotton Mill, donated the money that built the local hospital, and were considered very good and generous citizens, people whispered behind their backs about their carpetbagger history. Their youngest son, Roland, was my brother's best friend.

In a sense, the physical location of our house represented the economic status and ambitions of our family, straddling the middle and always trying to get ahead economically but deeply sobered and sometimes held back by duress; the Great Depression had an enormous impact on both of my parents' families, particularly that of Daddy. Our house in many ways also represented the social divisions in our community and the fact that our solidly middle-class upward-mobility status in Albany society seemed to be stalled for most of my youth.

When I returned to Albany as an adult and walked on that black asphalt pavement to 907 Fourth Avenue, I was surprised how small my childhood home looked. I remembered the hot, lazy summer days with the visible heat rising off the pavement. We were always barefooted, and the term "hot-footing it" meant crossing Fourth Avenue on a summer day . . . fast.

Insurance Man

"Here comes the insurance man," folks would say when they saw my daddy coming, briefcase in hand, tipping his hat to any ladies present and always ready with the latest joke and an easy smile.

Daddy's life seemed to revolve around something he called "the home office" in faraway Richmond, Virginia. I came to understand that his company was based out of Virginia, which required a lot of communication on Daddy's part. He was constantly mailing big fat envelopes to the home office filled with life insurance applications, medical forms, and silver metal tubes with urine samples. He would often tell my mother about a big case pending, and Daddy was always waiting for the home office to approve the insurance policy or turn it down if the customer was not in good health. I never understood what pee in a tube had to do with insurance and was worried that some friend might get in our car, find the aluminum tubes, and try to open one.

Every night after dinner, he took a stack of papers out of his brown leather briefcase with the gold letters "Life Insurance Company of Virginia" on the side, got on the phone in the hall—our only phone for most of my childhood—and made cold calls to people who appeared on a public listing he had gotten from the courthouse of people who had bought new homes and might need mortgage insurance.

Most folks hung up on Daddy or told him early in his spiel that they were not interested, but about one out of every twenty or thirty callers would respond with even mild interest, and my father would make an appointment to see them and explain the benefits of buying life insurance. When Daddy came home with an "application and specimen," it meant that his customer had been serious enough to fill out the paperwork and urinate into a metal container that would then be shipped off to Richmond. My Daddy worked very, very hard for our family.

Clothes Horse

I often heard noise from the kitchen—usually Hattie cooking bacon or doing the leftover dishes from the night before—as I came downstairs from my bedroom. Daddy, getting ready for work in the bathroom, would sing old favorites like "Old Mamie Reilly" or "I've Been Working on the Railroad" in his sweet tenor voice. He had a morning ritual, and I was happy to be a tiny part of it. When I knocked on the bathroom door, he'd ask, "Is that my Ham-toon?"

Worried that his "sleepyhead" son might topple off the toilet seat, Daddy would pull out with his foot the little four-legged wooden stool that sat under the sink. Perched on the stool, I looked up at him, in his white bedroom slippers, wearing long, dark argyle socks that stretched most of the way up his skinny, chalky legs to his knees, then white boxer shorts and an old-fashioned white T-shirt with straps over his shoulders.

He had a white bulky Sunbeam electric razor about the size of a triple-decker cheeseburger in his right hand and sometimes marveled, "I bet there aren't five men in Albany with this model!" He would pop open the shiny silver top covering the blades, take out the little black brush provided, and clean the whiskers from his previous shave into the sink. He would then put the top on, plug in the loudly buzzing razor, and lean forward over the sink, stretching and contorting his face at different angles with his left hand while guiding the chunky razor with the other as it gobbled up the standing whiskers.

When he was not in a big hurry, Daddy would pick me up in one arm and allow me to "shave" by quickly and lightly touching the buzzing, vibrating razor against both sides of my chubby cheeks. I can remember my head jerking when the warm, buzzing thing touched my little face. It was a bit scary but also thrilling.

Daddy would then open the cabinet over the bathroom sink, pull down his off-white porcelain bottle of Old Spice after shave with the thin gray plastic stopper in the top, splash a few drops in his hands, and rub them all over his face, the sweet aroma quickly filling the entire bathroom. Occasionally, he would touch his hands on both sides of my fat cheeks, leaving just enough of a scent so that I could still smell it for several minutes after leaving the bathroom.

I liked to follow Daddy into his and Mama's bedroom, where he would open the closet door and begin to assemble his outfit for the day. Just to give me something to do, sometimes Daddy would ask me for a weather report. I would run out the front door, stand on the front porch, hold out my hands, look up at the sky, take a few deep breaths, and then run back in, shouting out—even before I reached the bedroom—that it was clear or rainy, hot or cold.

By the time I got back, Daddy would be thumbing through—one by one—the six or eight suits that he owned, pausing for a second at each as he carefully contemplated his possible choices for shirt and tie. He usually wore white shirts but had a few that were light blue, which were considered more appropriate for the spring and summer.

But choosing a tie was a more serious matter and a greater challenge as he stared at the dozens of ties hanging from the tie rack in his closet. Daddy would carefully take three or four ties off the wooden rack, put them on the bed next to the suit selected, and then hold them, one by one, against the suit he had chosen. He might try three or four ties several times before making a final selection. Once he laid the suit of the day on the bed, Daddy would go to his closet and pull out two pairs of shoes and place them at the bottom of the pants legs hanging over the bed, step back, and see which shoes looked best with the rest of his outfit. He would then remove the shoetrees, hold up each shoe, and buff it with a shoe brush—one brush for brown shoes and one for black.

After putting on his pants, white shirt, and shoes, Daddy talked me through the steps of tying a Windsor knot. While this knot took more time, it was the only knot that did not slip, stayed in place all day long, and was symmetrical. Standing in front of the full-length mirror in their bedroom, Daddy would then put on his suit coat, make a last slight adjustment in his tie, button the middle button of his suit coat, and, finally, choose his hat for the day. "No well-dressed man steps out of his home without a hat," he said.

Hanging on the inside of the closet door was a wooden hat rack with several rows of protruding shafts, each with a hat hung on it. There was no doubt in my own mind that if that rack held fifty hats, Daddy would fill it up. Most were light or dark gray, deep blue, or black. "Never try to match your suit and hat—that doesn't work," he preached. "You want your hat to draw a contrast with your suit."

In the fall and winter, Daddy would select some shade of gray hat with a blue band around it or possibly a dark blue with a lighter band or a brown hat with a lighter contrasting band. In the spring and summer, it would be a light brown or tan or a favorite beige straw hat: a Panama.

Completing the ritual, Daddy would pull open the top drawer of the ornate mahogany dresser from his old home in Macon into which Mama laid out his handkerchiefs, pick out a white one, lay it out on the bed, and carefully fold it just right so it would have a point in the middle and was wide enough to fit snugly into the breast pocket on his suit coat. Then he would pat his hankie into the pocket, teasing the folded part until it stood tall in his pocket like a fresh white tulip.

Finally pleased with himself, he would walk into the kitchen and give Mama a big peck on the cheek. She'd walk him to the front door and wave as he loaded his briefcase full of insurance papers and urine samples into his dark-green 1948 Chevrolet. Like most folks, Daddy never locked the car, and we left our car keys in the ignition. I don't remember a car ever being stolen during my years in Albany. Completing the ceremony, Daddy would take off his jacket, hang it up in the backseat on a black wire hanger, lay his hat down carefully in the front seat, toot the horn a few short blasts, and smile and wave as he drove away.

"Goodbye Ad . . . love ya, Ham-toon."

I liked the way that my daddy looked when he went to work. Most other daddies on our street wore suits and ties and hats. Indeed, it almost looked like a uniform when several neighbors left at the same time. But for some reason, my daddy always looked a little bit "snazzier"—the word Mama used—than the others. I was proud of him.

■ ■ ■

One morning—I was probably four or five years old—after Daddy had left for his office and Mama was doing the breakfast dishes, I sneaked in the bathroom, closed the door tight, stood on top of the little stool on my tiptoes, opened the cabinet, and pulled down Daddy's electric razor. I plugged the cord in and—just as I had seen Daddy do so many times—ran the buzzing, vibrating razor back and forth across my face. Just like Daddy! But this time not just for a few seconds—I bravely "shaved" for several minutes. I got my chin, my neck, my cheeks, and the area above my lips, shaving just like Daddy. I was really proud of myself but started to worry that Mama might come looking for me and stopped. I somehow figured Mama wouldn't want me playing with this special thing. This was going to be my secret and mine alone.

And just as I had seen Daddy do so many times, I took out the bottle of Old Spice and poured the sweet liquid generously on my hands before splashing it all over my face. Instantly, my face felt like it was on fire, and I ran screaming into the kitchen. Mama, standing over the sink drying the breakfast dishes, looked up with a frightened expression on her face, and yelled back, "What's wrong?"

Scared and hurting too badly to respond, I just kept crying and Mama kept yelling, "What's wrong?" Her eyes scanned me head to toe to be sure that I had all my fingers, my eyes were okay, my teeth were still there, and there was no blood anywhere. When I finally calmed down enough to tell her, in between sobs and while rubbing my face, that I had been shaving and had used Daddy's Old Spice, she smiled a sigh of relief and quickly turned into my nurse, holding me on her lap and hugging and patting my puffy red face with a damp, cool washrag. She explained that Daddy's razor was for tough old whiskers—not soft baby skin—and that my "shave" had irritated my skin, made worse when I doused it with the Old Spice, which was full of alcohol.

For Christmas later that year, Santa Claus brought me my own toy electric razor, which was red-and-blue plastic and ran on two big D batteries. It had a string cord with a rubber suction cup that I licked to make wet and then stuck on the pink tile wall in the bathroom. When I turned my razor on, it made a loud buzzing sound. Nothing pleased me more in the morning than to be in the bathroom with Daddy, copying whatever he was doing with his razor. I didn't think much about it at the time, but when Santa gave me my own razor, Daddy was able to shave more quickly and did not have to spend so much time fooling with me! Maybe they were in cahoots.

My daddy was a very emotional and nostalgic man, and while he never said it explicitly—southern men don't talk about those sorts of things—I think it made him sad to see us grow up; I imagine that it was much to Daddy's dismay when I began to grow real whiskers in the seventh grade. I learned to shave with an old-fashioned Gillette straight razor. And while it smelled awfully good, no more Old Spice for me! Every time I saw an Old Spice bottle or smelled that familiar sweet odor, that fiery sensation was as vivid and real as yesterday, and my hand would often touch my face just to be sure it was a memory.

Chapter Three

■ ■ ■

POLITICS IN MY BLOOD

Today, people might say that, from the very first, I had politics in my genes. Back then—when "genes" would have seemed a misspelling of the Levi's I wore most of my boyhood—it was said that I had "politics in my blood." Indeed, politics was the lifeblood of Grandfather Hamp's existence, and he passed that on to me.

While I did not see it so clearly then, all southern politics flowed from the war. Not World War II, which had just ended and in which both of my grandfather's sons and both of his sons-in-law had honorably served, but the War Between the States, which had ended almost a century before. Hamp never called it the Civil War, believing that phrase to be a misnomer that suggested an internal rebellion instead of an effort to establish a separate and distinct nation. Nevertheless, if you grew up in the South that was the War. It was no mystery to us kids that it was going to take a long time before our folks and their folks forgot that war. When Annie would step in to refresh our glasses during these conversations, Mur would dab lightly at the corners of her temples with a cloth napkin and try to change the subject.

"My, it's warm in here."

On my early visits to Lexington, my grandmother presided over the meals, but Hamp was the emcee, guiding the conversation, telling the best jokes, kidding Mur, and talking about the weather and the farm. Hamp could also turn serious in a moment and start talking politics— and he often talked about "the War." He had about a dozen favorite war stories that he would tell over and over again, occasionally mixing in a new one, which might disappear from his rotation or be replaced by something better. Hamp had always said about my daddy, "I liked your father from the first time I met him." I recall my dear mother remarking once that Hamp may have liked Daddy the first time he met him, but he loved Daddy's family history even more since it added new material to his precious stories about the war.

My father's great-grandfather, General Alexander Lawton (my grandmother Jordan's family name), was from Savannah, fought under Stonewall Jackson, and served as the Quartermaster General of the Confederacy. After the war was over, Robert E. Lee, acting on a premonition that his own death was near, made the long trip to Savannah for the purpose of visiting nearby Cumberland Island, where his father, Revolutionary War hero Light-Horse Harry Lee, was buried. It was a great moment in our collective family history when General Lee spent two nights in Savannah at the home of my great-great-grandfather.

It did not take much urging to get Hamp to tell that story and to talk about Lee's visit. Even though Hamp was not there, he went on in great detail about what General Lee wore, what everybody said, and what everybody did. I never could figure out how Hamp knew all those things; Mama said that her daddy was just a good storyteller.

While Hamp knew a great deal about General Lawton—he was a candidate for Senate, the president of the American Bar Association, and appointed ambassador to Austria-Hungary—I learned many years later that Hamp had left out an important fact—that General Lawton had been relieved of his command by Stonewall Jackson after one major battle. My brother Lawton said that being "relieved of command" was the same as being fired, but I wasn't willing to believe that about my famous ancestor.

I was nine years old the summer of 1954 when our family went to Washington, D.C., on vacation. During my first visit to the nation's capital, I was all in a dither to visit the Civil War section of the Smithsonian Museum. We had heard so many stories over the years about this great conflict, and now I could see more for myself. I was more than a little excited to find a soldier named Walter McWhorter, almost certainly a cousin or uncle, who had won the Congressional Medal of Honor in 1865. As we read the citation that went with each medal, I was surprised and very disappointed to realize that this McWhorter fought for the North and had won his medal of honor for killing Southerners!

Hamp beamed with pride when I told him about our visit to the Smithsonian and my discovery that there was a McWhorter—almost certainly some kind of cousin—who had won a Congressional Medal of

Honor. Then I sprang the surprise—"But he fought for the North!"—and Hamp's jaw dropped. Hamp seemed almost speechless other than the expression he uttered that I had never heard before: "Holy shit!"

After asking if I was certain, he rose from his big chair and quickly left the room without saying another word. It was the only time that I ever remember seeing Hamp speechless or maybe even mad at me. I, of course, just about started to cry, because Hamp was the last person in the world that I would want to disappoint. But my mother hugged and comforted me, saying that I had learned an important lesson—that "the War" was simply not something to joke about with Hamp.

Gone with the Wind

In 1949, when I was barely five years old, and over the strong objection of Mur, Hamp took me to Atlanta to see *Gone with the Wind*, which was coming back to the Fox Theatre for the tenth anniversary of its premiere. We mounted the steps to the Trailways bus, which stopped just for him at the top of the long walkway. The driver had saved his usual spot for "Mr. Hamp" right behind himself, and the two older men fell into an easy conversation, trading local gossip and stories before getting around to their favorite topic, the prospects for the Georgia Bulldogs football team in the upcoming year.

It was about a two-hour drive from Lexington to Atlanta, and we stopped occasionally to pick up a rider. Black folks entered the rear door to the bus and moved quickly to the very back, leaving several rows separating themselves from the white riders. If there were more blacks getting on the bus than available seats in the very back, they would simply step back down off the bus and wait for the next bus. Who knows how many buses they'd been rejected from on busy hours and how many buses would come before they'd get a seat. As a small boy, I couldn't help but wonder how these people ever got where they wanted to go.

When we finally rode into Atlanta, we got off at the largest bus station I had ever seen and took a taxi down Peachtree Street to the Fox Theatre. It was also the biggest movie theater I had ever seen with its double balconies and gold railings. *Gone with the Wind* had held its worldwide premiere at the Fox ten years earlier with costars Clark Gable and Vivien Leigh in attendance.

Featured on a gigantic screen in Technicolor, *Gone with the Wind* was, even to a fidgety five-year-old boy, a wonderful (and yes, a little bit long) movie. Now, there was a lot that I did not understand, but I thought I understood *something* when I looked over to find Hamp dabbing his eyes with the white handkerchief he kept neatly displayed in his front coat pocket. I figured Hamp was sad because it was about Georgia. All the people in the movie who lived in big homes like Mur and Hamp were burned out by the Yankees.

Watching *Gone with the Wind* was also the first time I realized the South had lost the war. I had heard all the talk about great battles, heroes, acts of courage, and the constant theme of the South fighting against overwhelming odds. But no one had ever come out and said that we had lost.

On the bus ride back to Lexington, I asked Hamp about that. Hamp told me that there was no doubt about it—we had lost the war. But "they" had us outnumbered four and five to one, and we still almost beat them. He said the South had the greatest generals and the bravest soldiers. And we almost won. We almost won. Hamp drifted into one of his history lessons, which I had heard a dozen times before, about what had happened at Chancellorsville, Lee's almost successful invasion of the North, which would have brought England and France into the war on the South's side. From Hamp's point of view, this was a story about what might have been if Stonewall Jackson had not been accidentally shot and killed by his own soldiers. While I knew these stories almost word for word, I never tired of hearing Hamp tell them.

When I asked Hamp what it would be like today if "we" had won the war, he thought for a second and simply said, "Now, that's a good question for a little fella like you, Hamilton. That is a really good question." But Hamp never answered that question and never even tried. At the time, I thought he must not have known the answer. As I got a little older, I realized that Hamp probably knew the answer, but he just couldn't bring himself to say it.

■ ■ ■

Mur and Hamp lived on a well-traveled state road, and hardly a day went by that some visitor did not drop by to say hello to "Mr. Hamp," often dropping off a large bag of shelled pecans, a jar of preserves, or possibly even a big beautiful bouquet of roses wrapped in a newspaper.

Mur loved the roses best and carefully took them out of their paper, clipped the stems with her shears, and put them in a crystal vase on the dining room table.

Sometimes just one person and sometimes a delegation, visitors appeared at the front door without notice, possibly on the way to or from the state capitol in Atlanta. When it was purely a social visit, they sat in the living room with Hamp, and the rest of us were expected to join in the conversation and enjoy the visit.

Sometimes, however, when one of the visitors said something like, "Mr. Hamp, we want to talk to you about this governor's race coming up," or, "We need your help getting a little piece of road in our county," Hamp would simply say, "Boys, let's adjourn to the back." And they rose and followed him to his little office in the back of the house. They all seemed to know the way back there, indicating to me that they had "been to the back" before. Sometimes, I found a reason to go toward his office and listen at his door to the muffled talk, which always seemed to be about politics.

These meetings rarely lasted more than thirty minutes or an hour. The men usually came out laughing and talking, smelling a bit like they had had a taste of Hamp's Old Grand-Dad or Jack Daniel's whiskey. They would then pay their respects to my grandmother, who remained with the children and the other women in the living room, and then depart to Atlanta or to their hometowns.

While my parents told me that Hamp practiced law and was in "politics," I never really understood what that meant until I was eight years old and a Christmas present allowed me to see and understand politics a little bit better.

In 1951, Uncle Bill, my mother's youngest brother, gave Mur and Hamp a television set for Christmas. The first one anyone had ever seen in and around Lexington, the TV had a tall antenna mounted on the red brick chimney on the second floor that would, in perfect weather, magically receive signals almost eighty miles away from WSB-TV in Atlanta, one of the earliest NBC affiliates. Everybody knew that WSB stood for "Welcome South, Brother!"

Uncle Bill also bought an RCA color kit: colored sheets of plastic, blue at the top and green at the bottom, that could be taped on the television screen. These were designed to be used for shows like the many Westerns that dominated the afternoon programming—turning the black-and-white picture, however crudely, into "color." Once the six o'clock news or *The Jack Benny Show* came on, though, the two-tone faces looked silly. Finally my grandparents took the plastic sheets off altogether and only put them on when Uncle Bill was visiting to avoid hurting his feelings.

In the early days, there was not a lot of programming. The WSB test pattern would be on if you turned on the TV before the *Today Show* with Dave Garroway—Mur's favorite—which premiered in 1953 and came on at eight a.m. But the thing my grandfather enjoyed most was the national news and political coverage, so whenever we visited Lexington, we watched a lot of that.

In the summer of 1952, Hamp announced that he wanted me to watch the convention with him. I had no idea what a convention was, but I sprawled on the living room floor at Mur and Hamp's, pencil in my chubby little hand, writing figures down on the yellow legal pad as my grandfather called them out while we watched the fuzzy black-and-white picture flick and fade in and out. It was the first televised national political convention—Democratic, of course.

Hamp was supporting his friend from down the road, Senator Richard Russell, for president.

"The grrr-eat and sovereign state of Al-y-bam-y casts thirty-two votes for its neighbor and son of the South, the great Senator Richard B. Russell."

It was a long night for Senator Russell, who won support for his presidential nomination from every single delegate from the Deep South. But Russell failed to win a single delegate outside the South, leaving him far short of the votes needed to win the nomination, which ultimately was awarded to Governor Adlai Stevenson of Illinois, who had broad support of the party leaders in the large industrial states. Hamp was disappointed but loyal to his party. "Even though Stevenson is divorced and probably can't be elected, he is a Democrat. We've got no choice— we have to support him. Hell, I even voted for a Catholic in 1926!" (Al Smith of New York).

Growing up in rural South Georgia in the 1950s, there was nothing to be other than a Democrat, according to Hamp. I never saw a Republican (and only saw a couple of Catholics) back then. I guess there was *one* Republican, a local businessman in Albany. When I was a young boy, I often rode with my father down to the post office to get his business mail on Saturday morning. On one trip, when I was about ten or twelve, Daddy stopped and pointed to a well-dressed man crossing the street and said, "Take a good look at that man because you may never see another one. His name is Russ Kaliher, and he is a Republican." Mr. Kaliher looked pretty normal to me. But the way my father acted, he might've had a sixth finger on one hand or possibly a third nipple on his chest. Poor Russ Kaliher was a freak for sure—a Republican in South Georgia!

Following the Civil War and the bitter period of Reconstruction— which disenfranchised white southern loyalists to punish the South for its insubordination—each southern state created some sort of device to keep political control firmly in the hands of white men living in the rural areas and to discourage black participation in the vote. And just in case, the Ku Klux Klan, born out of the pain and suffering of Reconstruction, eliminated the race mixers and those opposing the system who occasionally reared their heads—you could find them later twisting at the end of a rope.

In Georgia, the system devised to keep rural whites on top was an indirect method of voting in statewide elections called the county unit system. In contests for statewide office, each county in Georgia was assigned a number of county unit votes depending on its population. But the allocation grossly exaggerated the voting strength of the rural counties and greatly understated the voting strength of the cities, generally, and Atlanta in particular. For example, in 1952, the smallest county in Georgia—Baker County, with 300 registered voters—cast two county unit votes in statewide elections, while Fulton County (the city of Atlanta) had about 150,000 registered voters but only eight county unit votes. With 159 counties, 95 percent of them small and rural, the overwhelming political power to determine who would be U.S. Senator, governor, as well as other statewide offices in Georgia lay in the hands of white voters in small rural counties.

Through most of the 1930s and 1940s, Eugene Talmadge was the dominant force in Georgia politics. Talmadge was a pure product of the county unit system, allowing him to play to the interests of rural white Georgians in the 1930s and 1940s, well after World War II, with the commencement of a steady migration of people from the farms—white and black—seeking industrial and service jobs in Atlanta and regional cities like Albany. Gene Talmadge's son, Herman, served as governor and went on to serve four terms in the U.S. Senate.

The county unit system made kingpins of wealthy farmers and local politicians in those rural areas—people like Hamp—who could control the votes in their small counties. Local "bosses" in Georgia's four smallest counties could offset the entire Atlanta vote for some other, usually more progressive, candidate.

Later, I came to understand that Eugene Talmadge was only a discount version of a more prominent and more colorful southern demagogue— Louisiana's governor, and later U.S. Senator and presidential candidate, Huey Long. Talmadge's campaign was light on populism—which was at the core of Long's appeal to working people—but heavy on racism. When campaigning, "Old Gene" wore the blue bib overalls of the farmer. When he dressed up, Old Gene wore brown working pants, a white shirt, boots, and red suspenders. Old Gene put his hands back against his chest and hooked his thumbs under the red suspenders, pulling them out occasionally and popping them to emphasize a point when making speeches. A shock of black hair fell across his brow as his head shook, and he gestured with his hands, slapping one against the other for emphasis, occasionally pausing long enough to brush the hair out of his eyes. Gene Talmadge was a spellbinding orator, and his message was plain, unequivocal, and consistent. He would certainly earn points from modern political pundits for staying on message.

For politicians campaigning in the 1930s and 1940s, before the time of television and even before many rural areas had radios or electricity, the outdoor barbecue was the staple of southern politics. Several days before an appearance, Talmadge supporters distributed fliers throughout an area, and a new-fangled speaker truck might come through some favorite local gathering spot blasting: "Come hear Old Gene Talmadge, the farmers' friend, speak Saturday afternoon."

Speaking from the back of a pickup truck or sometimes perched on bales of hay or cotton in the back of a larger flatbed truck, Old Gene, with the audience clapping and shouting all along, began the common refrain that had become his trademark: "The working man in Georgia has got three great friends," he would drawl, holding the last syllables of each word for emphasis: "Jesus Christ, the Sears Roebuck catalog, and Old Gene Talmadge!" The crowd clapped and yelled wildly. The men wearing their farm hats—called wool hats—whooped and waved them round and round over their heads in the air. "The working man in Georgia has got three common enemies," Talmadge said, pausing to sneer, "Nigger, nigger, nigger," dragging the words out at the end so as to fully enjoy their sound and the reaction. The crowd went wild.

This refrain of Old Gene's was so well known that the crowds usually joined in—particularly for the last part—spitting out the words "nigger, nigger, nigger" with disdain, as raucous laughter swept the crowd.

My grandfather Hamp, for a number of years, led the Democratic political opposition to the Talmadge machine—not on the core race issue but on issues of education and economic development. Make no mistake: Hamp was a strict segregationist. But he was not a hater or shouter. In 1933, Hamp was elected president of the Georgia senate (equivalent today to the position of lieutenant governor).

"Hamp should have been governor," I heard his friends say time and time again behind his back. They all said the same thing: "When Hamp McWhorter tells you something, you can take it to the bank. Hamp is a man with no enemies." Occasionally, one of his visitors would say it straight on. This compliment always brought a smile to Hamp's face. Sometimes he would chuckle as he protested, "Nope, nope, nope. My time is past . . . that just isn't in the cards."

And, indeed, it never happened. As a youngster, I often wondered why, as I had heard so many people say this. Was it because he was not a true and blue "Talmadge man"? No, I was told, there were "other things" that I just would not understand. It was years later before anyone would reveal to me what those "other things" were.

Lexington Reflections

Many years after that first viewing of *Gone with the Wind*, I realized that the film provided a context for understanding life on Hamp's farm back in the 1950s. Just like in the movie, every move, gesture, and utterance of Henry, Old Black George, and Annie was obsequious and seemed to affirm their supposed inferiority.

Nearly a hundred years after the end of the Civil War, and ostensibly the end of slavery, life on Hamp's farm was still only one half step removed: a group of poor and illiterate blacks—living in Hamp's housing, farming his land, and eating the food they grew on that land—were totally dependent on a white landowner (in this instance, a benevolent one) for their every want and need in life. These people were trapped in an economic system that arguably met their most basic needs but actively discouraged and prevented them from getting an education, keeping them tied to the land for mere survival.

During my youth, I was made to believe that my grandfather, his family, and his generation were as much slaves to this political and economic system—designed to "keep the Nigras in their place"—as were Annie, Henry, Old Black George, and their families. The enormous amount of time, resources, and effort spent defending, justifying, and maintaining segregation only served to limit the economic growth and political and cultural development of Hamp's beloved Georgia and the South.

The amount of change that has taken place would not merely surprise Hamp—it probably would positively overwhelm him. The promise of equality that Jefferson and Adams wrote about in the Declaration of Independence in the late eighteenth century was only beginning to be realized in the segregated South two hundred years later. These changes in attitude about race also stimulated other disadvantaged groups to seek their own justice and opened the door to the tolerance and acceptance of all peoples—even for people of different sexual orientations, a tolerance beyond just about anyone's wildest imagination in South Georgia in the 1950s and 1960s of my boyhood. We kids were encouraged to keep blinders on about such topics, and I ignored the ugly injustices of the world for about as long as I could. But the truth had its way of finding me—even if it was roundabout.

Time Magazine

When I got home from school on my ninth birthday, I made a beeline to the mailbox, hoping to find some presents or perhaps a fat birthday check from Mur and Hamp—usually ten dollars, since there weren't any toy stores in tiny Lexington for gifts for their grandchildren. Ten bucks would buy me a new football and leave enough for fifteen or twenty movies at the Albany or the State Theaters with popcorn and Coke.

I was disappointed to find nothing from Lexington, but I was surprised to get a letter addressed to "Hamilton McWhorter Jordan" and postmarked "New York City." I had never gotten a letter from New York before, so I opened it while still standing there at the mailbox. It was a typed letter from the editor of *Time* magazine to me. The first paragraph congratulated me and went on to inform me that "Mr. and Mrs. Hamilton McWhorter" had given me a one-year subscription to *Time* magazine. I was thrilled to get my very first subscription and mightily impressed that this important man would write to me all the way from New York City! Over dinner, Mama explained what a subscription actually meant. Every single week for a year, she said, I would get a new issue of *Time*. Daddy doubted out loud whether a nine-year-old would really appreciate an adult current events magazine.

Daddy was dead wrong.

Getting *Time* every week was a big deal to me, and it became a highly important ritual. When I got out of school every Tuesday afternoon, I could hardly contain my excitement as I stopped at the mailbox to find *my* magazine with *my* very own name neatly printed on the address label and usually some famous person's picture on the cover. (The first magazine I received had a cover story about Lewis Strauss, who was the first head of the Atomic Energy Commission.)

I couldn't wait to devour the magazine and, starting with the "Current Events" section, I proudly thumbed through the pages on the walk back to the house. It seemed nothing short of a miracle that this special magazine showed up in our mailbox every Tuesday with *my* name on it. Someone somewhere, it seemed, had written this magazine—chock-full of stories and juicy tidbits about politics and people—just for me. There were times, however, when my father objected to his young son reading *Time*, like when Dr. Alfred Kinsey, the "sex scientist," was featured on the cover. That same week, Kinsey was denounced as a "sex maniac" from the pulpit of the First Baptist Church by Dr. Leonard Stevens, who waved that same issue of *Time* magazine I had received with Kinsey's picture on the front.

Although Hamp thought that *Time* was too liberal and admittedly an unusual gift for a kid, he defended his choice, saying, "My grandson's got politics in his blood. He needs to keep up with the news!"

Ever since Uncle Bill gave Mur and Hamp that first television set in 1951, my grandparents both surprisingly became immediate and huge fans. Mur praised the educational value of some shows, and Hamp loved the news programs focusing on politics and public issues. Subsequently,

Politics in My Blood 45

Hamp soon bought brand-new RCA television sets for all of his children—or, more accurately, for his grandchildren. Mama said among our immediate family that all of Hamp's grandchildren benefited from something he was particularly trying to do for me.

In 1954, the first television station in Albany began broadcasting. WALB-TV was an NBC affiliate owned by the Gray family, who also owned the *Albany Herald*. At Hamp's urging, I started watching *Meet the Press*, hosted by a funny-looking man with a funny name—Lawrence Spivak—who asked questions of his guests, usually some politicians or famous people in the news.

Although launched in 1952, NBC's *Today Show*—on early in the morning on weekdays—only started to get ratings when a chimpanzee by the name of J. Fred Muggs came on as "cohost" to lighten up their stuffy news agenda. Women were almost invisible and only on air as "weather girls"; one of the most popular was a young New Yorker by the name of Barbara Walters. Long minutes of the *Today Show* were just music and pictures of fans waving at the moving television camera through the window at Rockefeller Center while towns, temperatures, and forecasts scrolled down the television screen.

In the morning, I sat in our small black-and-white tiled kitchen at the yellow breakfast table, drank a big glass of orange juice, and watched the *Today Show* while Mama cooked our favorite—cheese and eggs with bacon. When Mama was in a hurry, Lawton and I would eat either Corn Flakes or Rice Krispies, pouring milk into the little individual wax paper–lined boxes that served as bowls.

Palmyra Elementary was two blocks away, and unless it was raining, Lawton and I walked by ourselves down Fourth to Slappey, where an orange-vested police officer would stop traffic while we crossed the street and walked the last block to the school.

Hamp bragged to his friends that his young namesake—already following the *Today Show* and reading *Time* regularly at such a young age—was truly hooked on politics. Much of my grandfather's pride came, of course, from the fact that he had been largely responsible for the hooking. I think he saw possibility in me—the potential to venture the path down which he believed he was not welcome.

Chapter Four

■ ■ ■

THE FACTS OF LIFE

At the Post Office

Long-distance phone-to-phone calls were very expensive in the 1950s, and person-to-person calls cost twice as much. For that reason, Daddy got his good news and bad news from the post office, and on most Saturdays, I went with him. I rode in Daddy's lap to the post office, where he checked P.O. Box 1247 for mail from the insurance company's home office before heading down to his own office on the second floor of a two-story building on Pine Avenue right across from the courthouse.

After checking 1247, Daddy would find an excuse to go to the open window where Mr. Bob Pharis, a blind man, would be standing erect behind the window ready to sell stamps and envelopes to his customers. My first visits to see Mr. Pharis frightened me. He was a tall man with a big head on top of huge shoulders and a deep voice, and his eyes constantly flicked open and shut as I stood by Daddy's side with my hand grasped tightly in his. And when Mr. Pharis kept his eyes open for any length of time, the blind man's eyes rolled around in his head like he had no control over them. He reminded me of one of the scary characters in the picture show at the Liberty Theater, which played to a packed house of screaming kids every Saturday morning for a dime's cost of admission. Mama wouldn't let me go to see those horror shows after one bad weekend, when a Saturday feature left me so scared that I wet the bed and couldn't sleep for several nights!

Mr. Pharis took his job very seriously and executed it with perfection. While smiling and making small talk with his customers, he would effortlessly reach to grab prepaid envelopes and stamps (first class was one cent, and air mail was six cents), collect his customer's payment, and quickly dip his large hands into a worn cloth pouch that hung from his waist to retrieve the exact combination of coins to complete the transaction. When he handed the change back to his customer, he often offered a friendly challenge: "Catch my mistake, and the stamps are yours free."

Daddy said he had been in to see Mr. Pharis a million times and that he had never even once caught him in a mistake. I don't think anybody in all of Albany had.

About once a month, Daddy would stop at the bakery on the way to work or at the Coke machine at the post office and buy Mr. Pharis a doughnut or a Coke, which he would hand to the man with his stamp order. Without fail, Mr. Pharis gently protested, saying that Daddy shouldn't have done that, and then ask, "Mr. Jordan, what do I owe you?" as he reached into his pouch.

And Daddy would say something like, "From a satisfied customer," or "From one friend to another."

Then, Mr. Pharis would flash his pleasant smile, feel gently around the countertop for the Coke or doughnut, and quickly put it underneath the counter so that he could continue to conduct business.

Mr. Pharis must have had several hundred regular customers; he could recognize all of their voices. And if someone new came into the post office, he would listen to the unfamiliar voice and say something like, "I don't believe I have had the pleasure," and thrust his large paw forward in search of the stranger's hand, finding it and shaking it gently. He and the newcomer would exchange pleasantries, and at the next visit, the blind man would confidently call the new customer's name.

When he heard Daddy's voice and said his customary, "Good morning, Mr. Jordan," I could see him turn his head to the side so he could hear everything. If he had heard footsteps with Daddy, he would ask, "Is that Hamilton with you today?"

Sometimes, I tried to time my steps so that my feet would hit the shiny granite floor at exactly the same instant as Daddy's, hoping to sneak up on our blind friend and surprise him. Remarkably, he would greet us, saying, "Good morning Mr. Jordan," and, delaying an instant as a smile crept onto his face, "and Hamilton," with emphasis on my name.

Daddy would laugh out loud and kid me: "You can't fool Mr. Pharis, Hamilton!"

As a little boy, I realized from carefully watching Mr. Pharis that I was wrong about first impressions. Heck, he could change money without looking, tell one voice from two hundred others, and even catch me trying to walk in time with Daddy. For my money, Mr. Pharis was a genius and might have been the smartest man in all of Aw-ben-ny!

Daddy's Office

Daddy's office sat above Crowe's Drug Store on the second floor of a small two-story building called the Eatman Building. After driving down the alley, Daddy would park in the back, and we would walk up the dark stairs to the second floor. There was no elevator. I usually hung around for a while, banging on the Royal typewriter and exploring a large metal cabinet filled with tablets, gem clips, office supplies, and my father's "bag of tricks": a bunch of promotion and sales gimmicks he handed out to potential customers. For his established customers, there were "Life of Virginia" pen sets with the policyholders' names etched in gold, as well as beautiful calendars featuring the Natural Bridge of Virginia, which the locals proudly called "the eighth wonder of the world."

It was fun playing with the typewriter, typing out my name and address and learning to make copies as I typed. For this, I got several pieces of white paper, put the icky carbon in between them, typed, and checked to see if the copy came through. I learned that if I tried to make four or five copies, I had to strike the keys very hard or the fourth copy would begin to fade. I also learned that if I made a mistake, I had to go back and correct it on each of the copies, which, of course, was time consuming. So, whenever I screwed up, I would simply throw the copies away and start over. Although I could only hunt and peck at first, I actually learned to type well over time.

When I got a bit older, Daddy would take a break from phone calls and paperwork, come out of his little office in the back, reach down deep in his pocket, and drop the loose change into my hand. Normally it was mostly pennies, but sometimes there was a nickel or even a dime, and on a lucky day, a quarter might get away.

"I am not as good at this as Bob Pharis."

Clutching Daddy's spare change, I would race downstairs to Crowe's Drug Store as if they were going to run out of Cokes before I got there. Crowe's had one of the first automatic Coke machines in town. It was only a refrigerated metal box that opened from the top, but Cokes in green tinted bottles dangled from metal racks. After you put a nickel in, you grabbed the Coke by its cap and then guided it to the corner, where you could pull it out. There was only one kind of Coke back then, and it was delicious. If I had another nickel, I would buy a pack of Tom's salted peanuts, tear off the corner of the cellophane wrapper, and pour them into the Coke bottle. Then, after putting my thumb on top and shaking the bottle up and down until the cola nearly fizzed over, I would drink the sweet, salty, and bubbly soda, holding back and saving the peanuts in the side of my mouth. I savored those soggy morsels at the end, chewing slowly and enjoying every bite.

Sometimes, one of the young druggists would challenge me to play "far away." On the bottom of each Coke was the name of the town where the soda had been bottled. When you challenged someone to "far away," the person holding the bottle from farthest away won, and the loser had to pay for both Cokes. When three or four or more played, the losers each had to pay the winner a nickel.

More often than not, the Coke bottles had "Albany, Ga." written on them and had been made just down the street. The winning bottle might be from nearby Americus or Valdosta or Macon or even distant Atlanta.

Palmyra Pharmacy

While Crowe's had an okay comic book stand and a good Coke machine, there was no drugstore anywhere as good as Palmyra Pharmacy, which, fortunately for me, was on the corner of Slappey and Third—two blocks from our house.

Palmyra had a full selection of comic books that stretched all the way across the front of the store. Along one side of the store was a soda fountain lined with red vinyl stools that squeaked when you spun them around and six or eight red booths that held four comfortably but often had six kids squeezed into them. Most kids who wanted drinks, shakes, and sundaes sat at the fountain, while those at the booths ate hot dogs, hamburgers, and fries.

Until I was eight years old, I could only go to Palmyra Pharmacy with my older brother, Lawton. Mama stood on the porch and watched as Lawton held my hand and we started down Fourth Avenue. We'd continue for a few houses before cutting over to the alley between Third

and Fourth, which then took us up to Slappey Drive, where Palmyra
Pharmacy sat on the corner. Lawton looked back to wave goodbye to
Mama and then, when he was sure that she was no longer watching, he
would drop my hand and walk ahead. As we walked up the alley, we
often saw other boys playing in their yards, climbing trees, or tossing
a football or baseball; girls played hopscotch on lines drawn in the dirt
alley. Around dinnertime, you might see a car in the alley when the dads
came home from work, but it was rare to have to stop a football game
or hopscotch to step aside and let a car pass.

Once we passed Jack and Jill's Kindergarten and the Hudgens house,
Lawton and I came to the corner, where we took a left and walked past
Hutto's 5 & 10 and into the door of Palmyra Pharmacy. It was the biggest
thing in my life for much of my boyhood. Where else could you get
comic books, the latest toys, candy, baseball cards, great vanilla Cokes,
and chocolate shakes? It had everything I could possibly want!

Usually we were sent there on some mission—to get a prescription
filled or pick up something Mama needed. She almost always gave
us each a nickel but entrusted mine to Lawton. On special occasions,
she might even give us a dime or a quarter for one of their thick milk
shakes, served with a big pile of whipped cream on top and crowned
with a bright red cherry. Most kids would eat the cherry first thing,
but I always put it aside on a napkin. Only after I had sucked every
drop of the chocolate milk shake—signaled by the hissing noise of the
air in my straw—would I lift the cherry up by the stem, suck it dry of
every bit of sweet juice, and then put the whole thing into my mouth,
chewing ever so slowly to prolong the flavor and joy of the milk shake
for as long as possible.

But Palmyra Pharmacy was also serious business—helping people
with their health needs. "Dr. Durham," the head pharmacist, looked
just like an actor in the movies who was playing the role of a doctor.
In a lot of ways, he did play the role of doctor, doling out advice and
medications to the people of Albany. Wearing a white medical jacket
with "Dr. Durham" stitched over the pocket, he had silver gray hair
combed straight back; a quick and pleasant smile; black, wire-rimmed
glasses; and often a cigar hanging from his mouth. Standing behind
the elevated counter across the back of the drug store, the pharmacist
would peer into every nook and corner of the store. Customers—mostly
women—looking for something had only to pause for a second or say

"Dr. Durham" out loud, and he would quickly be down on the floor, helping them to find the right laxative, deodorant, notebook paper, or box of candy.

Lawton would always stop at the front of the store to read comic books, sending me to the back with Mama's prescription or a little note to Dr. Durham, asking for his advice or help. I had to stand tall on my tiptoes to reach high enough to slide the message or prescription onto the elevated counter, where Dr. Durham and his young associate, Dr. Dupree, worked. While waiting to have the prescription filled, I would usually wander back toward the comic book stand and take a good long look before deciding between a Superman comic, a vanilla Coke, or maybe even a giant chocolate shake if I had a whole quarter.

Dr. Durham was much, much more than just a pharmacist. People came in describing their aches, pains, and maladies, and Dr. Durham would usually respond with the classic, "I have got just what the doctor ordered," as if he were the doctor himself. But if he suspected that one of his customers had something serious going on that merited a visit to a real doctor, he would encourage them to seek medical help, often offering his opinion as to which physician was best for their ailment. Dr. Durham was one of the first people Mama called when Helen's legs started hurting—from what we would later find out was polio.

More times than not, when Lawton and I went to Palmyra, Mama would have to call Dr. Durham to ask if we were still there, requesting that he tell us that it was time to head home. We might hang around for a few extra minutes, but the combination of Mama's call and Dr. Durham's stare got us out the door swiftly.

Crazy Legs

When I was growing up in the Deep South, football was king. And for the first many years of my active boyhood, I was forced to sit on the sidelines in the sport I had come to love as much as Daddy and Hamp did. Even though I was walking much better over the years due to the help of my embarrassing yet effective metal leg braces, Mama still wouldn't let me play organized sports because of the continued warnings of my leg doctor.

The doctor's office was all the way down in Jacksonville, Florida, and we visited him once every year since I began walking so that he could examine the growth and progress of my bowed legs and flat feet. I didn't understand why we had to drive those long hours down to Florida when there was a perfectly good family doctor in Albany, but Mama explained to me that my leg doctor was a specialist who was very good at helping little boys like me get better at walking and running. If I wanted to be able to continue to get better at running like the other boys, Mama said, it would do me best to see the finest doctor around.

I guessed she was right.

Over the years, I came to begrudgingly respect the man, at least happy that he was doing whatever was possible to fix my legs—even if I hated those long drives and the uncomfortable, embarrassing braces even more. However, with each passing year, my heart always sank when he put the red light on the possibility of my playing organized sports. He was happy with my progress but said the same thing on each of our annual trips to Jacksonville—"Not yet, not yet. Let's wait one more year and see how his legs are developing."

While my classmates and buddies nearby were playing Little League baseball and official "Midget" football, I was left to organize make-shift games in the neighborhood—mostly tackle football—which we usually played in my backyard because we had a double lot. There were pickup games most fall afternoons when the other kids did not otherwise have real football practice, homework, or chores. My friends who played league football had formal coaching and a more in-depth knowledge of proper techniques than I did, but I had the single peculiar advantage of being accustomed to hitting and being hit without a uniform, shoulder pads, or helmet. Plus, I was a "gimp" with something to prove.

Fortunately, the years of daily exercises had made my young legs muscular and quick. I was still pigeon-toed enough to have earned the nickname "Duck" in the neighborhood, and my friends quacked loudly whenever I ran with the ball. But those bowed legs were strong.

One day after watching us kids play tackle football in our yard, my father observed over dinner that it might be safer and better for me to be playing football in an organized league than what I was doing in our yard most afternoons. "Have you ever noticed how physical they are?" he asked my mother, adding with a touch of pride, "Hamilton usually runs all over the other kids . . . even the bigger ones!"

After enduring much pleading, my mother agreed to bring this up with my doctor on our next visit to Jacksonville. She told him that I was rough-housing in the backyard anyway and asked if I could go out for Midget football in the fifth grade. Midget football was the brainchild of the famous Pop Warner, who had once coached at the University of Georgia and then started a football league for young boys—known today by the more politically correct title of Pop Warner leagues. My doctor reluctantly agreed to let me play.

Whereas most of my friends and classmates had already been playing for a couple of years, it was a big deal for me to be joining an organized team. Instead of wearing shorts or blue jeans, I had a real uniform, pads, and a jersey for my team—the Sharks—with my very own number. Most important, I had real football shoes with cleats instead of my clunky orthopedic shoes. I doubt if any kid was more excited or brought more intensity to the football field that first day than I did.

Because I was stocky and aggressive, the coach played me at defensive tackle. I learned that by being naturally aggressive, playing tough, and—most important—*acting* tough, that I intimidated the other players, and they were less inclined to take me on. I would constantly hustle, hustle, hustle for just a chance to tackle the ball carrier or sack the quarterback. After waiting for years to play, I was living my dream and did not *ever* want to lose; quickly, I became the leading tackler on our defense. I had never seen my daddy so proud.

One afternoon, when our best running back missed practice, the coach asked me if I would like to fill in for the absent player during a scrimmage scheduled with another team. It sounded like a great idea, but I got off to a terrible start, fumbling the handoff from the quarterback the first two times he called my play. After that second fumble, I could only figure I was finished as a runner.

When I returned to the huddle, most of my teammates just glared at me. One of the big guys ordered, "Hamilton, hang onto that ball."

I apologized to my teammates and—looking the quarterback in the eye—begged him to give me just one more chance.

It looked for a while that my apology had gone unnoticed, because the quarterback waited a number of plays before eventually calling the number for my play—for which he would lateral the football to me and I would run the ball wide to the right. When he pitched me the ball, I practically stopped dead in my tracks—determined not to fumble again—until I had that pigskin firmly in my grasp. Tucking it under my arm, I ran wide and deep to the right. But that instant of stopping to catch the lateral allowed a gang of defensive players to close in on me. Then I heard the coach yelling, "Run *up* the field, son! Run *up* the field! Don't run backwards!"

By this time, the defense was hot on my tail. I saw two or three guys waiting in front of me and heard the huffing and puffing of the other players chasing me from behind, getting closer and closer, so I made a sharp cut back against the grain and went the other way, running even wider and deeper to avoid the pursuers. By this time, I must have been at least twenty yards behind the line of scrimmage.

The coach went ballistic. "DON'T GO BACKWARDS," he yelled. And then, finally, "JUST STOP, FALL DOWN, SON, FALL DOWN!" he pleaded.

Then I figured that since I already was seconds away from the end of my career as a running back and since surrender was unacceptable, what did I have to lose? So I cut back one last time in the opposite direction. By now, the coach had stopped yelling and was just pacing the sidelines, probably muttering profanities under his breath. He'd given up on me.

But a funny thing happened. After this third deep and wide cut on the field, the hefty lineman fell farther and farther behind. Certain that I was about to be taken down for a huge loss by somebody, most of the defensive players stopped chasing me and were catching their breath or just running slowly. I was tired, too, but, more than anybody else, I was running on emotion, built up over years of being on the sidelines, unable to play. When I looked up field, there were only two or three defensemen standing between the goal and me.

I finally did what the coach had told me to do a minute earlier—I turned up field and headed toward the goal.

Out of breath and too tired to try to sidestep the defensemen— "juke 'em" is what we called it—I went right at them, just as I had done so many times in my backyard. The first kid saw me coming and tried to tackle me high by wrapping his arms around my arms, and so I just lowered my head, put my helmet into his chest, and heard him grunt out loud as I ran right over him, stumbling and almost tripping on his leg. But I didn't fall. Instead, I kept on running and was back to the original line of scrimmage!

I ran for another fifteen or twenty yards before two defensive backs hit me on about the five-yard line. They tackled me at the same time, one grabbing me high around the shoulders and the other around my waist. I paused like I often did in our backyard games—as if I were stopped and going down—just long enough for them to relax. Then I leaned all my body weight forward, started churning my legs up and down, pumping as hard as I could, and pushed with all my might until I stumbled across the goal line with both defensive backs hanging on.

It was only a scrimmage, but it was the greatest moment of my young life. My teammates swarmed around, slapping me on the helmet and on the shoulders. The coach flashed me a big smile of relief and then sent me right back on the field to play defense on the kickoff.

Coach probably thought my first run was a fluke, and so when we got the ball back, he sent in a play that ran me right up the middle. They were ready for me this time and gang-tackled me—but only after I had gained four or five yards. They gave me the ball again, and I ran right off center for another good gain and a first down. And the half was over.

In the second half, all the defensive players were gunning for me. Their coach was yelling, "Hit him low, hit him low!" The running got a lot tougher, but I loved every second of it! It was a great day, but not a perfect one—we lost the scrimmage. But in my debut as a running back, I had scored a touchdown and run for thirty or forty more yards. "Pretty good for a cripple," I thought to myself.

Daddy was so excited by my performance that he wanted to call my orthopedist in Jacksonville that very night and tell him about my success on the football field. But Mama was glad he could not reach him, saying that there was no reason to rub it in, because she knew the doctor still had reservations about my playing football with "those legs."

As word spread among my buddies about my success as a runner, my neighborhood nickname, Duck, reached one of my Midget football teammates. Pretty soon, whenever I had a good run, my teammates on the sidelines started making quacking noises. I never said anything about it because I knew that would only make the teasing worse. I didn't like people making fun of the way I ran, but I guess I was at least proud to have my very own noise.

At the end of the season, over the Thanksgiving holidays, I was selected to go to the Midget Bowl in Columbus, Georgia, as a member of the Albany All-Star Team for my age group. As the third-string fullback behind an older, bigger, and much better player, I didn't get into the game until the fourth quarter when we were losing by five touchdowns and the coach was just trying to get all of our players into the game.

On my very first play in the Midget Bowl, I was excited to hear the quarterback call my play—thirty-six—fullback off tackle. I was all hot and ready to run over the other team just like I did in our backyard. The moment I got the ball, a huge kid, who was faster and stronger than anyone I had played against in my backyard or in our league, broke through the blockers and hit me so hard around the midsection that I flew through the air backwards and landed with a "thud" on the ground, my right leg bent backwards under me. When I hit, I heard a popping noise. It felt like someone had chopped off my right leg.

I was in tremendous pain and was gasping for air but held back the tears until they put me in the makeshift school ambulance. I cried all the way to the hospital, not only because my leg hurt but also because I knew what my mama and doctor were going to say.

After taking an X-ray to be sure there was nothing broken, the ER doctor said that I had suffered a torn ligament and gave me some pain-killers. I sat on the backseat of the team bus with my leg wrapped up. I quietly cried myself to sleep on the two-hour drive home.

After reviewing the X-rays of my swollen leg and its torn ligament, my orthopedist called from Jacksonville several days later to give my mother very specific instructions for taking care of me during my recovery—including some exercises for me to do. Daddy got on the phone to ask the doctor if I would be able to play football next season. The orthopedist responded that I could play, if I wanted to be a cripple for the rest of my life, adding that if I continued to play after this injury, we could also find another doctor.

My father and mother waited a couple of weeks before they told me the bad news. I was terribly disappointed but not surprised. My football days were over.

Mama was right . . . I was going to have to find some other way than football to shine.

Daddy Buys a Sports Car

One of Daddy's great passions in life was cars. And while Daddy's love affair with the automobile was passed along to my older brother, I did not share it. Sure, cars were cool and a big part of teenage life, but I was primarily interested in them as a way to get girls—and to try to someday turn mine into a "bedroom on wheels," or at least a place to make out.

My father loved trading cars and was always trying to convince my mother that each and every trade was a good business deal. His favorite line was, "Adelaide, he made me such a good offer that we could not afford not to buy that car," couching his purchase as a good decision for the family. My mother would usually either flash a knowing smile or roll her eyes at us when Daddy was not looking. She often said that since he loved people, loved cars, and loved to talk, Daddy should have been a used car salesman.

A lot of Sunday afternoons, after going to Sunday school and church, followed by a lunch at Davis Brothers Cafeteria, we'd drop Mama off at home and spend hours riding up and down Slappey Drive, looking at all of the used car lots and making frequent stops so Daddy could inquire about any new arrivals that caught his eye.

Sometimes, Daddy would have a series of trades, one dependent on another. He would take a used car from one car lot for a spin and take it to another used car lot. Daddy would never lie to them—that wasn't his way. But he wouldn't tell them the whole truth either and let them believe that the car he was driving was his own. Daddy would have already identified a car that he was interested in at this second lot and see what kind of advantage he could gain through a multiple trade, swap, or sale. Usually, these deals would not work out, but occasionally, Daddy would succeed in trading up through his various maneuvers.

By the time I had started driving, my mother had a white 1956 Chevrolet, and I preferred to take it out—particularly on dates—to our other car. When I was younger, Daddy had bought Mama a used turquoise-and-white Buick Special. I will always believe he bought that car just because it had electric windows. I never will forget the day that he brought that Buick home, and the word spread through the neighborhood that Dick Jordan had a car with electric windows. We spent so much time that afternoon showing off the electric windows to the neighbors that the driver's side window broke and was stuck in the down position. My easy-going and lovable father was embarrassed and mad.

A thunderstorm passed through town that night, and I learned over breakfast the next morning that Daddy had gotten up in the middle of the night and taped cardboard over the open window. That was the one and only car with electric windows that Daddy ever bought.

In 1956, when I was in the eighth grade, Daddy called home and told Mama that he was on the way home and had bought a "foreign car" from an air force pilot at Turner Field who was being transferred overseas. I knew that cars were not a big deal to Mama (and I didn't care nearly as much about them as the other neighborhood boys), but I couldn't believe that she had forgotten to ask him what model he had acquired! I jumped immediately to the conclusion that this would certainly be a sports car and even a cool convertible that I would take on dates in two years when I got my driver's license. As Lawton and I and several of the neighborhood boys waited in the front yard for Daddy to zoom up, I tried to imagine what it would look like.

An MG—a British car—was pretty cool, and most MGs were convertibles, too. Or could he possibly have wrangled a deal for a Jaguar? They were very expensive, but Daddy was good at getting bargains. Of course, there was the German car, the Mercedes-Benz. I had only seen pictures of them, but I knew they were pricey, too. Daddy would have a hard time convincing Mama that we could afford a Mercedes-Benz.

I was growing increasingly excited as we waited in the front yard for him to get home and for me and my friends to see this wonderful new car. It was almost dark when we heard a beep-beep-beep and saw the small, low lights of a car turn onto Fourth Avenue and begin its way down the hill. When it got closer and I could make out the outline of the car, my heart sank. It looked like one of those little trick cars at the circus in which a clown drives to the center ring, six other clowns pile out, and you're left wondering, "How in the world did they fit all those clowns in that tiny car?"

My father was so excited about this little dark-green car that he stepped out of it, beaming, and looked like he halfway expected applause. Then he went right into a sales pitch, which I suspect was the same one the air force pilot used when he sold it to Daddy earlier that afternoon. To our question of, "What *is* it, Daddy?" he explained that it was a Volkswagen, which was German for "people's car." My brother made him spell it out for us as Lawton got behind the wheel and Daddy walked around the car talking.

Daddy said that in the early 1930s, Adolf Hitler had summoned the famous car designer Ferdinand Porsche and ordered him to build a car with these goals:

- It could be mass produced like the American cars;
- It would be inexpensive and affordable to the average German family;
- It would not require much gas and be reliable transportation; and,
- It would not be fancy, but would instead be the "people's car."

The war ended Hitler's dreams for his people's car, but afterward some German business leaders acquired the prototype designed by Porsche and began to manufacture the small car on a large scale. Cheap and dependable, it sold well in Germany, and in the early 1950s a few began to appear in the United States, brought to America by U.S. soldiers who had been stationed in postwar Germany. It sure looked to me like Porsche had been successful. It was about two years old and had no frills. None. It had no radio and no whitewall tires; there wasn't even a gas gauge on the dashboard. Just a speedometer. Daddy explained that the VW, as he had started calling it, got thirty-five to forty miles per gallon, and if you ran out of gas, you could turn a lever on the gas tank in the front, which opened up the auxiliary tank carrying two gallons of gas, and then you could go another eighty to ninety miles.

"A gas tank in the front?" we asked. Then we got our next surprise.

Daddy was clearly enjoying himself as we gathered around and he opened the front hood to reveal no engine! Instead, there was a spare tire in the front and a gas tank, which held ten to twelve gallons of regular gas, which Daddy quickly calculated would take you 350 to 400 miles before you needed to refill. He beamed with pride as we absorbed all of these amazing facts. For his final act, Daddy gathered us around the back of the car and opened what should have been the trunk. There, finally, was the engine, sputtering quietly and looking more like a lawn mower engine than one belonging to a car.

Daddy particularly liked the fact that every model of the VW was the same—a 1952 looked exactly like a 1953 and 1954!

We all stood there silently. I was happy that Daddy was happy. But we still had a car that looked like a toy. We also had—as far as I could tell—the very first and only Volkswagen on the West side of the Flint River in Albany. It would be years before I would see a second and third

Beetle in Albany. Everywhere we drove, people would stop and point and either yell out, "Look at the bug!" or laugh. While my father got a kick out of the attention he was drawing, I was embarrassed about it and sank even lower in the low seats to avoid being seen. The first couple of days Daddy drove me to Albany Junior High, kids would gawk and gather around our car and question me about it when I got out. On the third or fourth day, I made up some reason for being dropped off at the gym, where fewer kids would see me. I still had to walk an extra block to get to my homeroom, but fewer people saw me in the funny-looking little contraption.

In a few years, there were probably only four or five VWs or Beetles in Albany. But the Big Boys in Detroit were not worried, and Henry Ford II was quoted as calling the VW a "German piece of shit" when one of his executives recommended that Ford buy the German car company. But by 1960, the Beetle was doing so well that the big U.S. auto manufacturers began to take notice, and the next thing we knew, Chevrolet had built its own small car, the Corvair, a flawed vehicle (I know, since I had one), which resulted in many accidents and a generation of lawsuits by a young consumer advocate by the name of Ralph Nader.

Many of my friends my age made buying a car the biggest thing in their lives. One neighbor, Buddy Bethea, worked, scrimped, and saved all through junior high and high school to be able to buy a brand-new, dark-blue Pontiac with tail fins that swept out in back. That car was the envy of every boy in Albany. Another of my friends and classmates, Carey Webb, had one of the biggest paper routes in town and spent every afternoon throwing the *Albany Herald* first from his bike and later from his fire-engine red 1960 Chevrolet Impala. Carey was a nice enough guy, but I always thought that red Chevy was a major factor in his snagging Judy Hightower, a striking blonde, soon to be Miss Albany High and, later, Carey's wife.

While I liked cars in the abstract, I certainly did not want one badly enough to have a paper route like Philip Whitman or Carey Webb, spending several hours every day of the week delivering the *Albany Herald*. A darn car was not more important than sports or girls or fun. So, I guess I got what I probably deserved in the eleventh grade: a ten-year-old Simca Aronde station wagon that my friends promptly and properly named "the blue turd." With a bad paint job, a tinny body, an engine with no pickup, and doors and windows that didn't close tight or fit right, it wasn't much of a car.

Sex and Cigs

Sex. I can't remember the first time I heard an adult say the word. Maybe it was in seventh grade, when Albany Junior High's P.E. teacher Coach "Big Bob" Fowler screened a "health education" film for my junior high class. Boys and girls were to watch the notorious film separately. If a particular parent didn't want their own little Susie or Johnny learning about "such things," they could request their child be excused from the screening. But on the day I saw the film, few boys were missing.

At six foot ten, Coach Fowler was the biggest man I had ever seen. He was very popular with the students. The morning of the film screening, however, Big Bob had a very serious look on his usually playful face. It took only one sharp blast on the silver whistle around his neck to get all of us boys—who were sitting on the shiny wood floor of the junior high gym and chatting—to pay close attention.

Coach Fowler told us that the film we were about to see was very important—and he meant it. You could hear a pin drop as the lights went out in that gym. The old projector started whirring, throwing a black-and-white picture up on the screen. What unfolded was a confusing and frightening introduction to sexuality. The film was hosted by a stern-looking man with wavy gray hair wearing a white medical jacket and sitting behind a desk in a small office. Looking up from his paperwork and straight into the camera, our host advised that while America faces a lot of external threats—"international Communism" being the main one—the American family faces internal threats that are just as dangerous. One of those threats, he tells us, is "sexual misbehavior." According to the good doctor's word, any kind of adolescent sexual behavior was "misbehavior" and deemed strictly off-limits for respectable, healthy teenagers. This included a practice he called "heavy petting." (Was that like petting a dog, I wondered? A buddy explained that one later.)

Our host condemned the evils of adolescent sexuality while playing several different roles: a doctor (explaining that sex was "dangerous to your health," introducing a series of revolting and disturbing slides that exhibited grisly cases of "VD"), a lawyer (warning us that sex between minors is *illegal* in most states and punishable by jail time), and finally, a preacher (warning that sex was a sinful practice and that good teenagers should "save themselves" by remaining abstinent until marriage). The man finished his speech by advising young people to take their questions about kissing or sex to a trusted adult—"your physical education teacher, your school counselor, your coach, or your priest or preacher." Parents as a source of information or advice were not recommended by the good doctor—nor even mentioned.

The film ended with a series of shots of wholesome white American teenagers—well-groomed boys in varsity letter jackets and freshly scrubbed girls in pleated skirts that fell halfway down their calves—reading familiar Bible verses out loud to one another with upbeat music playing in the background.

"Do unto others as they would do unto you."

"Love thy neighbor as thyself."

It was a strangely cheery ending to such a disturbing and frightening film; for if we were to believe what our eyes had just seen, sex was a pretty scary thing. As the credits rolled, the light flashed back on in the gym, and Coach Fowler stepped in front of the screen. He didn't have to use his whistle this time to quiet us down—the film had done that. He quickly asked if there were any questions, pausing only a couple of seconds before dismissing the group of seventh-grade boys. He did not seem any more anxious to answer questions on the film than we were to ask them.

While the film we saw was called a "health education" film, there wasn't much educational about it. It mainly scared and confused the heck out of me, making sex not only mysterious but also dangerous and bad. Fear mongering—a looming theme of my adolescence.

The Birds and the Bees

While that "health education film" was probably the first time I ever heard an adult mention the word "sex," I had learned quite a bit about it—actually more than I wanted to know—a couple of years earlier.

One rainy Sunday afternoon, I was sitting with my good friend Eddie Mays, in Mama's green-and-white Buick Special—the first car on Fourth Avenue with automatic transmission. The car was parked in our driveway while our parents—also good friends—were visiting inside. I had just turned eleven.

Before the rain got too heavy, I got out of Mama's car, climbed up on the front hood, and pushed the greasy chrome antennae as high up in the sky as it would go so that we could hear Johnny Reb, our favorite local disc jockey. Known for his spontaneous and wild rebel yells, Johnny Reb played top songs from "The Hit Parade" like "Sh-Boom" by the Crew-Cuts ("Sh-boom, sh-boom, la da da da da da, la da da da da da, sh-boom, sh-boom, life could be a dream sweetheart"), "Oh My Pa-pa" by Eddie Fisher ("Oh, my pa-pa, to me he was so wonderful, oh, my pa-pa, to me he was so good"), or "Mr. Sandman" by the Chordettes ("Mr. Sandman, bring me a dream, make him the cutest that I've ever seen").

Although Eddie's father was president of the biggest bank in South Georgia—the C&S Bank—the Mays family lived on a working farm with horses, cows, and chickens. Because of her own rural childhood in Lexington, Mama always said you "grow up fast" on the farm.

She was right.

Heavy rain made it difficult for our parents to see us in the car, so Eddie crawled into the backseat and carefully took out a little plastic bag. At age eleven, Eddie was already sneaking smokes of rabbit tobacco—hand-rolled cigarettes made from a tall scraggly weed with blossoms that grew wild on his farm. Using a quarter page from the *Albany Herald*, Eddie poured out a pile of rabbit tobacco onto the newspaper and bravely rolled a cigarette on the backseat of Mama's car. He then leaned over the front seat and confidently used the car lighter on the dashboard to get the fat, homemade cigarette started. Eddie knew better than to offer me one. I had tried rabbit tobacco once at Eddie's behind the barn and choked on the putrid taste and smell and thrown up while Eddie just watched and laughed. He called me a "city slicker" after that. Indeed, that single experience with rabbit tobacco was the major reason that I never even tried to smoke as a teenager, when all of the boys and some of the girls were experimenting with cigarettes.

I turned my head away from Eddie to avoid both the smell and the memories as he lit up. After taking a big puff on the awful-smelling homemade cigarette and blowing smoke out the open side window out of view of our parents, Eddie casually asked me what I knew about sex.

I told Eddie that I knew just as much about it as *he* did.

"You know how to screw?" he asked.

I lied and told him that of course I did. But I turned stone silent when Eddie challenged me to explain "screwing."

A sly grin came over Edgar's face. He knew he had me. Eddie began to talk about "doing it," enjoying my shock while I tried—and certainly failed—to act cool about it. It was hard to conceal my surprise, though, when he went into grotesque detail about what my mommy and daddy apparently did *every night* after Lawton, Helen, and I went to sleep. I didn't say anything but didn't want to look Eddie in the eye and give him the satisfaction of seeing my discomfort. I just turned away and looked out the other side of the window to think about what I had just heard. I couldn't believe it.

But could it be true? I had a sneaking suspicion that Eddie, who raised calves and chickens on his farm, just might know what he was talking about. After a long silence, thinking about the process Eddie had described in detail, I wondered out loud when my "thing" would get hard, as he had explained happens to my daddy every night? Would it happen on my twenty-first birthday? Or maybe when I was sixteen and old enough to drive a car? Eddie smiled, put his hand over his zipper, and said his "thing" was always getting hard. At that point, I was ready to jump out of the car and get away from Eddie Mays—but it was raining heavily. Plus, I didn't want Eddie to know that he had succeeded in totally freaking me out.

Almost as if to reassure me, Eddie said that "doing it" felt real good for the man. Eddie swore that he was going to "do" somebody just as soon as he could. This was little reassurance, since I was still unable to shake the thought of my parents "doing it" in the way Eddie had described.

■ ■ ■

Later that afternoon, after the rain subsided, I returned home, only to dash upstairs in an attempt to avoid seeing either of my parents. I feigned sickness, yelling to Mama that I didn't feel well and was going to bed early. I couldn't bear to see either Mama or Daddy, for I might be forced to think about the awful things Eddie told me they did every night! I pretended to be asleep in my room, but I lay awake for a long, long time that night.

Learning about the birds and the bees only raised more questions. Eddie could probably answer a lot of them, but I wasn't sure that I wanted him to explain much more to me. I had heard enough weird stuff that day to last me for a long, long time.

Connie

It was only a few months after that talk with Eddie Mays that I got serious about Connie Cordell. Connie and I had been in school together at Palmyra Elementary School, but over the summer leading up to the sixth grade, Connie had gone from being just another girl to looking more . . . grown up. Mama said that Connie was "blossoming early." Whatever it was, I just started thinking more and more about Connie and couldn't take my eyes off of her.

By the social standards of the sixth grade at Palmyra Elementary, Connie was not a "goody-goody." Even though she was a Brownie Scout and active in her Sunday school, Connie Cordell would talk to boys at school and even on the phone. Most important, she was one of a group of girls who would play "spin the bottle" on those rare occasions when boys and girls got together outside of school, usually at birthday parties. (It was a while *after* we started "going out" before I got a peck from Connie, purely by chance and from a lucky spin-of-the-bottle at a birthday party.) Soon after we started "going steady"—celebrated by the exchange of dog tags and my purchase of a "real silver" friendship ring that I got her from Palmyra Pharmacy for $1.13—Connie invited me to go to a picture show. Mrs. Cordell took us to see *Twenty Thousand Leagues under the Sea* at the fancy Albany Theater. Mrs. Cordell surprised us both when she let Connie and me sit by ourselves a few rows in front of her.

We were barely through the opening credits when Connie reached over and grabbed my hand. It happened so quickly that it scared me; I had no idea what to do. I felt my heart racing and her hand clasped firmly in my own. I didn't dare to turn and look at Connie. I was petrified—what would I say or do? Just smile? I stared straight ahead at the movie, trying to absorb this strange thing that she had done.

My first worry was that Mrs. Cordell would be watching us. But when I looked around, I saw the theater was dark, and there was no way she could see us, sitting low in our seats. She might see Connie's black pigtails and my crew cut, but our hands—hanging down between the seats—were invisible to her. More important, I wasn't sure how this handholding was supposed to work and what I was supposed to do—so I just held on and squeezed back. It wasn't long before we both had clammy, sweaty paws. I made an excuse to go get Cokes and slipped into the bathroom, where I washed and dried my hands.

The instant after I returned to the seats and finished my drink, Connie grabbed my hand again then released it a little bit. All of a sudden, I felt fingers from her other hand walking up and down my lowered arm, pausing to stroke my arm. I was shocked, but I also was enjoying it. At some level, I realized that she was a real pro at this and knew more than I did about handholding, so I just started to imitate her moves.

I could feel and almost hear my heart beating faster and faster. One thought that ran through my mind was that this is what sex is all about. I remembered my talk with Eddie Mays. The last thing in the world I wanted was to have a lump in my pants while Connie's mother sat only a few rows back!

It was a long movie, and Connie and I touched hands the whole time, but I was relieved when it was finally over. I'd soon learn from my friends that it was very normal for girls and boys to hold hands—I guessed that the lovely Connie was more of a "goody-goody" than I had originally thought.

■ ■ ■

Along the way, I figured out that whatever I learned about sex was going to be from Eddie Mays, other boys, and from old copies of *Playboy* that some kids were able to sneak from their dads. But it sure was not going to come from my parents.

There was one time, however, when I was thirteen or fourteen that Daddy made a trip upstairs to my bedroom just before I turned out the lights to go to sleep. Daddy was not smiling—my first thought was that I was in trouble for something.

Daddy sat down on the side of my bed and gave me a big hug. Then he pulled back, hemmed and hawed, and finally blurted out something like, "Hamilton, you are getting to be a young man, and, uh, son . . . I just, uh, want you to know . . . that, uh, I am available to talk about girls and anything else you want to know." Daddy's discomfort over the subject matter made me nervous as well. It certainly did not make me want to ask him anything. I had barely thanked him for his offer before Daddy stood quickly, was out the door, and yelled, "Love ya, Ham-toon," as he skipped quickly down the stairs. He was as glad to leave the room and the discomfort of that conversation as I was.

■ ■ ■

This pattern of confusion, ignorance, and misinformation about sex was probably common for most teens in the 1950s—especially in a small southern Georgia town like Albany. It was challenging enough learning the ways of the birds and the bees as a young boy—we were spared the more rapid and dramatic physiological changes that the girls experienced. Thus, the young ladies of Albany had even more confusion on their hands, especially when the only real option for a doctor to help with their "female plumbing" was the firm, abstinence-championing Dr. Phil Robinson.

As many of my female friends later told me, their first period was closely followed by a visit to Dr. Phil, who would explain the workings of their "womanly systems." He would also admonish against the dangers of getting "knocked up," urging all young ladies to "keep their legs shut" and wait until marriage before engaging in any sexual activities. Understanding that not all of his patients were southern angels, Dr. Phil still told all of the young ladies to call him if their periods were late or if they began to feel heavy in their abdomen.

Famously, Dr. Phil would conclude all of his talks, "If you come in here pregnant under twenty-one years of age and expect me to deliver your baby, you better be married, as I did not go to school for ten years to learn to deliver illegitimate babies!" He also said that pregnant girls should only call him to confirm their pregnancy and eventually deliver the child—not to "fix things," as people called it. The girls of Albany had to go elsewhere if they didn't choose to play by Dr. Phil's rules.

Two "Ads" in Albany

Growing up, I really didn't think much about religion.

We regularly attended the First Baptist Church's Sunday school. Unlike "big church," Sunday school was not a total waste of time; I could be with my buddies, whisper gossip about football and girls, tell jokes, and pass notes while some well-meaning adult read Bible verses from the lesson—which none of us had read. Our teacher always tried to apply those lessons from the gospel to our young lives in South Georgia. It never worked.

When we got older, Mama and Daddy would take us after Sunday school to big church, which was just about as much fun as watching grass grow. Every Sunday, we counted the minutes and the seconds until the dull sermon was over. Lawton and I would pass the time by playing tic-tac-toe and passing notes (usually "knock-knock" jokes) written with little wooden pencils on the offering envelopes, which were stuck in a little rack on each dark-wooden pew so that parishioners could, in that emotional moment following the sermon, declare how much money they were going to give God that day. Once the gold-rimmed wooden collection plates had been passed around and filled with pledge envelopes, checks, and a pile of bills, the final prayer was offered, and the service finally came to a close. My impatient struggle, however, wasn't quite over—our family would join the long line of worshippers who shuffled slowly up the aisle to shake hands with Reverend Leonard Stephens and tell him how much we had enjoyed his long, boring sermon (a clear violation of the Ninth Commandment: "Thou Shalt Not Lie") before escaping to our car.

Every fourth or fifth Sunday, there would be Holy Communion, featuring saltine crackers and Welch's grape juice. Nobody I knew ever believed that stuff was really Jesus's blood! Holy Communion was good and bad—good that it shortened the sermon and broke the monotony, but bad because it made the church service even longer.

Most everybody we knew were Baptists. I would guess that the Baptist population of white Albany was 80 to 90 percent. There were a few Methodists and Presbyterians, but it was considered a big deal for a Baptist to marry a Methodist or a Presbyterian—Mama called that "marrying outside your religion."

There were even a handful of Episcopalians in Albany and a very small Episcopal church. Daddy called them "whiskey-palians" because they served real wine at Communion and were tolerant of their members drinking alcohol in social settings, just like Catholics. Daddy said that Baptists drank just as much as, if not more than, the "whiskey-palians" but just didn't talk about it so much, which left me thinking that drinking beer and alcohol was even worse than lying and hypocrisy. But marrying an Episcopalian was considered just about as bad as marrying a Catholic (which was just not done in South Georgia in the 1950s and 1960s), because Episcopalians called their preachers "Father," dressed them in ornate robes and hats, and had high-falutin' services, allegedly in Latin—just like the Catholics.

Later on, I would learn that there were even Jews in Georgia and that almost every little southern town had a few Jewish families, often dry-goods merchants or in other forms of retail.

In Albany, there was Bennie Prisant's Shoe Store, which featured an electronic gizmo that allowed you to try on a pair of shoes, stick your feet under the machine, look through a scope, and actually see your feet and toes through the shoes. You could wiggle your toes and see how tightly or loosely the shoes fit. It was like something from outer space that you would see on television! A doctor told me years later that using that crude gadget a single time exposed you to the same amount of radiation that one received from about two hundred X-rays.

Walter Goldsmith owned a popular clothing store, Goldsmith's, staffed mostly by high school seniors and college kids; it was *the* place for boys and men to buy clothes in Albany. Walter himself was a good-looking and likable guy, always sporting the latest in men's fashion. He hired the coolest kids who were sharp dressers—popular boys and football stars who guaranteed a steady stream of friends dropping by to see them and buy clothes. Walter paid low wages but gave his salesmen 20 to 30 percent discounts on all purchases. Most of the sales team at Goldsmith's were students who were constantly using their discount to charge more Gant shirts, Bermuda shorts, suede belts, Bass Weejun loafers, and Madras shirts—becoming imprisoned by their work and their account balance.

My father passed along to me a lot of his interests, but I never was a sharp enough dresser to get a job at Goldsmith's.

The largest Jewish-owned store in Albany was Rosenberg's department store, which was two stories, covered most of a city block, and earned the great compliment of being called Rich's South—a nickname that came from the Atlanta retail store Rich's, which was famous for its broad selection, good prices, great service, and no-questions-asked return policy. Just like at Rich's, a Rosenberg's customer could purchase a jacket or dress on trial, wear it once or twice, and return it—no questions asked. Purchases at Rosenberg's—whether cash or check (there were no credit cards then)—were placed into a pneumatic tube by the clerk and sent through a chute to the second floor, where a table of clerks double-checked each order and quickly returned a receipt and change through the tube.

But the first Jewish person I really knew was Alfred Blum, who became my friend in the sixth grade. Aside from having the same weird name as Alfred E. Neuman of *Mad* magazine fame, Alfred—slim, likable, and very smart—was just another kid in junior high. Well, maybe he was a *little* bit different—at least for the Deep South. One friend who spent the night with Alfred reported that his family listened to "fancy pants music." But when I asked what that was, he could not explain. I soon found out for myself when Alfred invited me over one Saturday afternoon to play and spend the night.

I was unsure what a Jewish house might look like, but I was happy to find that the Blum residence was not very different from any of my other friends' houses—they actually had some pretty cool stuff. The Blums had a big yard with a fat rubber tire that hung by a thick rope from the limb of a giant oak and swung back and forth. They also had a huge playroom upstairs that stretched the length of the house and featured a Ping-Pong table, boxes, books, and old pieces of furniture that were great for hide-and-seek. There was a lot of fun to be had at the Blum residence, but Alfred's parents were also very serious about some things. Before dinner, Mrs. Blum marched Alfred and me up to the bathroom, where she supervised our brushing our teeth and washing the sweat and grime away from the afternoon play. Finally, she ran combs through our hair before we could go back downstairs.

Blanche Blum was a tall, slender woman with curly black hair. Very kind and with a deep, rich southern accent, Mrs. Blum was obviously smart and well educated. For reasons I could not quite put my finger on, she reminded me very much of Mama. Mr. Blum was a tall, distinguished-looking man with a prominent nose and wavy black hair, which he combed straight back. I was quite surprised when he stuck his hand out and introduced himself as "Ad Blum." I told him that was my mother's name, too—an abbreviation for Adelaide.

Mr. Blum smiled and commented that it was, indeed, a small, small world.

We did not say the usual blessing ("God is great, God is good, let us thank Him for this food") or any blessing at all before eating dinner, but the food tasted pretty good anyway. Unlike our family dinners, which were filled with jokes, neighborhood gossip, and inside family pranks, dinner at Alfred's was more formal as we sat around a large mahogany table in their dining room with fine linen napkins across our laps, eating from fine china, and using silver forks and knives.

Mr. Blum—still wearing his business suit and tie—sat at the head of the table and presided over the meal, playfully questioning Alfred and his sister, Barbara, on their school day, their homework assignments, and current events. He smiled when they reported As, frowned at the mention of Bs, and glared at Alfred or Barbara when they reported a rare C.

From that one meal, I could see that Alfred's parents—particularly his father—expected a lot from their children. I decided then and there that while I liked Mr. and Mrs. Blum a lot, I'd rather have my Ad as a parent than Alfred's Ad!

After dinner, Mr. Blum suggested that we move to the living room and enjoy some music, suggesting that Alfred and I pick out something to play. While I certainly didn't expect Mr. Blum to have "Heart Break Hotel" or "Hound Dog" by Elvis in his collection, I was hoping to possibly hear Dean Martin's "Memories Are Made of This" or Tennessee Ernie Ford's "Sixteen Tons."

The Blums' record collection consisted of all long-playing classical music recordings kept in cardboard sleeves. Most of the covers had foreign names, and there were *lots* of numbers in the titles of their records—but no "Sixteen Tons." Alfred finally picked out an album with "1812" on it, featuring a picture of a fierce battle on the sleeve. Very carefully removing the disc, Alfred held the LP by its outside edges, being sure not to touch the black part. He wiped each record with a smooth cloth that the Blums used before and after each listening session.

We sat and listened as Mrs. Blum served coffee for her husband and herself and dishes of sherbet for Alfred, Barbara, and me.

"So *this* is fancy-pants music," I thought to myself as I listened. "You can't dance to it, but it ain't bad," I thought. "Not bad at all."

Mr. Blum occasionally talked over the music about the history of the particular concert that we were listening to, telling us about the Russian composer with a big name who wrote this music to commemorate Russia's defeat of Napoleon in 1812. His story made the music even more enjoyable, too, as I could imagine and even hear cannons and guns firing, drum rolls, fighting, and ultimately—victory.

Unlike my home, where everyone talked at the same time with the loudest voice prevailing, there were huge gaps in the conversation at the Blums' when no one talked. Mr. Blum occasionally leaned his head back against his big chair, his eyes closed and his hair flopping back, lost in his music.

When I got home, Mama and I had a big laugh over Mr. Blum's having the same name as she did. I told her that I could not understand any parents naming their son Ad! Mama said that there was a good reason for his nickname and that Mr. Blum's full name was Adolph, a common German name, but also the name of the monster Adolf Hitler, who started World War II and killed millions of Jews.

Why in the world, I asked, would a German Jewish family name their son after Hitler?

My mother smiled and explained that "Adolph" in Germany was a common name like Fred or John or Bob in our country and that Mr. Blum had been born in the 1920s, a long time before Hitler came to power. Regardless, it certainly became a great shame for a Jew *anywhere* to share a name with that evil man; Mr. Blum's American nickname avoided that unpleasant fact.

I told my Mama that I had a very good time at Alfred's but that the Blums seemed a little bit different from other friends. Mama said that the Blums were a "wonderful Jewish family." She explained that Jews were just like us, and that Jewish families consisted of great people who believed in education and culture and were always wonderful members of the community. She mentioned that Alfred's grandfather (Mrs. Blum's father) was both chairman of the Board of Education for Albany and chairman of Phoebe Putney Memorial Hospital.

I asked Mama if the Blums were rich. Mama sidestepped my question but said that they were "prosperous" and that Mr. Blum had a factory near Albany where he manufactured colored hose for women. My mama and her friends sported hose all the time, but they wore a variety that were light brown or tan and made their legs look smooth and perfect. I had never seen a single pair of colored hose and asked Mama if she intended to buy some from Mr. Blum. Mama laughed and said that Mr. Blum's hose were "a bit over the top" for South Georgia and that most of Mr. Blum's customers were Yankees—mainly New Yorkers—and even some movie stars in California.

As Alfred and I spent more and more time playing together and got to be friends, Mr. Blum would occasionally send me home with a box of his latest fancy hose for my mother, who would promptly sit down, take out her special stationery with her engraved initials on it—AMJ— and in a handwriting that was close to perfection, write him a thank you note for the "beautiful hose." But I never ever saw her once wear a single pair of those colored hose.

Indeed, one time when she was cleaning out her closet, she gave several boxes of these hose to our black housekeeper, Hattie, who seemed thrilled to have them. I asked Mama if she was worried about Mr. Blum running into Hattie wearing the distinctly colored hose that he had given her. Mama laughed and said it was not likely that Ad Blum would ever be down in Harlem Sunday morning and see Hattie wearing Mr. Blum's hose on her way to Antioch Baptist Church!

Alfred remained my good friend all the way through high school. Even though I had learned why he was a little bit different, I pretty much forgot about it.

Part II

··· ·

FEAR AND THE FIFTIES

Chapter Five

■ ■ ■

ARE THE RUSSIANS COMING?

I first heard about Communists while sitting on Hamp's lap in Lexington, watching Channel 2 (WSB-TV) from Atlanta. The Atlanta CBS affiliate would have a proud history in television news; many great newsmen, such as John Palmer and Tom Brokaw, did stints there early in their career.

Hamp was very interested in this Senator McCarthy, and on one visit to Lexington, we watched hearings in which Senator McCarthy was sniffing out possible Communists. McCarthy had a secret list of over two hundred who had "infiltrated" our own government. Hamp explained that Russia, who had been our ally in World War II against Nazi Germany, was now our global enemy and was the only other nation in the world with atomic weapons. On a globe he had in his den, he showed me Russia. When you looked at the Atlantic Ocean, which separated America and Europe, Russia seemed like it was halfway around the world, but on Hamp's globe, it was no farther away than my little thumb over the top. Hamp explained that the Russians could fly a plane with an atomic bomb over the Arctic and drop it on our country. I was sure glad to know that Senator McCarthy was finding those Communists.

At first, Hamp said McCarthy was an American hero. But as time went on, Senator McCarthy's charges got more reckless and more irresponsible—he never did reveal his secret list, and Hamp dismissed McCarthy as a publicity hound who had gotten "too big for his britches."

During that same period when Senator McCarthy was chasing Communists in the State Department and throughout the federal government, we exploded a hydrogen bomb "Ivy Mike" in the Pacific on November 1,

1952. The *Albany Herald* said that this bomb was seven hundred times more powerful than the bombs we dropped on Hiroshima and Nagasaki, which had killed 150,000 to 200,000 people. This frightening news and these staggering numbers boggled my mind. I had seen pictures of the huge mushroom cloud following an atomic explosion, building and climbing higher and higher above the clouds, and I could not imagine a bomb or a cloud being seven hundred times bigger than that! If we had a bomb like that, who knew what the Russians were cooking up!

Even in the second and third grade, I found myself keeping up with news, particularly on the A-bomb, reading the *Albany Herald* every afternoon when I came home from school and asking Mama and Daddy a lot of questions at dinner. Our country had entered an age of fear that stretched all the way to 907 Fourth Avenue. My interest in news and politics meant that I was more aware and, consequently, more scared.

It was one thing for Hamp to merely *talk* about Communists, but when I was in the second grade, we had a sobering school assembly in the cafeteria. Our principal, Miss Willye Powell—a short, stout lady who seldom smiled and usually wore a stern look on her face—announced that we were going to watch a "public service film" that the school was showing at the request of our president and the Dougherty County School Board. The way Miss Powell said it, we might think that President Eisenhower himself had asked us to look at this film.

The lights were turned off, and as the film began, we were surprised to be watching a cartoon entitled *Duck and Cover*, starring Bert the Turtle. Bert walked upright, had a big smile on his face, and sported a sailor hat. He walked by a tree and a playful squirrel climbed out on a limb, lowering a lit firecracker right over his head. Bert, sensing the danger, ducked into his natural shell. The next scene showed the tree scorched and burned from the explosion of the firecracker—but the turtle shell was unharmed, and Bert soon emerged from his shell, smiling and safe.

So, this fear and possibility of nuclear war was the reason that we started having air raid practices and watching films like Bert's *Duck and Cover*? Our teachers told us, not very convincingly, that this would "probably" never happen. However, in the "unlikely event" of a nuclear attack, if ever we heard a shrill siren, we should immediately duck and—just like Bert the turtle—cover our heads.

Since we didn't have shells like Bert, it meant that we should quickly crawl under our desks on our knees, put our hands and arms over our heads, and bend down with the top of our bodies curled up against our legs. There were large glass windows in almost every classroom, and some teachers thought (if there was enough warning) that it was best to lead their children out into the hall to avoid the shattered glass from the windows flying through the room. I asked Miss Powell if the schoolchildren in Hiroshima crawled under their desks when we dropped the A-bomb on them. She appeared flustered by my question, said she did not know, and told me to pay attention to her directions.

As an additional safety measure, our teachers recommended—again, if we had adequate warning—to file quickly and quietly in single file past the sink in the back of the classroom, remove a brown paper towel, and put a towel over our heads after we had ducked and covered. I did not understand. I had seen many pictures of the aftermath of the bombs dropped on Hiroshima and Nagasaki—both cities were flattened piles of black rubble. And a brown paper towel on my head was going to save me?

Later that year, each child at Palmyra Elementary was issued dog tags that were actually pretty cool. These little silver tags—just like the ones worn by soldiers in combat during World War II—came personalized in tiny font with each student's name, address, birth date, and even blood type! The boys put a chain through the tiny hole in the dog tags, proudly wearing them around their necks. The girls did not like to wear them as much, and most chose to wear the tags under their blouse or sweater—probably so that boys couldn't pull on them.

We were told at school that this was simply to protect us if we were ever lost or kidnapped, but I knew from listening to the radio and reading the *Albany Herald* that these dog tags were going to be used to identify bodies after the nuclear attack—an attack which seemed more and more likely with each passing month as tensions continued to rise between the two antagonistic global superpowers.

While I had gotten a good chuckle at the stupid cartoon about Bert the Turtle at school and made jokes to my classmates about the drills and dog tags, the daily "red scare" headlines in the *Albany Herald* really got me thinking—and worrying—about the Communist threat. When I went to bed at night upstairs in my little bedroom, tucked under the sloped roof, I started having trouble going to sleep. My mind would race, and I started waking up in the middle of the night, usually after some dream or nightmare about Communists and atomic attacks.

I felt terribly alone and helpless in the middle of the night, and Lawton—who was a sound sleeper—didn't want to bother with me. When I occasionally got the nerve to wake him up, he called me a "baby" or "sissy" and told me to go to sleep and leave him alone. I'd go downstairs and stand by Mama and Daddy's bed. Mama would usually walk me back upstairs, sit on the side of the bed, and pat me on the back until I went to sleep.

"You Commie"

Growing up in Albany in the early 1950s, about the worst thing you could call someone was a Communist, or "Commie" as most put it (I suppose you could have called someone a "nigger lover," but the practice of "race-mixing" was so rare that it would be years before I ever heard anyone sling that terrible slur!).

The fear of Russians and atomic bombs seemed all the more real when the Civil Air Patrol began construction of a watchtower on a vacant lot on Fifth Avenue right off of Slappey Drive, about a block from our house. Made of wood and never painted, it looked like the towers along the highway driving to Mur and Hamp's house that forest rangers used to spot forest fires. The tower had a shiny tin top on it and yellow-and-black Civil Defense Alert triangles nailed to the wooden posts at the bottom. It only took a few months to build the two-story wooden structure, and I was just thankful that the Russians had waited until the tower was up to try to drop an A-bomb on us.

There was a big ceremony when the watchtower opened. Several hundred civilian families, city officials, law enforcement officers, and military personnel from the bases gathered around the base of the tower to hear Mayor Taxi Smith "open" the tower by cutting a red, white, and blue ribbon across the bottom steps while members of the Albany High School Band played Sousa marches and patriotic songs. As usual, the loudest cheers went up when they played "Dixie."

The center of attention, however, was the local Civil Air Patrol members, who were dressed in their uniforms and wore binoculars that hung on straps around their necks. Betty McNabb, wife of the Albany High School principal and the only woman in Albany to have a pilot's license, was among them. Marching mostly out of step, they carried the American flag to the bottom of the tower, where four proud CAP members climbed the steps to the very top. When the "cadets" reached the small square enclosure at the top surrounded by a deck with metal railings, each took his or her post on one side, put their binoculars up to their eyes, and started looking for Russian bombers. The crowd clapped, watched for a few minutes until the ceremony was over, and then melted away, probably feeling a lot better and safer about making it through the night with the CAP on duty.

That was the first and last time that I ever saw many people at the tower other than kids like me from the neighborhood who would play football and fly kites in the vacant field where the tower stood. For the first few weeks, volunteer "watchers" would regularly occupy the tower, but only during the daylight hours. I guessed the Russians were gentlemen and would not bomb us while we slept.

I knew about our dropping the bomb on Hiroshima—we had not given the Japanese any warning. I learned later that Truman had been petitioned by some of the key scientists who developed the atomic bomb *not* to use it on Japan, but to first try it in a demonstration project. Truman never personally received those petitions, but following his meeting with Stalin and Churchill at Potsdam, he included a public statement calling for the Japanese government "to proclaim now the unconditional surrender of all Japanese armed forces" and warned that the alternative was "prompt and utter destruction." President Truman thought he had hinted at the atomic attack that was forthcoming, but who could have actually imagined the massive destruction that was to come?

The Japanese did not respond to the declaration, and Truman had not expected them to. So, the specially configured airship, *Enola Gay*, dropped the atom bomb on Hiroshima on August 6, 1945, killing an estimated 150,000 Japanese, destroying 90 percent of that city, and bringing the general staff and the emperor (considered a god-king by his people) to their senses—and ultimate surrender. But before the surrender, while the issue was still debated between the general staff with an increasingly vocal emperor, a second bomb was dropped on Nagasaki three days after Hiroshima, killing another 50,000 Japanese.

The emperor, whose voice had never been heard by his people, personally broadcast a declaration of Japan's unconditional surrender— although he did not use that humiliating term publicly.

Based on our surprise attack on Japan with atomic bombs, what were the chances that old Joe Stalin, rumored to have killed millions of his own people, was going to give us polite warning or any notice before blowing all of us to smithereens?

For a long time, I simply avoided walking or riding my bike up Fifth Avenue, since I figured the Commies might drop an A-bomb right on top of the *highly* important watchtower. Over time, however, people quit talking about it, and there was a sharp drop-off in "watchers." Six months after the grand opening, it was rare to see someone in a CAP uniform, binoculars pressed against their eyes, walking around the top of the tower, sweeping their binoculars from side to side, looking for nuclear-armed Russian airplanes. Indeed, after a while, you were much more likely to see neighborhood kids playing on the stairs or flying kites from the top of the tower. I even heard stories about neighborhood teens that took their girls up there for a kiss or a smoke.

As appealing as that sounded, I never went up there myself, as I was scared of high places. That was part of the so-called "worry gene" that I had inherited from my mama and especially my daddy, who was prone to anxiety and terribly afraid of heights.

Eventually, it was probably even more likely that you would see an actual Russian bomber flying across the South Georgia skies than a CAP on watch at the Fifth Avenue tower. Over time, I wondered about the benefits of the tower at all. While it did put the "watcher" above the tops of the trees, long-distance bombers flew at 30,000 to 40,000 feet above the clouds, so the 30-foot advantage from the top of the tower gave the watcher a mere millisecond to notify someone if they spotted a Soviet bomber or an atomic bomb head down on top of us. I often wondered who they would call and what they would do? How would the watch tower actually change anything?

As the Communist threat further infiltrated my thoughts, my troubles sleeping only got worse, so Mama finally took me to see Dr. Mack Sutton about my fears. We talked for about fifteen minutes without much progress before he told me that I was clearly too big and strong and smart to be scared of the dark or booger bears—what was *actually* bothering me? I finally confessed that I was really more scared of Communists than those things. Dr. Mack asked me if I had ever actually seen a Communist, and I told him only on television but not in Albany.

"Then why in the world," Dr. Mack asked, "would you be scared of Communists?"

"Why are we having air drills at school all the time?" I asked. "Why are we wearing these dog tags? Why have they built a watchtower a block from my house?"

Dr. Mack chuckled, shook his head, and said, "Son, you may know too much for your own good!"

But then he went on to say something that made a lot of sense. "We can blow them up, and they know it. And they can blow us up, and we know it. So, the way I figure it is that chances are that neither one of us will start a war . . . unless by accident."

I wished Dr. Mack had not told me that last thing. But I did start sleeping better after our talk. Mutually assured destruction, as terrifying as it sounded, was a strangely comforting concept.

Chapter Six

■ ■ ■

THE REAL TERROR

Sis Is Sick

I was playing with my four-year-old baby sister, Helen, in our backyard one hot afternoon in April 1953. I was nine years old. Helen started crying, complaining that her legs hurt.

"Don't be a crybaby," I said. "My legs hurt all the time."

But calling her "crybaby" didn't seem to help, and little Helen finally just plopped herself down on the ground, wailing uncontrollably, tears running down her pudgy cheeks. While I was used to her attempting such stunts to get the attention of our parents, she didn't usually try to pull this kind of thing with me. Maybe she really is hurting, I thought, so I told her that if she would shut up, I would carry her to the house.

While she continued her quiet sobbing, I tried and failed to pick her up. Finally, I got down on my hands and knees like I did when we played horsey, Helen climbed on my back, and we slowly made our way to the back steps. Mama rushed out and asked if there had been an accident, but I told her that Helen was just being a crybaby.

Mama picked Helen up, carried her inside, gave her early dinner, and put her to bed. When Helen woke up the next morning and said that her legs still hurt, Mama called Dr. Durham at Palmyra Pharmacy. He told her that several kids in the neighborhood had developed those symptoms and that she should take Helen to Dr. Mack Sutton right away.

I knew something was up later that afternoon when Mrs. Sheppard, my third-grade teacher, asked me to go to the principal's office, where I found my father waiting. Daddy sometimes dropped us off in the morning, but he had never, ever picked me up after school. Besides, this was the middle of the day.

When he squatted down to hug me, his eyes were red and puffy like he had been crying. "We're going home. I'll explain in the car."

My father then thanked Mrs. Sheppard, who handed me my book sack and suggested that I try to finish reading several books. As we walked out, she said that she would be praying for my family.

As we walked to the car, my father said simply, "Sis is sick," and pulled his handkerchief from his coat pocket, pretending to blow his nose, but I could see he was using it to wipe away tears. When I asked what was wrong with Helen, Daddy said that the doctors were not sure yet, but they were afraid that she had polio.

Polio.

I had heard the word before on television but had no idea what it meant. But I learned a lot about the virus in the next twenty-four months, since Albany had an epidemic, and stories were featured on the national news calling Albany the "polio capital" of the United States.

"Why are you taking me out of school?" I asked my daddy.

"Because some people think that polio is contagious," he said. Seeing the confused look on my face and realizing that I did not understand that word, Daddy said that polio is "catching," a term used at the time. "I am sure you won't catch it, though," he quickly added. "We are just being extra careful."

After a minute of silence riding in the car, I asked Daddy a question I would ask my parents over and over again in the weeks to come—if Helen was going to die. And over and over, Mama and Daddy told me that my sister would *not* die. Helen might have trouble walking, they told me, and her legs might shrivel up, but Helen was not going to die. I never quite believed that they could really be so sure.

Shortly after I got home from school, several ladies with masks on their faces knocked on the door, loudly announcing that they were from the Public Health Department. They walked through the house, spraying the sinks, the bathrooms, the toilets, and the tubs with a foul-smelling disinfectant that lingered for days. As the team was leaving, they posted signs on the front and back doors of our house and nailed more to the telephone poles around the house. In big red letters, these signs read,

Notice!!
Polio Quarantine!!
Stay Away!!
Dougherty County Public Health Department

After the signs went up, a few neighbors still came to our house, but they did not knock or try to come in. They just left casseroles, covered dishes, cakes, cards, and notes on the steps or the front porch, swiftly disappearing as quickly as they had arrived. If we didn't bring the food in quickly, ants swarmed all over it. After a while, I noticed that our neighbors were leaving only paper plates—they didn't want dishes back that might have polio germs on them. Somewhere along the way, I shifted from being scared for Helen to being scared for myself. "Am I going to catch polio?" I wondered to myself, and repeatedly asked my parents. While Mama and Daddy offered me reassurance and lots of hugs, they never could promise me 100 percent that I was not going to catch polio. I had to weigh their words against the awful fact that within several weeks, five other families who lived within a hundred yards of our house were also struck with polio.

Courtney Thomas, the older brother of my first girlfriend, Cecelia, developed the most serious strain of polio and almost died. Stan Glass, who lived next door to Courtney, came down with polio several weeks after he had. Then Jackie White, who lived two doors down from Courtney on the other side, was diagnosed, followed by my sister Helen, and then David Campbell, who lived one block over in the other direction.

There were stories in the *Albany Herald* and the *Atlanta Constitution* about the "polio epidemic" in Albany, as well as random speculation about how it spread. One scientist noted that one family's swimming pool was used by many of the neighborhood kids who had developed polio.

Many families in our neighborhood took their kids out of school for the rest of the year and would not even allow them out of the house. One old wives' tale was that sleep helped prevent polio, so lots of kids were put down for afternoon naps. Other parents became fanatical about their children washing their hands throughout the day so that they wouldn't get polio. My only contact with the outside world for those first several months was the telephone. One family in the neighborhood would not even let their son talk to me on the phone! His mother later admitted to Mama that she was simply paranoid and thought it was tempting fate even to talk to our family on the phone; suppose the polio virus could be transmitted through telephone lines?

Mama stayed at the hospital with Helen night and day for many weeks. It was strange to be cooped up inside our home and not have Mama there. Lawton was in charge while Daddy was at work, but there was nothing to do but read or watch television, which was only on for a few hours each day. We usually argued about what to watch—he wanted to watch *Gunsmoke* and other Westerns, and I wanted to watch cartoons, sports events, and the news.

My parents didn't say too much about Helen those first few weeks other than to reassure us regularly that she was "okay" or "doing well." Whenever I asked Daddy about Helen, his eyes would become damp, and he would turn his face away.

Sometimes, I woke up in the middle of the night or early morning to find Mama standing over me. She would come home from the hospital, shower, and change clothes before heading back to Helen. If she knew I was awake, she would smother me with hugs and kisses before tucking me in and telling me to go back to sleep. Years later, she confessed that she was constantly looking for signs, wondering and worrying that Lawton or I had also contracted the dreadful disease.

After a few weeks, my brother and I were finally allowed to visit Helen at Phoebe Putney Hospital. She had been placed in the wing of the hospital that had quickly become known as the polio ward; all guests and staff had to wear protective masks, and ominous "quarantine" signs were posted all over the walls and doors. Just like on the day Helen was born, I found myself wearing a mask and peering through a thick glass window at her. My father leaned into the glass and forced a smile, waving and trying to get Helen's attention. She usually smiled back, but sometimes she just stared with a pained expression. Daddy then waved and quickly stepped to the side, out of Helen's sight, wiping his eyes and trying to compose himself before reappearing in front of the glass, once again forcing a smile and waving to "Sis"—the same pet name he had called his only sister.

Helen came home after about eight weeks, and several weeks later, the "quarantine" signs were removed—but it didn't make any difference. While our house had once been headquarters for neighborhood fun and games, with kids dropping in all the time, now it was very quiet and very, very lonely.

On our brief outings to the post office on Saturday mornings, Daddy inevitably ran into friends who would ask about Helen. Some cautiously stood back a few yards, avoiding the possibility of shaking hands with Daddy. They did not say anything, but their actions told me that they were afraid. Daddy always forced a smile, put on a good face, and said that Helen was doing "as well as could be expected." But the longer Daddy talked about her, the more likely his eyes would fill with tears—at which point he would turn his face away and try to change the subject.

I didn't realize then, as I do now, how violated and vulnerable polio had left our family. What had we done wrong? What had we done to deserve this? We said our prayers every night and went to Sunday school—well, most Sundays. Why had this happened to Helen? Why had it happened to us?

Warm Springs

While Helen had a serious bout with polio, her case was diagnosed early—thanks to Dr. Durham's and Dr. Mack's urgings—and was treated aggressively and effectively. I would learn later that there was never any serious doubt that she would survive the attack. The larger question, instead, was the quality of her life in the long run. Would her arms and legs function and even be useful? Would she be confined to a wheelchair for the rest of her life?

The local doctors treating Helen agreed that her chances for a strong recovery would be greatly increased by taking her to nearby Warm Springs, Georgia, the world center for both treatment and research on polio. The warm waters there even attracted FDR after he had been struck down with polio as young man. After his election to the presidency, President Roosevelt made regular return trips to Warm Springs, staying in a favorite cottage there, which became known as "the Little White House."

The good news was that Warm Springs would accept Helen as a patient. The bad news was that she would have to stay there for several months by herself. Families were not allowed to stay on the grounds and were even discouraged from staying nearby. Besides, Lawton and I had to go back to school soon, and Mama had to turn her attention to taking care of Daddy, Lawton, and me.

It was a dark and terrible day when my parents came home after leaving four-year-old Helen off at Warm Springs Hospital that first time. My father could not even talk about what it was like to leave her there. Mama said she was brave at first, not wanting to further upset Helen, but then started to cry when it came time to say goodbye to her baby girl. Later, Mama said she heard baby Helen "screaming her lungs out" the entire time she and Daddy were walking down the long hallway to the parking lot—even though the door to Helen's room was shut tight. How could a little girl understand being left alone in a strange place like that?

"Leaving your sister there is the toughest thing I have ever done," Mama told Lawton and me that day.

Those difficult first trips over to Warm Springs every weekend were emotional roller coasters for us all. Little Helen lit up when we walked in with presents, books, toys, and chocolate chip cookies. But it was always very, very tough when it came time to leave. On the ride home, Mama and Daddy put their best faces on, trying to cheer each other up by talking about how good Helen looked, the progress she was making, and what a wonderful place Warm Springs was! They constantly reassured one another that they were "doing the best thing for Helen." What kept all of us going was the fact that Helen's doctors believed she was making a strong recovery. Plus, Helen had become close to several of her nurses, so leaving her got a little bit easier each visit.

On our third or fourth weekend trip to Warm Springs, my father took my brother and me to visit Roosevelt's Little White House, a cottage in which he stayed during his treatments there and in which he ultimately died in 1945.

My grandfather Hamp loved to talk about how FDR "saved our country from the Nazis, the Japs, and Wall Street," so there was something magical about being able to walk through the presidential cottage at Warm Springs. As a young boy, I found it surreal to be walking in the very building where a former president had fought through the dark days of his battle with polio. I was able to see and sometimes even *touch* the chairs where he had sat, to stand in the room where he had died, and to read famous letters written to and from him postmarked "Warm Springs, Georgia." It was very impressive.

One of the things I remember most vividly from the Little White

House was a prominently displayed photograph of Graham Jackson, a famous black Georgia musician, crying as he played accordion and sang "Goin' Home" at President Roosevelt's funeral.

Every time I went to Warm Springs, I insisted on returning to President Roosevelt's former residence. Fascinated, I went through that same tour over and over again, eventually becoming a familiar face to the National Park Rangers who led me time and time again on the tour. My appetite for politics, already strong because of Hamp, was whetted considerably by those visits to the Little White House, which piqued my interest in the president I felt kinship with as a fellow (if only part-time) "Georgian." With Senator Russell's failing bid for the Democratic nomination in 1952, Hamp said that Roosevelt would probably be as close as Georgia would ever get to having one of our own in the White House.

After five months at Warm Springs, it was time for Helen to come home. In the words of her doctor, she had made a "remarkable recovery," and while it was unclear if she might have some permanent leg damage, she had avoided permanent damage to her lungs and upper body and had a decent chance of full recovery of the use of her arms and legs. This would depend largely on her continuing a vigorous physical therapy.

Mama, joking that she was a "trained physical therapist" from working on my feet and legs for years, toiled away at Warm Springs learning very specific exercises for Helen from the staff. Twice a day, in between meals, she laid a double-thick layer of blankets and sheets over our kitchen table, where Helen would lie while Mama "did her exercises," stretching and bending my sister's arms and legs up and down. Over and over and over again. Hamp offered several times to pay for a professional physical therapist, but Mama insisted that no one could ever care for her daughter better than she could.

Helen and our neighbors Courtney Thomas and David Campbell were the lucky ones; they were diagnosed early, received excellent treatment, and made complete recoveries. Other family friends Stan Glass and Jackie White, however, were not so lucky; they were left with damaged muscles, steel braces, and lifelong challenges.

Less than a year after Helen got polio, a big announcement was made that Dr. Jonas Salk had discovered a vaccine that would prevent polio; he had even tested the vaccine on himself and his own family.

There were stories all over the country about people waiting in line for hours and hours to get the "Salk vaccine." Mama had no intention of waiting for the injection to make its way to Albany and—through Hamp's contacts—found a doctor at Emory Hospital who had Salk's seemingly magic medicine. The next day, Mama, Lawton, and I boarded a Trailways Bus for Atlanta and headed straight to Emory as soon as we arrived. We were the first kids in Albany—and probably throughout South Georgia—to get the vaccination. I never quite understood how one shot protected us, but I was happy to know that I would probably not have this terrible disease that had struck Helen.

Chapter Seven

■ ■ ■

UNCLE FRANK'S SHELTER

RUSSIA LAUNCHES SPUTNIK!

The ominous headline was emblazoned across the top quarter of the *Albany Herald* in huge black letters. It was October 4, 1957. My mother said it was the biggest headline she had seen since the atomic bomb was dropped on Hiroshima. A smaller headline declared, "Russians First In Space." We quickly learned that Sputnik was, in fact, a satellite, about the size of a watermelon, which had been carried into orbit by a powerful Russian rocket. It circled the earth 1440 times.

Hamp had told me time and time again that part of being an "educated man" was reading the newspaper every single day of your life. I started with the local newspaper, reading a quote from a Pentagon expert who claimed, "The world will never be the same. We live in dangerous times."

So what's the big deal about an orbiting watermelon, I wondered. Why all the fuss?

I asked my seventh-grade science teacher, Coach Gordon Dixon, who was really a basketball coach disguised as a science teacher. Coach Dixon was a good guy but also the kind of person who, when he read the newspaper, began at the sports section and then—if he had time—read the comics, then the movie and television schedules. There was little evidence that Coach Dixon ever made it to the front page. Not surprisingly, Coach Dixon knew less about Sputnik than I did. He was a lot more worried about the upcoming game with our traditional football rival, Riverview High, than the Russians. He declared Sputnik was "no big deal" and encouraged the interested students to read the newspaper on their own time.

The next issue of the *Albany Herald* explained that the same technology that had allowed the Russians to put the small satellite into orbit could also launch a nuclear weapon and put it down "anywhere in the world."

A few days later, the commander of nearby Turner Air Force Base—which housed long-range bombers capable of delivering nuclear weapons anywhere in the world—spoke to the Albany Kiwanis Club. In response to questions about Sputnik, the commander—a real no-nonsense ace who downed near fifty German planes in World War II and was awarded the Distinguished Flying Cross—explained that Albany was "blessed" with more than its share of military assets, due largely to the fact that Georgia's Richard Russell, chairman of the Senate Armed Services Committee, had sprinkled military bases all over our state. Two of the biggest were Turner Field and the Marine Supply Corps Center. He pointed out that both the Marine Supply Depot Headquarters—described as the largest military supply center in the world—and Turner Field were within ten miles of the Albany Courthouse. The high-ranking officer, almost boasting, said that Albany was a "prime target" for the Russians, probably one of their top ten in the United States. Suddenly, Sputnik was transformed from a flying watermelon to something that was about certain to blow Albany and the surrounding area to smithereens.

The next day, in a follow-up to the commander's speech, the *Herald* featured a giant map of the southeastern United States on the front page with a bombardier's grid overlaid and Albany in its crosshairs. Scary.

"They shouldn't put something like that in the newspaper," my father complained. "It's alarmist . . . but it's probably true."

While most of us were fretting and wringing our hands about this new Russian threat, a few were acting on it. Daddy's brother, whom I knew as Uncle Frank, was a prosperous peach farmer who lived down the road in Talbotton, Georgia. Frank was a can-do guy who was not going to just sit back and wait for the Russian missiles to arrive and the Russian troops to march straight into South Georgia. He ordered plans from the Civil Defense Bureau in Washington for a bomb shelter. Then, using a tractor from the farm, Uncle Frank dug a fifteen-foot deep hole the size of a large bedroom next to his house. Uncle Frank and his sons poured a concrete floor, built wooden walls, and laid a triple-thick layer of aluminum siding over the top, which was then covered by a foot of gravel, sand, and grass—all to repel the radiation. When Uncle Frank realized how much more of his yard he would have to tear up to build stairs to the shelter—which would include taking down the hundred-year-old oak that dominated the front yard—he decided to dig a tunnel from the basement of the house to the shelter, facilitating his family's escape directly from the house to the shelter without any exposure to atomic radiation. Because the basement floor of the house was ten or twelve feet below the thick concrete floor of the shelter, the evacuee had to climb up a step ladder in the basement to reach the tunnel, barely large enough for the average person to crawl through.

Closely following the directions in the handbook from the Civil Defense Bureau, Uncle Frank planned an evacuation drill to access his shelter and timed it—just like it called for in the Civil Service booklet. It took Uncle Frank less than thirty seconds to descend to the basement, climb up the ladder, and quickly crawl on his hands and knees to the shelter, where he then turned on the single light. His wife, my aunt Elizabeth, who was spry for her age, easily mounted the ladder in the basement but said she preferred not to have to crawl on her knees through the tunnel and risk ruining her new hose.

Once Uncle Frank added a couple of folding chairs and a short-wave radio so that he and his family would know when it was safe to depart the shelter, the job was done. Several months after he finished the shelter in early 1958, a large front-page article appeared in the *Columbus Enquirer*, the nearby newspaper, with a picture of Uncle Frank standing in the shelter, his face peering into the tunnel. The *Enquirer*'s article, however, failed to mention that the local champion was never able to convince all of his family to join him in the shelter during his self-scheduled nuclear drills. Aunt Elizabeth and Uncle Frank's daughter Gladys politely refused.

Forty years later, after Uncle Frank and Aunt Elizabeth were gone (both dying of natural causes, not killed by Russians), one of Uncle Frank's children, Raines, widened the tunnel significantly, making a more comfortable passage so that a normal-sized person could stoop down low and actually walk from the basement to the shelter. Raines put in refrigeration and turned the moribund bomb shelter into a wine cellar.

Part III

■ ■ ■

GROWING UP: BEFORE THE DELUGE

Chapter Eight

■ ■ ■

ALBANY HIGH

Miss Dobbins

Miss Dobbins, our beloved Latin teacher, was what we called, kindly, a spinster. Her life and passion was Latin. I struggled in her class, but I loved the old lady. I also learned that her soft spots were the two special projects each year, which counted for one-third of our semester grade. By spring of my sophomore year, I had a high D average in Latin—due to the 65s and 70s I regularly brought home on Latin grammar tests—and was worried that my Latin grade could keep me from getting into a decent college. I put all my chips on the special projects.

My mother struggled for a week sewing the red velvet cape. A neighbor helped with the round shield, which I painted gold and sprinkled with glitter. Hattie used a can of gold paint to convert a pair of my father's old leather sandals. I had pretty much farmed out most of the project to family and friends.

My classmates could hardly contain their snickers when I marched into Miss Dobbins's class as "the Centurion."

Miss Dobbins looked up from her desk, where she was grading papers. When I started speaking in Latin, Miss Dobbins stood up, seemingly in a trance, as if transported to an earlier time. Clasping her hands together, she sighed audibly; I thought the dear old lady might faint. I had talked a girl named Virginia—one of the smartest students in our class—into composing a two-minute speech in Latin for the Centurion to make. I'd practiced it over and over and over. Although I had no idea what I was saying, I kept glancing at Virginia, and she kept nodding her head up and down, indicating that I was doing okay. When I finished, I drew my sword with a flourish and lifted it high, looking up into the heavens and making the proudest statement that people of that age could make, "Civis romanus sum" (I am a Roman citizen). Thank God, I thought. It was over.

When I turned to Miss Dobbins, she was so excited that I worried the old gal would have a heart attack. She clapped and clapped, muttering a Latin phrase I assumed meant "congratulations" or "good job." A number of my friends joined in the fun, mocking me and yelling out "bravo" with sarcastic grins on their faces. They realized that I had pulled it off.

Miss Dobbins clasped her hands together and started speaking back to the Centurion in Latin. She was obviously ad-libbing, gazing up at the ceiling, moved by this special moment, as she spoke. While I listened hard and caught a couple of words, I had no earthly idea what she was saying. I just stood there and occasionally nodded my head up and down like I understood. Out of the corner of my eyes, I could see my classmates were giggling quietly, enjoying my obvious predicament.

When Miss Dobbins finished, she turned to me, as if expecting a response back in Latin. It was close to the end of the period, so I pointed to my watch, proclaimed loudly, "O tempora, o mores . . . finis," made a grand bow in Miss Dobbins's direction, grabbed the "SPQR" banner made by my neighbor in his woodshop class, and quickly marched out of the room just as the bell rang.

I was the laughingstock of my class the rest of the week.

"Ass kisser!" a classmate said after class.

"Yo Centurion . . . what a suck up!" another yelled from a passing car.

I never knew what Miss Dobbins had said back to me in Latin, but it didn't matter. I got an A+ for my special project, which when averaged in with my D+, should have given me a solid C for the semester. Miss Dobbins gave me a B instead. I figured she knew a good Centurion when she saw one.

Listen to the Music: The Sophomore-Sophomore of 1960

When I answered the phone, I heard a squeal, then an excited voice: "Billy Ivey has asked me to go to the Prom!"

It was Jeanie Cross, the best-looking girl in the sophomore class—hell, the best-looking girl in the entire Albany High School student body of two thousand. A natural beauty with huge brown eyes and an amazing body, Jeanie had "Playmate of the Month" potential and was the

object of many locker room conversations and fantasies, including my
own. (*Playboy* had been out a few years but had just come to South
Georgia. But you couldn't find it on the regular newsstand, and no
self-respecting family would risk a subscription and possibly have the
mailman tell your neighbors. The rumor was that if you were old—say
thirty or forty—and asked Dr. Dupree at Palmyra Drug Store, he would
go into the back, slip a copy into a brown paper bag, and sell it to you
for about four times the cover price of one dollar.)

"What did you tell him?" I asked Jeanie.

"What do ya mean, Hamilton?"

"Are you going?"

"Are you crazy, Hamilton? Of course I'm going! No girl in her right
mind would pass up a chance to go to the prom with the captain of the
football team!"

"Then why in the world are you calling me?" I asked.

"Connie wasn't home. I had to tell somebody!" she blurted out. Then,
sensing she had chosen the wrong words, said, "I just wanted you to
know, Hamilton, since you are my best buddy."

Best buddy—bullshit! Jeanie had no clue what she was doing to me.
Or maybe she knew *exactly* what she was doing to me. While I thought
of her as a secret girlfriend and a certain future conquest, it was pretty
obvious that Jeanie thought of me only as a good friend—someone to
gossip with when her girlfriends weren't around.

Well, that was okay. I would hang in there as a friend, and someday it
would happen. Someday we would be riding around in the "Blue Turd,"
or we would be at the Slappey Drive-In watching a horror movie and
drinking a beer that I had snuck, and it would happen. Someday, she
would put her hand on my knee or rest her head on my shoulder and
snuggle close, and Jeanie Cross would be all mine. Would I ever get up
the nerve to make the first move? Or should I just wait for her?

I hadn't worked up the nerve yet but figured I had better hurry up
and make my move. Old Billy Ivey, a huge tackle known for being "fast
off of the ball," was probably hoping to be fast onto Jeanie. He sure
as hell was not going to wait for me to make his move on the beautiful
Miss Cross.

In the next few weeks, the rest of the sophomore guys learned in
short phone calls and notes slipped during class that just about every
decent-looking woman in our class was going to the Junior-Senior Prom.

Even my best friend Jay's steady girlfriend, Julie, broke up with him just so she could go to the prom with a senior (they got back together right after the prom).

We were all mad as hell, but there was not a darn thing we could do about it. The Junior-Senior was a big deal. On prom night, the AHS gymnasium was always decorated in the orange-and-green school colors of the Albany Indians. Each year had a theme. The year before, the prom committee erected a giant tepee at the front door and each couple entered the dance through the door of the wigwam. With the boys in their white summer tuxedos and the girls in flowing formal dresses with corsages, the prom signaled the end of the school year and the beginning of summer.

As always, the band would be Wayne Entrekin and the H-2-Os, led by our chemistry teacher, Dr. Entrekin, who played the saxophone with several other old teachers in their thirties and forties. They specialized in playing popular songs that were five or six years old at half speed. They sounded awful and looked worse: a group of old white guys in faded, powder-blue summer tuxes, playing Pat Boone hits like "April Love" or "Tutti Frutti" in slow motion. It was worse than trying to dance to Lawrence Welk.

But it was the prom, and none of us sophomore guys were going.

Our regular gang was hanging out at the Dairy Queen after school, sitting on the hoods of our cars, radios blaring, sipping on vanilla Cokes, and griping about all the sophomore girls deserting us when it hit me: "Let's have our own party the same night of the prom!"

There was a ho-hum response until I said, "We'll call it the Sopho-more-Sophomore and make bad stuff out of the Junior-Senior. They send out engraved invitations—we'll do ours on postcards. They called the prom a 'formal' and wear tuxedos—we'll call ours an 'informal' and wear jeans. The prom will spend hundreds dressing up the old gym. We'll spend $25 on crepe paper. They have a bunch of old fuddy-duds for a band—we'll get some really cool band." Before the afternoon was over, the First Annual Sophomore-Sophomore was born.

I knew the band I wanted to play: Johnny Jenkins and the Pinetop-pers, a hot, all-black rock 'n' roll band from Macon we first heard at a Christmas dance at the Elk's Club, which had been sponsored by a college fraternity. They had made quite an impression on me that night. Arriving in a shiny black hearse, the Pinetoppers emptied out one-by-one, wearing yellow suits. Just when it looked like the last person had exited, out popped a skinny, white kid with curly hair, all dressed up in a black suit. This kid started shaking hands all around and handing out cards that read, "Phil Walden, Agent, Macon, Georgia." Smooth talking and cocky, he couldn't have been over twenty years old, but he had his own business cards! I was impressed. It was also the first time I had ever seen a white person act so familiar with blacks; this Walden guy was joking with the band, whispering in their ears, and putting his arms around their shoulders. I was just not accustomed to seeing white folks behaving that way around black folks. The Pinetoppers played out of their minds for hours, performing current hits as well as their own songs. Everybody agreed they were the coolest band ever to play in Albany, Georgia.

When I got home the afternoon we invented the Sophomore-Sophomore, I found Phil's business card in my drawer and reached him at the Phi Delta Theta fraternity house at Mercer University in Macon. Barely sixteen myself, I called him "Mr. Walden" and reminded him that we had met in Albany. While he pretended to remember me, I could tell he had no idea who I was. I told him that we needed the Pinetoppers for the Sophomore-Sophomore. He chuckled at the idea but said the Pinetoppers were "hot," cost $200, and would expect us to supply booze for the band. "Nothing cheap . . . good stuff," he added.

"But I heard the Pinetoppers charged only $150 when they played here last time," I protested mildly.

Walden replied, "That was then and this is now." It was the high season for high schools and colleges, where they had a lot of offers. Plus, he told me, the Pinetoppers' lead singer was going to be a big star.

Yeah, yeah, yeah, I thought. He was just trying to do a snow job on me.

I finally bargained him down to $180 with $20 for "gas money." Phil guaranteed that they would be on time and would set up and begin playing by eight o'clock sharp. When I bragged about the good deal I had struck, one of my buddies pointed out that we still had to pay $200, Phil's original price. I began to see why this guy was such a good agent.

No one could believe it the next day when the word spread that the Pinetoppers were going to play at the Sophomore-Sophomore. Before the week was over, everybody was talking about it, and some of the upperclassmen started asking for details, indicating that they might drop by after the prom, which ended at eleven. The Sophomore-Sophomore had become a really cool thing.

But it wasn't very cool the night of the dance at about eight-thirty p.m. when I was standing in the middle of the toilet paper–draped floor at the Garden Center with fifty couples milling around and no Pinetoppers. I kept assuring everyone that the band was on the way, making frequent trips outside hoping to see the big, black hearse pull up. By eight-forty-five p.m., a few people left, and others started to complain. We were only minutes from people starting to demand their money back. Just when I thought I was going to be in serious trouble, Phil Walden came bopping in with a cigarette hanging from his mouth, a couple of the Pinetoppers staggering in behind him. Walden was loose and had been drinking himself. He advised me to relax and said it was "cool" to be late and have the audience really hungry for the band. I was so relieved to see him that I forgot my anger and quickly took him to the back to give him four bottles of Jim Beam bourbon for the band, purchased for a premium from a guy who tended bar at the country club.

The Pinetoppers were even better than we remembered, and their late arrival was soon forgotten. By nine o'clock, the Garden Center was rocking, full of sophomores in jeans and shorts. By ten-thirty, the prom crowd started to drop in. Couples in jeans and tuxedos and formal dresses mingled together. It was packed, and I started to dream of clearing a couple of hundred dollars—really big money for the times!

But the highlight of the evening was when Jeanie made her entrance around eleven o'clock in a daring, low-cut, white, flowing dress. I was willing to bet that Mr. Cross, a gruff little man who watched over his only child like a bulldog, hadn't seen her in that dress. Jeanie had her long brown hair piled on top of her head in a bun, which meant that her beautiful tanned face and long neck seemed to be rising out of her bosom. She looked absolutely stunning. Although the Pinetoppers were in the middle of playing "Love Twist," every guy in the place had their eyes glued on Jeanie as she made her way through the crowd to where several of us were dancing right in front of the band.

"Hot damn," one of the Pinetoppers said, loud enough to be picked up by the microphone, "That gal in white is a looker . . . what a body!" Jeanie laughed out loud as she hugged me and congratulated me on the "cool party." The hug didn't last for long as I saw the scowl on Billy Ivey's face and pulled back quickly. The captain of the Albany High Indians didn't seem to think the Sophomore-Sophomore was so cool.

Jeanie loved music and attention and so I knew she was dying to get out on the dance floor and rock with the rest of us—particularly after having to listen to the H-2-Os for the last couple of hours. While old Billy Ivey was great on a football field, he wasn't much on the dance floor and didn't have the guts to try. But I wasn't about to get punched in the nose. When the Pinetoppers played "Let's Twist Again Like We Did Last Summer," most of the male heads turned in hopes of seeing Jeanie drag Billy out on the floor. But Jeanie just sat there and watched, unsmiling, with Billy's bearish arm draped around her.

Phil Walden was right about the band. They were hot, and their new lead singer—Phil said his name was Otis—was terrific. Just when the whole place was really rocking, the band told me their time was up. They promised to play one more song while I scurried around and found Phil, who was sitting in the back, cigarette hanging out of his mouth, talking on the phone in between occasional sips from a fifth of Jack Daniel's.

"They were late," I protested. "Can't they play a little longer?"

"You're right. I'll give you a special deal and try to get them to do another hour for $50 . . . it's normally $100."

"It's a deal!" I said, certain that we had more than enough profit to pay for the extra time and anxious to get back and be part of the fun.

The Garden Center was still rocking well after midnight when the security guard began to switch the overhead lights off and on, signaling the dance was over. I slipped him $25 to let the Pinetoppers play a few more songs. When their last song—"Save the Last Dance for Me"—was over, our gang of friends gathered in a circle with our arms around each other, stomped our feet in unison, chanting "sophomore-sophomore" over and over again while the rest of the crowd drifted away. A few of us hung out with the band as they packed up their instruments and mopped themselves off with large white towels. Then we counted up the money.

I was positive that we had cleared a couple of hundred dollars, but it didn't quite work out that way. I learned that Jay had gotten drunk and quit selling tickets at about nine. Half of the sophomores got in free, and none of the juniors or seniors paid. Instead of having a nice profit, I found myself standing there with only $85 and Phil Walden swearing he would not leave Albany without their $250. Fortunately, my home was only three blocks away. I woke up my dear father. He sat at the kitchen table in his seersucker blue-and-white-striped bathrobe, half asleep and rubbing his eyes as he wrote a personal check for $165. He was usually a good sport but sounded kind of angry when he asked, "Who in the hell are the Pinetoppers?"

Check in hand, Phil Walden and the band loaded up. Johnny Jenkins and the Pinetoppers, thoroughly smashed, piled in the very back of the hearse. We couldn't see them behind the tinted windows but could hear them yelling loudly and laughing. Phil slipped in behind the wheel, and the long black hearse pulled out of Albany, headed for Macon. It was a strange looking spectacle, a white kid in a black hearse, driving a bunch of black men in the Deep South.

We all got a big chuckle the next day when the Sophomore-Sophomore was described on the society page of the *Albany Herald* as "a wonderful party. A gay evening was enjoyed by all the young couples in attendance." Without telling me, my mother had called Louise Whiting, the society editor, and told her about our dance at the Garden Center. Mrs. Whiting deemed it such an "adorable idea," but she obviously did not personally "cover" the dance, as her story did not mention that we had decorated the Garden Center with rolls of toilet paper, that a hard-drinking black band had played "Hot Nuts" four or five times in a row, or that Lenny Stephens, the Baptist preacher's son, barfed all over the fancy green sofa in the foyer. The whole episode left me thinking that it was pretty easy to get a good story in the paper.

I had to work double shifts for several weeks as a lifeguard at the Elk's Club pool that summer to pay back my father and to reimburse the Garden Club $75 in damages. It was the first and last time that my gang was allowed to have a dance there. That was also the first and last Sophomore-Sophomore held in Albany, Georgia—or anywhere else, as far as I know. The next year, we were all juniors, so it was our turn to cherry-pick the best-looking sophomore girls to take to the prom.

That year, we entered the gymnasium—one couple at a time—through a big arc decorated to look like a giant class ring, paused for a photographer to take our picture, and then tried in vain to dance to the music of the H-2-Os. The big window fans strained, but it was like a sauna in the old gym. The band members—under the lights—were drenched in sweat, and I started calling them Wayne Entrekin and the Drips, a name that stuck with all of us that year and again the next year when we came back for our swan song senior prom.

There were the usual rumors about prom punch being spiked with vodka, but that was hard to imagine, as Miss Bessie Dobbins—my beloved, seventy-year-old, silver-haired Latin teacher, clad in her best blue taffeta dress with a giant bow on the waist—ladled green punch from the cut-glass bowl filled with ice into orange paper cups.

In the years that followed, we had the Pinetoppers at over a dozen dances, getting to know them and their music well. I also learned Otis's last name—it was Redding. In a few years, he was one of the biggest names in rock 'n' roll and the basis for Phil Walden's new record label, Capricorn Records, which became a highly influential record label in the late 1960s and 1970s thanks to the success of artists like Redding, the Allman Brothers, and Lynyrd Skynyrd.

Almost twenty years later, when I was working to get a peanut farmer and former governor of Georgia elected president, Phil Walden and Capricorn Records were an important part of that effort. Phil—at the very top of his profession—was responsible for introducing Jimmy Carter to the music and entertainment industry, including the stars. Phil's advocacy of Carter helped to overcome some of the stereotypes of Carter, the Baptist. At a practical level, fundraising concerts for Carter with the Allman Brothers and Willie Nelson were huge publicity events and major sources of campaign funds.

Phil Walden became and remained a close friend of Jimmy Carter and of mine. He died of cancer in 2006 at the young age of sixty-six.

■ ■ ■

After the Sophomore-Sophomore, it became obvious to me that music was not only a way to have fun and make a little money (that is, if someone other than my buddy Jay Beck was handling the money). It was also a great way to meet girls.

For several weeks at Albany High, my classmates and even the upperclassmen talked about the Sophomore-Sophomore almost as much as they did about the Albany Indians football team, which was on its way to a regional championship! The girls in particular were interested in talking about the dance. It was considered "really cool" to have gone to the Sophomore-Sophomore. With this "experience"—one dance under my belt, underwritten by my daddy—and my contact with Phil Walden to the world of rock 'n' roll, I organized dances for the rest of my time in high school. Due to the slight damage from the Sophomore-Sophomore, we were barred from renting the Garden Club, but I was able to rent the pool area at the Radium Springs Country Club on their off nights. When Daddy started calling me "the impresario," I had to go to the dictionary to find out what "impresario" meant!

Johnny Jenkins and the Pinetoppers—featuring the yet unknown Otis Redding as lead singer—were regulars. By their third or fourth performance, I knew the band members by name. At the end of each dance, they would thank me over the loudspeaker for the gig or dedicate songs to me. I tried to pretend I was embarrassed by their attention, but I was just as proud as if I had scored the winning touchdown in the championship game. Mama was right—there were other ways to shine.

At the end of one dance, Otis Redding himself thanked me: "Our exclusive local promoter, Mr. Hamilton Jordan." The next day, I went to a local printer and had business cards printed, reading,

Hamilton Jordan, Promoter
Bands & Concerts
Phone 21017

I thought about using the term *impresario* but realized that most folks in South Georgia, like me, would not know what I was talking about. I got five hundred business cards and never used more than twenty of them, but I carried them around in my pocket for most of the next decade, mostly using them to impress girls I met. The cards didn't work very well.

But far and away the biggest gig of my "career" was when I booked Doug Clark and the Hots Nuts for a summer jam in 1961. The Hot Nuts were one of the hottest bands anywhere: an all-black group out of North Carolina that made its reputation playing fraternity parties at the University of North Carolina at Chapel Hill. Good musicians who were known primarily for their raunchy songs, they would save their signature number—"Hot Nuts"—until the beer was flowing, the party was really rocking, and the dancers were chanting, even demanding, "Hot nuts, hot nuts!"

Only when the whole crowd was roaring would the Hot Nuts play their familiar refrain:[1]

> "Nuts, nuts, red hot nuts,
> You get 'em from the peanut man,
> Nuts, nuts, red hot nuts,
> Get 'em any way you can."

Then they would go into one of their regular ditties:

> "See that gal,
> Dressed in green [pointing to a girl on the dance floor]?
> She goes down,
> Like a submarine.
> Nuts, nuts, red hot nuts,
> Get 'em anywhere you can!"

The crowd would go wild and they would do another one.

> "Nut, nuts, red hot nuts,
> You get 'em from the peanut man,
> See that guy
> Long and tall?
> He ain't got
> No nuts at all!"

And another one,

> "See that babe
> Dressed in black?
> Makes her living
> On her back."

As the night dragged on, the Hot Nuts would stick the microphone in front of the people dancing, who would improvise lyrics of their own—mostly flops—but it was considered a proud moment to create your own verse and localize it.

Sometimes, one of the Hot Nuts would stop and tell a joke, appropriate for their audience. If they were at a frat dance with a lot of Kappas present, they might ask:

1. Used with permission of publisher, Rhinelander Music.

"Do you know the difference between a rooster and a Kappa Kappa Gamma?"

Of course, no one did.

"A rooster, he says, 'Cock-a doodle, do-o-o!' A Kappa Kappa Gamma, she says, 'Any cock will do!'"

After the Hot Nuts played at Radium Springs Country Club, I could have been elected president of AHS by my classmates, but I would not have gotten any votes from the adults, as word quickly got around town about the "Hot Nuts." My daddy found it amusing, but not Mama, who questioned me about the name of this "outrageous band." I explained it away, saying that they were musically "hot" and acted kinda crazy, hence the name "nuts." That didn't work for long, as Mama continued to hear stories about their "filthy antics."

■ ■ ■

In the summer of 1962, Phil Walden put me in touch with one of his New York City booking agents who was trying to book a "brilliant, young folk singer" who was scheduled for Emory University, in Atlanta, and looking for other gigs in the South. He told me that he had written "Blowin' in the Wind"—the song that made Peter, Paul and Mary famous. He mailed me a copy of his new 45. I listened to it, expecting to hear some lilting folksong, but instead heard a kind of whiny, scratchy voice singing lyrics with a strong political message. I talked to the New York agent on the phone and told him that we were not interested. He gave me the usual stuff, claiming that this guy was going to be big. I told him we were looking for a band that I could promote and sell tickets to—not a folk singer. Plus, I said that I would get run out of town by bringing this guy to Albany. "This is the South, man," I said. "The Deep, Deep South."

So I missed his client but heard him a couple of years later at a concert at Emory. He was good. His name was Bob Dylan.

But it was Bo Diddley, not Bob Dylan or even the Hot Nuts, who brought an end to my days as a promoter. And it happened as a result of a gig in Albany that I had absolutely nothing to do with! Bo Diddley played a style he called "jive," but most whites just considered it "nigger music." His biggest hit—"Gunslinger"—came out in 1959 and had a terrific rhythmic beat that was great to dance to.

Bo Diddley came to Albany only a few weeks after the Hot Nuts played at the country club, but Bo and his band played at an all-black club in south Albany. Within days of leaving town, rumors started to circulate among my mother's friends that Kay Reynolds—the rebellious, good-looking, eighteen-year-old daughter of a prominent white doctor—had run off with Bo Diddley.

It was almost unbelievable to think that this could have happened. A few weeks later, the story spread that Kay Reynolds had actually married Bo Diddley, making her Mrs. Diddley! People in Albany could not believe this, and they were so embarrassed for the Reynolds family that they tiptoed around this very sensitive family issue. My mother regularly played bridge with Mrs. Reynolds but reported that the status and whereabouts of Mr. and Mrs. Diddley never came up. Later, we would all learn the truth: they *did* get married, and Kay had become one of a string of Bo Diddley's white wives and girlfriends. They did not stay married long, but it was long enough to have twin boys named Rocky and Rolly.

The Diddley-Reynolds scandal pretty much did it for black bands performing in Albany in the late 1950s and early 1960s. It was one thing for black bands to entertain white audiences, but another thing altogether to "entertain" and even marry "our" white women. The manager of Radium Springs Country Club told me that he would be fired if he allowed another black band to play there.

I looked around town but was unable to find a venue for future dances. My days as a promoter were over.

Chapter Nine

■ ■ ■

MEET THE GOTTHEIMERS

Every Sunday night while attending the University of Georgia, I called home to talk to my parents. Long-distance calls in the early 1960s were a big deal—rare and very expensive. Most families carefully reviewed their monthly phone bill from Southern Bell—the only choice—for long or unusual calls, making sure no one had charged an unauthorized call to their number. So, when an "urgent" note slipped under the door of my dorm room read, "Your mother called and wants you to call home immediately," I was frightened. Why in the world would she call me so late at the dorm and in the middle of the week? Something must be really wrong—it was unusual and disturbing. A couple of friends had recently lost their fathers to heart attacks, and as the operator placed a collect call to our home phone number, 21017, my first impulse was to think that the call was about my daddy.

The line was busy for a long time, only adding to my anxiety. Mama finally answered the phone and—obviously struggling with her own emotions—simply told me, "Mur passed away late this afternoon." I was devastated. This was the first time any close member of my family had died. When I asked for details, Mama said that Mur's health had deteriorated over the last month, that she blacked out at home earlier in the week, and that Uncle Hamilton, her oldest son, who lived with them, had to revive her with mouth-to-mouth resuscitation. She stubbornly refused to go to the Athens hospital for additional tests and passed away in her own bed. Hamp and Uncle Hamilton were with her when she died.

Mama said that she, Daddy, and Helen would leave South Georgia for Lexington early the next morning, arriving in the afternoon. Although grieving for her dear mother, dead only a few hours, Mama had already turned her thoughts to Hamp and his health, wondering out loud, "What will Daddy do without Mama? I don't know how long he can last without her."

Having never lost anyone in my immediate family, I was only able to think about all of this in the abstract. Numbed by the very idea of Mur's death, I got up the next day and drove the eighteen miles from Athens to Crawford and on to Lexington, along the familiar winding road, thinking about all sorts of things. I could not imagine walking into Mur's house without her being there to greet me with a big hug. I also began to be nervous about seeing Hamp. He had been married to my grandmother for sixty years, and now she was gone. My mother's concerns became my own as I tried to imagine him without Mur. What could I possibly say that would comfort him? How could I face him? I felt so bad for Hamp and began to understand for the first time the fear of "growing old alone" that I had heard older folks often express.

Having learned to slow down the instant I saw the Lexington City Limits sign in order to avoid overrunning the small town, I turned right onto the country road that ran along the side of the big familiar house, soon coming on the scene of so many wonderful memories and happy times, the likes of which would never be replicated. Couples were arriving and leaving the porch that surrounded the front of Mur and Hamp's house, many carrying covered dishes and a few with homemade floral arrangements. Cars were already parked on both sides of the road in front of the modest wooden houses where the hands and their families lived—all the way down to the barn, more than a hundred yards from the big house. I took a deep breath before getting out of my car; this was not going to be easy.

To avoid the crowd, I came in the back door of the house and entered by way of the large dining room, the site of so many wonderful meals, so much laughter, and countless political discussions. Hamp would sit at one end and preside over the conversation, and Mur, at the other end, would smile as she presided over the meal, ready to step in if Hamp started too much "foolishness" with her grandchildren.

On this day, the room was crowded with a number of familiar-looking, silver-haired Lexington ladies dressed in their Sunday best, hovering over the table and fussing over each new dish to arrive as one—clearly designated to keep track of who brought what—made careful and detailed entries in a black notebook. These were women with a method and a purpose. I wouldn't be surprised if thank-you notes on behalf of the family were mailed out before we even buried our dear Mur!

The dark wooden table that dominated the dining room was already loaded with pies, casseroles, homemade breads, biscuits, cheese rolls, and jams. Pies were cut into neat slices and placed on fine china plates, steaming casseroles had large silver serving spoons scooped into them, hot coffee and fresh cream were available, and huge pitchers of iced tea had been poured into tall, frosty glasses with lemon wedges stuck on the rims. The mere volume of wonderful food produced overnight confirmed how fast news spreads in a small community; the Lexington women and their help were up way before dawn, cooking to honor Mur and her family with their favorite recipes.

Several of these ladies now circulated among the mourners in the living room, each carrying silver trays and offering up—and in some cases, forcibly pressing—fresh samples of their efforts on the guests. A small cloud of cigar smoke hovered over the room already thick with people as groups of three or four, mostly men, huddled together, talking quietly, swapping stories, and laughing softly.

Over in the corner of the large living room, I finally found Hamp, sunk low in his favorite red leather chair, wearing a dark blue, double-breasted suit, his Masonic pin in the lapel, and his red tie loosened at the neck. He was chewing on the ever-present unlit cigar. When no one was talking directly to him, Hamp stared straight ahead with a blank expression on his face.

I had never seen him like this.

A ritual had developed. Folks who dropped by to pay their respects were greeted at the door by one of the local ladies and asked to sign the guest book, which rested on a little wooden stand, both items furnished by the funeral home. Guests were then brought into the living room, where they first exchanged pleasantries with Uncle Hamilton or Uncle Bill and eventually my mother and her sister, Sydney, who would both arrive later. Finally, folks would make their way over to see Hamp.

"Daddy," one of his children announced softly, "you remember Judge Knox from Thomson," or "Sarah Jernigan from Athens," or "Bill Friar from the Planters' Bank," or "Senator Brown from Elberton." Many of the visitors were old political friends and acquaintances from out of town, usually dressed in dark suits, occasionally mixed in with a local farmer in overalls or a local merchant in khaki pants and a short-sleeved shirt, all of them expressing their condolences at the loss of "Miss Helen" to "Mr. Hamp."

I stood back and watched for a few moments as Hamp's long face brightened at the sight of these old friends from politics, and he usually struggled to stand up to shake hands before getting motioned down or discouraged from rising by the guest or one of his sons. When these old friends offered some personal comment about my grandmother, Hamp got teary eyed then struggled to regain his composure, mumbling his gratitude for their visit and moving quickly to some distraction about another mutual friend or memory. Before long, Hamp and the visitor would be smiling, even chuckling, together.

Obviously, Hamp found some relief in reminiscing with these old friends instead of focusing on the reality of Mur's marked absence from her nearby favorite rocking chair, where she spent so many years knitting, reading, or working on a crossword puzzle while Hamp visited with the constant flow of friends who would drop in without notice.

When I gathered myself, took a deep breath, and came on into the living room from the dining area, I immediately caught my grandfather's eye. Hamp, in a voice loud enough to catch the attention of those around him, called out, "This is my namesake, Adelaide's boy, Hamilton *McWhorter* Jordan. Come over here!" he demanded. "Helen was so proud of this young man!" he continued as I walked in his direction. And then the tears just started to flow.

Fighting to control my own emotions, I knelt down on one knee in front of his big leather chair and looked right into Hamp's reddened, baby blue eyes. Feeling that folks around us were watching, waiting, I struggled to find something to say. But Hamp just reached out with his frail arms and drew me to him, pressing my head up against his shoulder, where I stayed while his body just shook, his chest heaving. He quietly sobbed and sobbed for what must have been a minute or so. Finally, he held me away, pulled his handkerchief out of his suit pocket, wiped at his own eyes, and handed it to me.

Having regained his composure, Hamp began to call old friends over, introducing me loudly and stressing to each that I was Hamilton *McWhorter* Jordan.

It was easier for me after seeing Hamp that first time. He and I shed tears for Mur together; some of my tears were for him. Word of Mur's death—coming to me only hours before in a late-night phone call—had seemed almost surreal, but once I reached Lexington, saw the tears, and felt the grief, I knew that she was really gone.

Hamp looked very old and tired to me that day. His suit seemed to swallow him, and his collar, even while buttoned, was hanging loose around the neck. My grandfather seemed to be wasting away. He was eighty-four years old, suffering from advanced prostate cancer, having had one serious heart attack, and now having lost his partner of sixty years, and his remaining time with us was probably short. So, even as we mourned our dear Mur, the attention of our entire family turned to helping Hamp through the difficult two days, greeting hundreds of family members and friends and burying his wife.

My mother and Aunt Sydney finally arrived that afternoon after long drives from South Georgia and Virginia. The daughters took over greeting duties from their brothers and finally talked Hamp into taking an afternoon nap, which he badly needed. His children met with the hired funeral home folks from Athens, making it plain that they wanted the service to be very simple and fast—Hamp was clearly under enough strain as it was, and most of the mourners would be older people.

Worried that Mur's death could have immediately devastating effects on her father, my mother sent me in to peek at Hamp from time to time to be sure that he was breathing. The old man was sleeping soundly. I could see the rise and fall of his chest.

While my mother and her siblings put forward a good front for Hamp and for their own children, it was not until I went into the kitchen that I felt the full depth of grief and loss that gripped this Lexington home. Annie, the family cook for over sixty years, was by this time close to eighty years old. I found her dressed up in her finest white apron with a crisp, white turban wrapped around her head, sitting on a stool in the corner, next to the large, black iron, wood-burning stove, site of tens of thousands of wonderful meals. There was Annie, all bent over, hands on her head, sobbing uncontrollably. Her daughters, Cat and Nookie, stood on each side, patting her on the back, trying to console her.

When she heard me call her name, Annie looked up, exclaimed, "Mister Hamilton," stood to hug me, and just said over and over again, "I'm gonna miss Miss Helen so much . . . I'm gonna miss her so much, so much. Miss Helen was so good to me and my younguns. What am I gonna do without her? What am I gonna do without Miss Helen?"

The grief of the rest of the family in the living room was profound yet restrained. But among these folks in the kitchen who had known and worked closely with Mur for so many years, the emotion was raw and had no limits.

The white folks in the living room were grieving. Annie and her extended family in the kitchen were truly mourning, pouring their whole souls into the feeling of my grandmother's death.

■ ■ ■

Mur's funeral, held the following day, was attended by a mostly older crowd. It was a beautiful spring morning for the graveside service, which was conducted at the small cemetery only several hundred yards down the road from Mur and Hamp's residence.

We drove the short distance in shiny black Cadillacs provided by the funeral home—Hamp and his four children in the lead, followed by several black limos with the rest of the family. By the time we arrived, several hundred people had already gathered around the outer edges of the small, green tent, filled with rows of white, wooden folding chairs for the family.

Several dozen blacks who worked in Mur's home or on the farm stood behind the very last row of seats where the family sat. Wearing their "go-to-meeting clothes," the women were in their Sunday finery. George, Henry, and the men looked uncomfortable in their ill-fitting suits with ties hanging around their necks. I couldn't help but think how much closer they were to Mur and how much closer their lives had been intertwined with hers than most of the white folks sitting in front of them and under the tent. A seat of honor with the family was saved for Annie, next to my mother and Aunt Sydney. She wore a black dress with her hair done in a permanent. It was the first time I had ever seen her without an apron and with a hat on her head instead of her usual white turban.

All of the six grandchildren piled out of our shiny limos, walked on a path through the crowd, and filed into the second row of folding chairs sitting on the artificial green carpet. We remained standing as the rest of the cars unloaded. We sat waiting for Hamp so the service could begin. The dark wooden casket containing Mur's body, resting on a platform, was right in front of us, fresh dirt piled to the side of the hole in the ground that the man from the funeral home called "her final resting place." I was surprised to see a tiny grave marker in front of the large marble McWhorter headstone. Later that day, I learned from my mother that the tiny grave was Mur and Hamp's first child, an unnamed son, who lived only a few days.

But that was not the only surprise.

My eyes wandered as we waited for Hamp. Less than five yards to the right of Mur's burial site, I couldn't help but notice a large, weathered family marker with the name Gottheimer chiseled into the stone. Two dark, long slabs lay side by side in front of this marker. The writing on the slabs was not easy to read, but I could clearly make out the name "Gottheimer" at the top and the word "Germany" in the inscriptions on both. I had never seen nor heard that name before. It sure looked German to me, and it sure sounded Jewish to me.

Standing just behind me was one of my Uncle Hamilton's oldest and dearest friends from childhood, Cliff Brooks, owner of the Chevrolet dealership in nearby Crawford. I turned and whispered in his ear, "Cliff, who are those Jews buried next to my grandmother?"

Cliff looked surprised at my question. After looking around, Cliff cupped his hand over his mouth, leaned forward, and whispered quietly in my ear, "Those are Miss Helen's parents." Then, after a pause, he added, "Your great-grandparents!"

I was stunned. My great-grandparents? The Gottheimers? How could that be? I had never even heard the name before!

My mind was spinning. Who were these people?

It sure sounded *Jewish* to me!

But Cliff had no reason to mislead me. If Cliff was right, that would mean that Mur was the child of a Jewish couple, which meant Mur was Jewish! And if Mur was Jewish, I figured that meant my mother was half Jewish! And if my mother was half Jewish, I figured that meant I was a quarter Jewish! (Later I would learn that "Jewishness" is determined through the maternal side of a family. As my grandmother was Jewish and my mother was the daughter of a Jew, I am—by birth—Jewish.)

How could this be? Why has this critical fact about our family and its heritage been hidden all these years? My mind was still racing until the sight of our dear Hamp startled me back to reality. Supported under each arm by one of his sons and followed by his daughters, my grandfather was walking slowly—and with great difficulty—toward the green tent, finally taking his place with his children and Annie on the front row.

But everything that was happening in front of my eyes collided with this jarring discovery about these people called the Gottheimers. The Baptist preacher stood up, the crowd was quieted, and he began to read the scriptures in a melodious voice. I tried to think about Mur as I heard the familiar words of the Lord's Prayer but could not keep my eyes off the large marker and the word GOTTHEIMER chiseled in stone.

Was Mur now technically a Baptist? Had she ever joined the Baptist Church? I thought of all those times when we visited Lexington, her dressing us up and inspecting us Sunday morning before sending us off to church. I could not remember a single time she went to First Baptist with us, but I had always attributed this circumstance to her fragile health and the fact that she rarely went anywhere far from her home.

Thoughts bouncing back and forth, I glanced at Hamp, struggling to hold his head high and maintain composure. Occasionally, he dabbed at his watering blue eyes with a white handkerchief. Still, the mysterious headstone with the strange name on it loomed larger and larger in my vision and in my thoughts. In my confusion and my grief, I just couldn't reconcile things. I wanted to ask somebody, anybody, what did it all mean?

Everyone who had attended the funeral dropped by the house to pay their respects, and so a whole new group of Lexington ladies once again took over with a huge table of new food choices. Tired and confused, I did not feel like seeing anyone, and so I went upstairs and locked myself in one of the bathrooms, staying there just long enough for my mother to send my older brother looking for me. I asked Lawton if he had seen the Gottheimer marker next to Mur's grave, and I was surprised to learn that he knew all about it.

"They were Mur's parents, but Mama and Hamp and his children just don't want to talk about it . . . we have to respect that."

Obviously, the aftermath of Mur's funeral was no place for me to ask questions about this discovery, but as I headed back to Athens the day after the funeral, my sadness over Mur's passing was clouded by my own frustration and the feelings of anger at the deception practiced by my family. Why, I was wondering, did it matter? What was the point of "respecting" this apparently dark family secret?

I vividly remembered Hamp regularly holding forth in his chair about our McWhorter family and our ancestors, the annual—indeed man-datory—trip to the McWhorter reunion at the old cemetery in nearby

Greensboro, Georgia, the burial site of the McWhorters from whom we were all descended. We ate barbecue, drank iced tea in the hot sun, met new relatives, and renewed ties with cousins, aunts, and uncles from all over Georgia and the Deep South. Every year, we were introduced to one or two new cousins or encountered some obscure branch of the family, occasionally a few rare Yankee McWhorters, the odd ones, whose parents had gone astray and left the South.

Hamp was president in perpetuity of the McWhorter reunions, and each year a different cousin would prepare some speech that probably exaggerated the accomplishments of one or the other famous ancestor. Awards were given for the McWhorter who had come to the most consecutive reunions (Hamp was not eligible because he would have always won), the McWhorter who had traveled the longest distance to be there, and so on. These half-day reunions ended with several of the oldest members of our family standing, encouraging the younger ones to continue this tradition of the reunions (and admonishing them if they seemed uncommitted to the cause), and to never, ever forget what it meant to be a McWhorter in America. Traditionally, a McWhorter preacher sent us all off with a prayer for a safe trip home, good health during the year, and a safe return to next year's reunion.

Never, now that I thought of it, had there ever been a single word about Mur's family from Hamp or my mother or her brothers and sister. Our family had done as good a job of hiding the Gottheimers as they had of celebrating the McWhorters. I realized that, throughout all of those years, my family had never acknowledged the presence of the Gottheimers in the lives of my mother and grandparents—and not even a mention of their names; I had to stumble across them at the mouth of my own grandmother's grave!

The Jewish blood that flowed through our veins must have been a huge issue for my family in 1908 when Mur and Hamp married. It was obviously still a big issue a half a century later but something that apparently had to be hidden from their children and grandchildren and simply not talked about.

Years later, one of my mother's dearest friends, Olivia Beck (and mother of my best buddy since kindergarten, Jay Beck), who lived near her in Albany, talked to me about my mother's background but only when I asked her specific questions. Mrs. Beck, an artist and a magnificent socialite, had studied at Parsons (an institution teaching art,

governor of Georgia, largely on fame won as the man who prosecuted Leo Frank. Populist Tom Watson, author of vitriolic and inflammatory anti-Semitic, anti-Catholic articles in his Georgia newspaper that demanded the death penalty for Frank and applauded the lynching, was credited by most (and blamed by only a few) for inspiring the mob action that led to Frank's lynching. Watson was elected to the U.S. Senate a year after the trial.

It was not until 1982 that Alonzo Mann, one of the key witnesses whose eye-witness account had led to Leo Frank's conviction, made a deathbed confession that he had seen Jim Conley carrying Mary Phagan's body. On his deathbed, Mann said that Conley had been the murderer of Mary Phagan and threatened him with death if he ever spoke of what he had seen.

In 1986, nearly seventy-five years after the lynching of Leo Frank, the Georgia Pardons and Parole Board granted Leo Frank a pardon.

■ ■ ■

This was the same anti-Semitic, anti-Catholic political and social climate in which Hamilton McWhorter and Helen Gottheimer had courted, fallen in love, married, and started their family in rural north Georgia. Their farm in Lexington was only sixty miles from the site where Mary Phagan was murdered and Leo Frank, falsely accused, was lynched by a mob from a tree.

As I sat in the University of Georgia library, mulling over the circumstances of the Frank case and the hostile social climate in which my grandparents had fallen in love, there were so many questions that raced through my mind. Had Mur's and Hamp's parents opposed their marriage? Before they married, did Mur and Hamp talk about these issues and how they would raise their children? By the time they married, Hamp was already interested in politics and was a local judge. Was Hamp blind to public opinion or so much in love that he did not care?

Had this anti-Semitic feeling in Georgia discouraged Hamp from running for statewide office? Was this why he never did it? His old friends and family members had made a habit of confiding in me mysteriously: "You know, Hamp could have been governor," without ever supplying the reason that he was not. Did Hamp ever talk about these things to his children? Growing up, were my mother and her siblings ever targets of bigotry and prejudice? Or did they grow up in the protected cocoon of the small town where the McWhorters and Gottheimers were among the respectable handful of well-to-do families in their community?

What was it like to renounce your faith and live in the South, known for its intolerance of other religions? Did Mur ever practice Judaism in nearby Athens?

Unfortunately, most of these questions would remain unanswered for the rest of my life. If I wanted to learn anything about the perceived "dark side" of my heritage, I'd have to take matters into my own hands.

■ ■ ■

Decades later, I learned that my great-grandmother Adelheit Stern Gottheimer, who died in 1896, was buried in a Jewish ceremony in Athens. Only later was she moved to Lexington and buried next to her husband and my great-grandfather, William, when he died in 1919. I found the obituary of Mur's mother in the newspaper archives back at the University of Georgia library. Written in the stilted, exaggerated style of the day, the headline in the *Oglethorpe Echo*, which served all of Lexington, read:

AFTER SHORT ILLNESS, MRS. WILLIAM GOTTHEIMER
PASSES TO THE GREAT BEYOND

One of the saddest deaths that has ever occurred in Lexington was that of Mrs. William Gottheimer at her home in this place at 5 o'clock on Friday evening. All that the best of medical skill and loving ones could do was done for her but to no avail. At the hour given, she passed peacefully away.

Mrs. Gottheimer was, before her marriage to William Gottheimer, Miss Adelheit Stern of Athens, her family being one of the most esteemed Jewish families of that city.

Upon taking up her residence in Lexington, she at once won her way into the hearts and esteem of everyone and no lady of this town was ever more beloved than she. She was a sincere friend, a kind neighbor and her remarkably sympathetic nature brought her always to the aid of any and all who were in distress and in trouble. That she should be struck down while yet in the full bloom of womanhood is a dispensation of Providence which casts a gloom over the entire community.

The remains of the deceased were carried to Athens on Sunday evening and interred there at 6 pm after appropriate funeral ceremonies at the synagogue in that place.

The little newspaper story told me so much that I had never known and that my family had never shared with me: my great-grandfather had had to raise his two very young daughters by himself. My great-grandmother had died when she was only forty-eight years old. My grandmother's family had practiced Judaism to some extent, as Mur's mother was "interred" in Athens after her death, following a service in the synagogue. My mother, whose name was Adelaide, was named for her grandmother, Adelheit Gottheimer.

I also learned that the same wonderful obituary for my great-grandmother Gottheimer—stressing her kindness—could easily have been used for Mur.

Finally finding out about my mother's ancestors was fascinating, but it was frustrating to have to get that information from old newspapers, when my very own flesh and blood could have given me far more insight and knowledge. I felt hurt and confused to realize that information that had once been public knowledge had been swept under the rug and shielded from younger generations for so many years.

I learned even more when I found the issue of the *Oglethorpe Echo* announcing the death of my great-grandfather, William Gottheimer, twenty-three years later. The *Oglethorpe Echo* proclaimed in a small headline at the top front of page 1:

LEXINGTON LOSES ITS MOST ESTEEMED CITIZEN

The happy Christmas spirit of every citizen of Lexington was turned into sadness when at about twelve o'clock on Christmas day, it was announced that Mr. William Gottheimer, than whom Lexington nor the county claimed a more highly esteemed citizen, had passed away at his home in this place.

The deceased was a native of Germany, having been born in Felane, Germany, on January 19, 1845. At about the age of seventeen, he came to this country with three brothers and then he came to the South and to Athens. From that city, they sold goods through this section for two or three years, during which time he gained by his always honest dealings, the confidence of the people of this county.

In 1873, he opened a store in Lexington, being joined soon after by his brother and they, for a number of years, did a thriving business together.

No man ever had a higher sense of honor and integrity than did Mr. Gottheimer. From his first coming among us, he held the highest of esteem and confidence of everybody and no man among us was more beloved for his excellent trait of character.

We had no more public spirited citizen than he, and in his modesty, he gave every worthy public cause his endorsement and aid. He was identified and took active interest in practically all of our public enterprises and to his wise counsel and attention can the success of most of them be attributed. He was all that one could ask for as a citizen, a friend and a man.

When his daughters were but babies, Mrs. Gottheimer died and to the father fell the task of reassuring his daughters, a task he performed lovingly and so successfully as to rear them to be among the most popular women of our town.

We feel the loss of this good citizen and man, and individually we feel the loss of a friend than whom we have none we more highly prize to whose advice and example we owe much of what success we made of life. There are hundreds of others to join us in this feeling of deprivation.

The irony that my great-grandfather Gottheimer, a Jew, died on Christmas Day (and the fact that this was the introduction of his obituary in his hometown newspaper) was not lost on me. But was he still a Jew? It said that a local Methodist preacher spoke at his funeral, and he was buried in a Christian cemetery. I wondered if he had truly abandoned the faith of his mother and father or had just bowed to the conventional wisdom of the day.

■ ■ ■

While trying to absorb all of this, I was also trying to be a good grandson, which, in this case, unfortunately meant keeping my thoughts, questions, and research to myself. Every couple of weeks following Mur's funeral, I drove down to Lexington from Athens to visit with Hamp. I toyed with the idea of asking him about Mur's family, but I did not have the nerve. How would Hamp, who actively hid the truth about the Gottheimers from his grandchildren for twenty-five years, react to such a question? Would it upset him? Embarrass him? Suppose it brought on another heart attack? I could never forgive myself if my selfish curiosity about this family secret killed my dear Hamp.

When I arrived at the home, my grandfather would be sitting in his regular chair, chewing on his unlit cigar. His face always lit up the moment I walked in and gave him a big hug; he would then ask me about school, the Phi Delta Thetas, and the prospects for the Georgia Bulldog football team.

But no matter what small talk was drummed up at the onset of each meeting, it wouldn't be long before he got all teary-eyed, talking about his dear Helen. It never seemed a good or right time to bring up my questions about the Gottheimers—and I never once got the nerve to do so. I determined that it was simply not fair to expect Hamp to discuss the subject with me, deciding that it was much more realistic and fair to expect my own mother to help me.

I went to Albany several weeks later for the sole purpose of finally talking in greater depth with my mother about Mur's family. I was going to ask her—I felt determined and justified in my objective. We had just finished a good home-cooked meal, my father was making a business call, and my little sister, Helen, was in her bedroom doing her homework. I helped my mother clear off the dishes from the dinner table and simply opened with, "Mama, can you tell me about your Gottheimer grandparents?"

I was surprised at her reaction. Freezing in her steps, almost dropping the stack of plates she was carrying to the sink, Mama turned her back to me, mumbled some excuse about needing to use the bathroom, and disappeared. She was gone for at least five minutes. When she returned, her face was flushed, but she had regained her composure. She calmly sat down at the kitchen table, motioned me to sit across from her, looked me right in the eye, and said, "Son, I understand your curiosity and will talk to you about that someday—as much as you want to hear and know. But it is complicated and also painful. Most of all, it is just too soon after losing Mur. Give me some time, okay?" she said, reaching across the table to grab my hand.

What could I say?

And that was the end of that. She changed the subject and started asking me questions about school and my courses for the quarter, a subject I had no desire to talk about. What was I to do? Chastise my dear mother? Try to make her tell me? Upset her?

I raised the subject of her family history with my mother on two other occasions over the next few months. The first time she said that she knew she "owed me that conversation," but then she changed the subject. But the second time, she rebuffed me gently and then effectively cut it off. "Sometimes we have to let sleeping dogs lie."

I talked about the mystery of our heritage over the years with my cousins who, while curious like me, also did not want to either embarrass or upset their own parents. At various points in time, we cousins would talk amongst ourselves about this unknown lineage in our backgrounds, resolving to confront our parents about it.

But we never did, and our collective hesitation came from the same source—a certain awareness and concern that we could be opening up something *so* painful or embarrassing or upsetting for that generation of the McWhorters that it could cause legitimate humiliation, create some rift in the family, or even bring about a heart attack or some stress-related health tragedy.

Some years later, when my own dear mother died, we were going through boxes of old family pictures when I found one photograph that caught my eye. It was a picture of my mother with her three siblings, dressed for some fancy occasion. They looked to be in their early thirties.

As I looked at the photo for the first time with my knowledge of our Jewish grandmother, I realized that I was looking at what my parents or their friends might say was a "nice-looking Jewish family."

That was my family, about whom—even today—I know very little.

■ ■ ■

In retrospect, it is interesting how I chose to deal with this family secret when I became privy to it. While frustrated with my own family's lack of candor and honesty with me, I admittedly did not rush to tell my friends about this discovery. Through the years, as I tried in subtle ways to learn more and more about this "dark secret," I seldom volunteered this information to anyone outside of my own family.

The first time I ever dealt with this publicly was many years later when I thought it might be helpful to me in the context of a news story.

In 1978, I was White House chief-of-staff and in charge of organizing a campaign to win support for the sale of sophisticated U.S. fighter jets to our ally Saudi Arabia, which was vigorously opposed by the government of Israel and their active lobby in this country.

Jack Anderson, the muckraker heir to Drew Pearson, and a totally scurrilous and irresponsible journalist himself, reported in his widely read column that I made anti-Semitic comments at a Georgetown cocktail party I had not even attended and used this alleged comment as the basis for the supposed "anti-Israeli" attitude of the Carter Administration. These charges were false, but they had turned into a serious story that had to be confronted. When a friend at the *New York Times* called me for a quote in response to allegations of my anti-Semitic attitude, I mentioned for the first time that this story was not only untrue but also preposterous, as Jewish blood flowed in my veins. That factoid appeared in the story with a comment from some "source" who was quoted as saying that the allegation stood that I had made anti-Semitic comments and that "Jordan is obviously one of those self-hating Jews."

As it is always impossible to win a public relations battle against anonymous sources, I chose not to respond.

An early portrait of Hamilton's grandmother Helen Gottheimer McWhorter, or "Mur."

Hamilton's grandfather Hamilton "Hamp" McWhorter sitting in the Georgia State Capitol.

Helen Gottheimer McWhorter, or "Mur."

Hamilton "Hamp" McWhorter, far left, eats watermelon alongside friends.

Cover page of the *Atlanta Journal*, January 15, 1933.
From left to right: Governor Eugene Talmadge, Hamilton
"Hamp" McWhorter, Senator Richard Russell, and Georgia
Speaker of the House E. D. Rivers.

Hamilton's father, Richard, and his family ride in the Confederate
Memorial Parade in Macon. From left to right: Corrine, Carrie Mae,
Robert, James, Richard.

Hamilton's father, Richard Jordan, in uniform. He served as a second lieutenant in the Quartermaster Corps of the U.S. Army.

Hamilton's mother, Adelaide Jordan.

Richard Jordan (left) with his two brothers, Robert (center) and James (right).

Above left: Hamilton's mother, Adelaide, tending to Hamilton in his carriage. *Above right*: Hamilton with his mother, Adelaide, outside Hamp and Mur's house in Lexington. *Left*: Baby Hamilton with his grandparents Hamp and Mur.

OPPOSITE: *Upper left*: Hamilton with his brother, Lawton, and Annie's daughter Cat in the backyard of Hamp and Mur's house in Lexington. *Upper right*: Hamilton and his cousin Albert play while being watched by Cat, Annie's daughter. *Lower left*: Hamilton pushing Lawton across the front yard of their Albany home. *Lower right*: Hamilton and Lawton playing on the Albany sidewalk.

Hamilton riding through Albany with training wheels.

A young Hamilton frolicking outdoors.

Hamilton in his Easter best in front of his childhood home in Albany.

Hamilton, his mother, Adelaide, and sister, Helen, on their porch in Albany.

Young Hamilton appraising the camera.

Hamilton posing with his brother, Lawton, and father, Richard, on an automobile display.

A picture of all the boys at Palymyra Grammar School in Albany in 1953. Hamilton is in the third row, fifth from the right.

Pretending to play football for the photographer, Olivia Beck, in her front yard. From left to right: Bill Arnold, Hamilton Jordan, Jay Beck, Richard Stalvey, Bobby Boesch, Buddy Dial, and Ronnie Cannon. (Unable to identify boy in foreground.)

Hamilton and his younger sister, Helen, goofing off.

Hamilton with his father, Richard, and mother, Adelaide.

Hamilton and Lawton with their father, Richard.

Hamilton holding the Confederate flag.

Family dinner out. Seated at the table (from left to right): Mur, Lawton, Hamilton, Hamp, and Uncle Bill.

Hamilton in fifth grade.

Hamilton poses for a portrait in middle school.

Hamilton with his eighth-grade class at Albany Junior High in 1957. Hamilton is in the second row, second from the right. Alfred Blum, Hamilton's "first Jewish friend," is third from right in the same row.

Hamilton with his girlfriend, Marylin Barfield, in 1960.

A photograph taken to commemorate Jeanie Cross's victory in the Miss Georgia pageant in 1962. She autographed it for Hamilton's best friend, Jay Beck.

High school portrait of Hamilton.

VOTE FOR

HAMILTON
JORDAN

PRESIDENT

FRESHMAN CLASS

Card from Hamilton's campaign for UGA freshman class president in 1962.

Hamilton poses for a class portrait at
the University of Georgia.

Part IV

■ ■ ■

OVERCOMING THE PAST

Chapter Ten

■ ■ ■

TWO, FOUR, SIX, EIGHT,
WE DON'T WANT TO INTEGRATE

It was already hot enough that summer of 1961, but the temperature went up all over town when the civil rights struggle came to Aw-ben-ny.

Dr. William Anderson, an idealistic black physician, organized the Albany Movement to test the city's willingness to integrate public facilities. The organization's actions were aimed specifically at eliminating the "White Only" signs at bathrooms and water fountains—the most powerful symbol of legal segregation throughout the South—and to give black Georgians access to the local bus system and trains. Unfortunately, the good intentions of Anderson were not enough. While Anderson had energized the black community, he had no plan for translating their activism into leverage with the white authorities. After several months of public marches and the subsequent arrests, trials, and releases, there was little evidence of legitimate progress. The word on the street was that the movement was floundering, losing steam, and having trouble finding fresh marchers, since many locals could not afford more time in jail or fines. In addition, there was a growing sense of competition between locals and outsiders for leadership of the Albany Movement. The leadership of the Student Nonviolent Coordinating Committee (SNCC), which had sent key national leaders into Albany, was increasingly concerned that other civil rights organizations might be invited in.

While the movement dominated the headlines and gripped the local community, nothing was really happening: there was no dialogue with the public officials and no strategy. The white community, in the

Sections from this chapter originally appeared in Hamilton Jordan's 2000 memoir, No Such Thing as a Bad Day.

daddy came up from behind and lifted him under his arms onto the box. The crowd went wild.

The young boy said in a loud and confident voice and in a thick drawl, "Thanks very much folks . . . my name is George Wallace Jr." It was hokey, but it sure worked. Young George delivered what was obviously a carefully prepared intro, inviting the crowd to "give a warm Eufaula welcome to my daddy and the next governor of the great state of Alabama . . . George Corley Wallace!" Wallace's compact body supported a rather large head, further exaggerated by that full head of black hair. Although he occasionally smiled when delivering a punch line, it seemed forced and unnatural. Wallace's smile looked more like a sneer, which seemed almost fitting as he denounced the federal government and the U.S. Supreme Court as being "out of control and trying to tell us down here in Alabama how to raise and educate our children."

"This George Corley Wallace sure is a bundle of emotion," I thought. Wallace spoke without notes, but his lines were carefully rehearsed, and his hands chopped the air with each catchy phrase.

But where was the southern liberal I had heard so much about from the 1958 campaign? His message was certainly not what I had expected based on his earlier race, which had earned the support of black Alabamians and progressive whites. George Wallace's message this time around was plain and unequivocal—aimed at rural white Democrats who hated Washington and feared blacks going to school with their children, taking their jobs, and marrying their daughters.

As we drove home that afternoon, I reflected on what I had seen and heard. George Wallace was certainly effective as a candidate. He obviously had had a convenient "change of heart" and was going after the redneck vote. Sure, every person I knew—except for my uncle Clarence Jordan—was a segregationist: Hamp, my parents, my neighbors, my schoolmates, and my friends. But there was something hard, mean, and raw about George Wallace. The reaction of the crowd to Wallace's message was unsettling. They came in happy and left angry, feeling threatened and wanting somebody to do something about it. Even though he had this crowd of Eufaula homefolks solidly behind him, I didn't think a candidate like George Wallace with just a straight racial appeal could be elected governor of Alabama—not in the 1960s!

One year later, George Wallace won the race for governor by a landslide.

had come pouring in town. The KKK responded by calling for a rally in Albany, declaring an "alert," and asking its chapters to send "white militia" to Albany, prepared to fight.

We couldn't see them yet, but we saw the advance guard of policemen on motorcycles, which preceded the marchers. Necks craned. People stood on tiptoes. We began to hear a quiet noise that became a chorus as it got closer and closer. Finally, we could make out the words:

> We shall overcome.
> We shall overcome.
> We shall overcome someday.
> Oh, deep in my heart,
> I do believe
> We shall overcome someday.

The protesters rounded the corner, coming into full view as they filled Pine Avenue. I was surprised—most of the marchers were high school and college aged with a sprinkling of kids who were barely teenagers. It was easy to pick out the familiar face of King in the front line, marching in locked arms with other men who looked like clergy. Particularly noticeable was a toffee-colored, handsome young man marching next to King, probably not much older than me . . . hell, he even looked young enough to be in high school. I would later learn that he was a preacher from Thomasville, Georgia, named Reverend Andrew Young—a key advisor to King who would later go on to serve as mayor of Atlanta, a congressman from the Fifth District, and the U.S. ambassador to the United Nations.

Someone else in the crowd had noticed the light-skinned marcher as well and shouted, "Go home, you high-yellow nigger!"

A farmer in overalls standing nearby voiced the ultimate fear, "That's what happens when you integrate . . . niggers will marry our daughters!"

"Over my dead body!" another retorted.

"Go home, Commies!"

"Get a job, you lazy niggers!"

"Two, four, six, eight . . . we ain't gonna integrate!" a group of teenagers methodically chanted, time and again.

The group kept marching down Pine Avenue. "My God," my father muttered as he held up his hand and pointed, "there's Hattie!"

Sure enough, bringing up the rear were several rows of black women in their Sunday best, and right in the middle was our housekeeper of over fifteen years, Hattie Jackson. In her sixties, Hattie was a proud, quiet woman. I was shocked.

What did this mean . . . "our" Hattie in a protest march?

The crowd moved at a quick pace on down Pine Avenue until they reached the area of City Hall, only to be met by a phalanx of big policemen in riot gear: tall black boots, white helmets, and black leather jackets. They chatted nervously among themselves, standing across the street about five feet apart, twirling their billy clubs.

Positioned in the middle to "receive" the leadership of the Albany Movement was Police Chief Laurie Pritchett. Looking down at the top of King's head, the chief blared over his bullhorn, "You are violating the laws of our city by marching without a permit. You have two minutes to disperse . . . you have two minutes to disperse, or you will be arrested!"

There was no response from the crowd. King and another marcher knelt in prayer. After a minute, the light-skinned young man pulled out a bullhorn and stuck it in front of King. Avoiding the chief's glance, King said in a strong, clear voice, "We are exercising our constitutional rights to peacefully assemble. We are marching today to protest the failure of the City of Albany to allow its Negro citizens and taxpayers to use the public facilities. We have broken no law and seek no trouble. We only request that you enforce the law of the land, Chief Pritchett, and allow us to exercise our rights."

There was no reply, and the chief looked around nervously as a television camera crew pressed through the crowd with a microphone extended, trying to pick up the exchange. Chief Pritchett studied his watch . . . waiting for the two minutes to expire. Things were going according to plan. The marchers knew they would be stopped, the chief knew that they would not disperse, and the group expected to be herded into the area between City Hall and the jail, where they would be led one-by-one up the stairs to be booked and put in jail.

The protest marchers waited quietly for what seemed like eternity. Most stared straight ahead at Chief Pritchett. The chief finally looked up, pulled out his bullhorn, and said calmly, "You have refused to obey my orders, and you will now be arrested. Do not resist arrest, and you will not be harmed."

The large crowd moved quietly into the area between the city jail and the courthouse, which were connected by a large, brick building, thus surrounding the group on three sides. The policemen took their billy clubs, gently prodding and poking until all the demonstrators had squeezed into the small space. The marchers had started to sing again, but you could hear the voices of some starting to talk or complain out loud. One or two of the children began to cry.

I was never sure what happened next . . . whether the demonstrators stumbled and tripped or were pushed to the ground by a nervous or overzealous cop. But people began to pile up in the narrow alley, and several ear-piercing screams penetrated the winter air. A couple of the onlookers laughed, and one man standing with us yelled out, "Looks like a bunch of niggers in a sardine can!" I saw the light-skinned young man and several others lock arms and circle King to protect him. Soon, the entire crowd had dropped to the ground, the singing had stopped completely, and screams and cries echoed out of the enclosed area. The white onlookers began to shout their approval, enjoying the discomfort of the protesters.

I looked anxiously for Hattie but could not find her in the sea of black faces. It turned out that a young lady had fainted and was being passed above the crowd to the outside, where some medics could attend to her.

My father, a normally gregarious man, watched in silence, then suddenly tugged at my arm and said, "Let's go!"

I was gripped by the spectacle in front of me and just stood there. I felt another hard tug. "Listen to me, Hamilton, we are leaving," my daddy said sternly. "Right now, do you hear me?"

He was silent for a while as we drove away. Then, he started talking . . . angrily. "Those people ought to be ashamed of themselves . . . getting those children into that mess. I'll be glad when they all leave town."

"What about Hattie?" I asked.

"Hattie better be careful, or she's going to be looking for work somewhere else."

My father harbored no sympathy for the protesters and repeated the argument that the good, local "colored folks" had been brainwashed by these "outside agitators." But my father was a gentle man who would never harm another human being. I could tell that he was uncomfortable, even troubled, with what we had seen that day—the ugly mood of the crowd, the raw hate that we could see and hear and almost feel.

Reading about the protesters in the local papers, I, too, felt threatened. These people were apparently out to destroy our way of life! But seeing it up close was entirely different, and witnessing the march that afternoon and seeing the faces of those people quietly fighting for their rights had an impact on me. I felt real shame for the first time in my life, standing by and merely watching while decent people—including our own dear Hattie—were herded into the alley and treated like animals.

Later, I would mark that day as a moment of moral failure in my life. I had an opportunity to take a stand, to risk something—instead, I had just stood there. And like so many other "decent" white southerners, I kept my outrage and my shame to myself.

We worried that Hattie might be in jail. When she did not answer her phone, I begged my father to call the jail and check on her.

He was resolute. "This is none of our business, Hamilton. Hattie got herself into this mess, and I am not going to interfere. If she calls and needs bail, I will help her, but I am not going to stick my nose in this civil rights business!"

We were surprised the next Monday morning when Hattie, who regularly rode the six o'clock bus across town to be at our house by seven, slipped quietly into the house, like always, wearing her crisp white maid's uniform. She even gave me a good-morning hug, something she used to do every day, but less often now that I was a teenager. Later, I would wonder if that hug was a way of forgiving all of us and Hattie's way of bringing King's message into our home: I love you even though you have mistreated me and my people. That hug, coming just two days after the march and Hattie's arrest by the Albany Police Department, stuck with me the rest of the day.

Hattie followed her usual routine: she took the garbage out, cleared off the dining table after breakfast, and assumed her usual place at the sink to wash the dishes before she went room to room, making up the beds and gathering clothes to be washed and ironed. My father appeared in the kitchen, dressed in a dark suit, ready to go to work. He looked surprised to find Hattie there, and I wondered what he would say . . . or if he would take her aside and scold her for getting involved in the march.

"Good morning, Hattie," he said.

"Good morning, Mr. Jordan."

"Nice day, isn't it?"

"Sure is, Mr. Jordan. Sure is." Somehow I knew then that my father was confused by all that was happening and felt the same shame as I did. Something had changed, and none of us knew what to do or think about it! No one in our family ever said anything to Hattie about her marching, and she never mentioned it to us. She did seem to be spending more time at "church activities," which was a clear signal to us that she continued to be heavily involved in the Albany Movement.

It was through Hattie's quiet commitment that I slowly began to appreciate the depth of the civil rights struggle. I was sure that all over the South there were "good colored folks" playing the same game as Hattie—working in the homes, restaurants, garages, and businesses of white people for meager wages but slowly and surely putting aside their fears to become the foot soldiers of the movement.

A few years later, Hattie surprised my mother when she announced that she was taking the day off so that she could get people to the polls to vote in the 1964 presidential election. It was as close as she ever came to acknowledging her political activism to the Jordan family.

■ ■ ■

Martin Luther King came back to Albany several times in late 1961 and during the summer of 1962. My older brother and I went to see both of King's hearings. As boys, we had been to the courthouse many times in the company of Hamp—who had been a trial lawyer and judge—and were well aware of the high drama that sometimes played out there. Plus, it was free.

The courtroom was packed, but we knew some ladies in the clerk's office who slipped us into a row in the back just as the judge called the court to order. In one section, we saw twenty or thirty people scribbling furiously on pads, most of them probably members of the national press.

Judge Abner Israel presided.

I knew Judge Israel well; he was one of my father's regular golfing partners in his Sunday game. As he sat on the raised bench in black robes, the judge peered over his glasses and out at the courtroom. He did not look happy as he glared first at the section where the press was sitting and then at the group of blacks standing and huddled around a table. I half stood, hoping to see King in the group, but was unable to find him.

Judge Israel softly tapped his gavel a couple of times, and the blacks standing around the table quickly took their seats. Several of the men in the press area were still turned around in their seats and talking, so Judge Israel banged his gavel about ten more times. There was absolute silence.

"In the event some of you have not had the occasion to appear in this court," he drawled, "I will expect order and respect." Unable to hide the sarcasm in his voice, the judge forced a slight smile and looked at the area where the press was sitting. "To our friends in the press who may not be accustomed to southern courtesies, you are welcome here, but the very same rules apply. No talking, no outbursts, and no noise."

He paused. "Clerk, read the charges."

A wiry little man who always wore a black suit, white shirt, and red bow tie stood up and read the charges, concluding with "*City of Albany v. M. L. King* . . . organizing a march without a permit, refusal to obey an officer's order, and general disobedience."

"Mr. King," Judge Israel snapped. "Stand up."

King wore a tapered, dark suit that fit him snugly. He looked quite dapper.

"Mr. King, you have heard the clerk read these charges against you . . . how do you plead?"

"Not guilty, Your Honor," King said in a deep, clear voice.

"Alright," the judge said. "Let's proceed."

The city prosecutor slowly lifted his large, pear-shaped frame and waddled toward the judge. "The city calls Chief of Police Pritchett."

The police chief took the stand, took the oath, and slowly recounted King's offenses: that he had led a march that was not authorized by the city, had disrupted traffic and commerce in the downtown area, and had refused his repeated requests that the marchers disperse. After several minutes of questioning, the prosecutor turned to the judge and said, "Your Honor, the city rests."

The judge turned in the direction of King. "The defense will now be heard."

An elegantly dressed black attorney rose and started to speak. I remember thinking that this was the first time that I had ever heard a black man talk like a white person. "My name is Donald L. Hollowell. I have been retained by Dr. King to represent him. I am an attorney for the NAACP and am licensed to practice in New York State, Washington, D.C., the State of Georgia, and have argued before the U.S. Supreme Court. Assisting me is the Honorable C. B. King of Albany and Miss Constance Baker Motley of New York State."

C. B. King rose briefly, acknowledging the judge, who just glared, and sat back down. I had to stand to catch a view of this lady Motley; she was a small, attractive woman well dressed in a dark suit. I had never seen a female attorney in my life—much less a black one from New York!

"I know C. B. King," the judge said snidely, seeming to enjoy the fact that he had withheld the simple courtesy of a "Mister." "I do not know this lady lawyer and do not know if she is licensed to appear before this court."

"But Your Honor," Hollowell protested, "I would like to bring to your attention that Miss Motley has practiced before the Supreme Court, participated in the landmark *Brown vs. Board of Education* suit—"

Abner Israel started banging his gavel and, almost shouting, exclaimed, "Order, Mr. Hollowell, order! I don't care where else you claim she is licensed to practice, you have not made the proper arrangements for her to practice in my court, and she will not be allowed to speak here today. Mr. Hollowell, don't waste this court's time. I have ruled. Proceed with your defense."

Hollowell went back to the table where King was sitting with the other black lawyers, picked up a handful of paper, turned around, and held up a document. "Your Honor, if it pleases the court, I would like to read some selected portions of the United States Constitution. The Thirteenth Amendment reads—"

BAM, BAM, BAM. Israel was red in the face and banging his gavel over and over and over again. I thought he might explode, he looked so angry!

"Miiiiiiiister Hollowell," he dragged the name out mockingly. "You are in the City Court of Albany, Georgia. I do not need instruction from you or anyone else in the U.S. Constitution. Do you understand?"

"With all due respect, Judge Israel," Hollowell quickly countered, "the Constitution of the United States is *the* ultimate authority. The city's refusal to permit Dr. King and his people to peacefully assemble are a violation of their Constitutional rights under Article—"

Judge Israel was now standing. "Stop, stop, stop, Mr. Hollowell! You will not make speeches to *me* in *my* court about the law!"

"Your Honor, the defendant has a right to a reasonable defense," responded Hollowell. "Is this Court not aware of the following Supreme Court cases," he continued, proceeding to read cases in a loud voice while the judge, his face beet-red, banged on his gavel nonstop.

"Guilty, Mr. Hollowell, guilty," Judge Israel shouted. "This court finds your client guilty on every count! He is sentenced to pay one thousand dollars and serve thirty days in jail."

Hollowell, in a loud voice, continued to cite case law that supported his position as the judge turned and walked toward the door leading to his chambers. He stopped at the door, turned, glared at Hollowell, and warned loudly, "One more word, Mr. Hollowell . . . one more word, and you will find yourself in contempt of this court and spending the night in jail."

This time Hollowell stopped. Israel smirked as he put his hand on the door and started to leave. A hush settled over the courtroom, and Israel turned to see King standing up with his hands outstretched, asking for quiet.

"Judge Israel, neither I nor my attorneys mean any disrespect to you personally. But this is a court of law. How can our very own Constitution and the rulings of our highest court be of no interest to you or no relevance to this court? Can you answer that question for me, Your Honor? Do you recognize the U.S. Constitution and the rulings of the U.S. Supreme Court?"

The judge froze. King's deep voice rang out again, "Answer me please, judge. Do you recognize the U.S. Constitution and the ruling of the U.S. Supreme Court?"

With a rage-shaken face and a quivering voice, the judge—trying to control his anger—quietly seethed, "Take him away . . . take him away."

City policemen quickly surrounded King, who continued to say in a loud voice, "Answer my question, judge . . . please answer my question!"

King was in jail for only a couple of days before an anonymous person paid his fine. King objected to someone paying his fine and refused to leave, but the officials put him out on the street. King faced a skeptical national press who questioned his leaving jail and what the Albany Movement had accomplished by his presence. King did not give convincing answers and would later remember Albany as one of the low points of the early civil rights movement.

The word on the street—widely believed among Albany whites—was that the American Communist Party had paid his fine. The King haters also circulated stories (obviously untrue) that King had spent his entire time in jail crying and begging to be released. A more likely story was that a couple of prominent white merchants, worried about shoppers staying away from downtown during the upcoming holiday season, had paid King's fine.

The Albany Movement was one of the few abject failures of the 1960s civil rights struggle, but it provided important experience and rich lessons for King and his group moving forward. The local black leadership thought that King's presence itself would assure success, but it did not. There was never a strategy for King to engage the white leadership in negotiations and never an exit strategy for King to leave Albany with a victory. King marched two more times in Albany, was arrested again, and found himself free again, courtesy of some anonymous party.

After his last march in our town in July 1962, Martin Luther King left Albany under a cloud, never to return. The regular marches continued for several weeks, becoming smaller and smaller in size until they were reduced to occasional gestures, covered only as a local story. King moved on to Birmingham, Selma, Montgomery, Chicago, and Washington—where I would see him again—and finally, to Memphis.

■ ■ ■

Change came hard to the South—and to the Jordan family. My father could never bring himself to say "Negro" properly, but he stopped saying "nigger" around us and usually used the words "colored" or "nigra," which was the "polite" compromise between "nigger" and "Negro."

In the late 1960s, the reality of integration again hit close to home.

A proud veteran of World War II, my father was serving as the local draft board chairman, a thankless volunteer job that he treated very seriously. With the Vietnam War raging, the Johnson Administration was pushing hard for these local boards—which exercised considerable authority over the fate of young men of draft age—to add black mem-

bers in symbolic recognition of the increasing number of black draft-
ees and volunteers. After much discussion, the board invited Thomas
Jenkins—the tall, dynamic president of Albany State College (the local
predominantly black college, which was part of a network of thirty-four
predominantly black colleges all over the South)—to serve on the board.
Jenkins, a shrewd and gregarious leader, knew how far to push for what
he wanted without permanently alienating the white elites. He made
quick friends with the white members of the draft board and quickly
became a force in their deliberations. It was not long before my father
was telling us that Tom Jenkins was a "good man" and a "good example
for the colored race."

My father was more shocked than touched, however, when Dr. and
Mrs. Jenkins, unannounced, dropped off a pecan pie at our home for
the Christmas holidays.

Hattie seemed to take special delight when she walked into the family
room where my father was reading the afternoon paper to announce,
"Mr. Jordan, Dr. and Mrs. Thomas Jenkins are at the *front* door."

My father—flabbergasted to have a black couple at our front door
paying a social visit—maintained enough composure to exchange pleasantries and invite them in. He seemed surprised that they accepted his
invitation and were soon sitting in our living room. He offered them a
drink, and before long they were sipping on bourbon-and-water and
making small talk. Later, laughing at his predicament, my father said,
"I suppose if I had invited them to spend the night, they would have
slept over."

The Jenkinses' visit was a landmark in my father's life. Although he
told people about it in a joking way (I always thought, to preempt or
dispel any notion around town that he had actually invited them for
a social visit), I could tell that he took a secret sense of pride that the
black educator had chosen to visit our home. Many years later, in 1970,
when Dr. Jenkins was appointed by Governor Jimmy Carter to be the
first black person to serve on the State Pardon and Paroles Board, Tom
Jenkins invited my father to attend his swearing-in ceremony in Atlanta.
My mother was sick and unable to go, but Hattie—who still worked
for my parents all those years later—heard them talking about the trip
and asked my father if she could ride up with him, since Dr. Jenkins
attended her church and was one of her "personal heroes."

While my father didn't want to have to accommodate Hattie, neither did he have the heart to turn her down. So my father—with Hattie riding in the backseat, where blacks always rode when traveling in a white person's car, even in 1970—drove all the way to Atlanta. My mother made sandwiches for them to eat in the car so that my father would not have to deal with the complicated issue of the two of them eating at a public facility. My mother could not resist kidding my father later that, as they drove away, it looked like a black woman had a white chauffeur. He did not find her observation amusing.

Upon his return, my father reported that he learned more about Hattie in that drive than he had learned in fifteen previous years. Trapped in the car for six hours, they talked about things never before mentioned, and that time alone together changed their relationship forever.

I often wondered if my father ever thought about the irony and contradictions of that trip to Atlanta: he in the front seat and Hattie—part-time maid, part-time civil rights worker—in the back, driving to Atlanta to see his friend sworn-in, the first black man appointed to an important state board, and the first black person ever to come to our *front* door for a social visit. My father was very proud of Jenkins's success. He loved to tell friends that Jenkins's service on the draft board, which demonstrated his effectiveness in dealing with whites, had been a major factor in his appointment to the important statewide position.

Years later, I made the trip home to Albany to attend Hattie's funeral at the church where she sang in the choir for forty years. I was the only white person there. My mother and father stayed home. They loved Hattie and appreciated her years of loyal service, but they simply could not bring themselves to attend a black church. What would the good white people of Albany say if they heard that they had gone to a black funeral? It was just too much change too fast for my parents, who grew up in a very different time and place. But that didn't stop them from being wrong.

George Wallace: Standing in the Doorway

I heard about a young "liberal" politician in Alabama in the late 1950s—not from *Time*—but from Jerona.

I started dating Jerona Trammell in my sophomore year at Albany High. She was definitely a late bloomer. I hardly remembered her from junior high: a chunky, pleasant-enough-looking girl with braces, long hair with bangs, and thick, black glasses that framed her chubby cheeks. Today, it would be said that Jerona had a makeover somewhere along the way. Back then, we said that Jerona had blossomed, losing baby fat, developing a great figure, getting a pixie haircut, and wearing contacts and very short skirts.

Jerona overnight became cute and bubbly enough to be elected a cheerleader at AHS by the student body, a big deal at a school with over two thousand students.

But "Jerona"?

A lot of southern gals have unusual names, *especially* the many brotherless young ladies (or eldest daughters) whose fathers were lacking male offspring at the moment of their birth. It was Jerona's fate to be the first daughter of a man, Jerome Trammell, who was hoping for a son and a namesake.

This unfortunate phenomenon was repeated next door to us, where Will Mason, our neighbor for most of my childhood, had no sons and insisted on incorporating his name into those of his two daughters: Willette, who was my age, and Twilla, who was older. These lovely young ladies carried a considerable burden, as the names Willette, Jerona, and Twilla stuck out like sore thumbs among the Nancys and Bettys of the neighborhood.

Jerome Trammell was a good man and a good father with not a lot to say—and probably not a lot of opportunities to do so, as he was the only man in a house with four strong-willed, talkative women: his very attractive wife, Edith, his eldest daughter, Jerona, and her two younger sisters. Mr. Trammell, as I called him, had the same hopes and dreams for his family as everyone else I knew growing up. He was a hardworking salesman for Wynn's Friction Proofing, a product sold at service stations that was designed to prevent engines from knocking. To promote and distribute his products, Mr. Trammell drove a vibrant red-and-yellow van with the words "Atom Smasher" emblazoned across the side and with a gizmo erected on the front bumper—covered with plastic to protect it from the elements—that he could use to demonstrate the wondrous properties of Wynn's fluid.

The Atom Smasher was usually piled high with boxes of Wynn's Friction Proofing. As my romance with Jerona flourished and we looked for places to indulge in a little teenage intimacy, we sometimes climbed into the back of the Atom Smasher when we were sure her parents had gone to bed. The vehicle, usually parked on the side of her house, was out of sight of her parents' bedroom. We usually moved around a few cases of Friction Proofing before rolling around on the floor of the van, making out.

Mr. Trammell, a stocky man with a thick southern accent and wavy reddish hair, hailed from Eufaula, Alabama, a town in southeast Alabama much smaller than Albany. He was one of six Trammell brothers, one of whom was a lawyer quite active in Alabama state politics. When I started dating Jerona in 1960, Mr. Trammell's brother, Seymore, was already working for the campaign of an ambitious, young Alabama judge by the name of George Wallace.

A few years later, Wallace—nicknamed "the little fighting judge"— would become *the* national icon for defying the federal government and opposing forced integration. But growing up in southwest Georgia in the 1950s and early 1960s, George Wallace was just one more ambitious young politician, trying to claw his way to the top. At age sixteen, Wallace had proudly proclaimed that he would be governor of Alabama someday. Eleven years later, he was elected to the legislature at the young age of twenty-seven. By the time he was thirty, Wallace had been voted in as a state circuit judge.

Wallace's first race for governor, in 1958, reflected his public service to date—he was a populist and a racial moderate who even earned the support of the NAACP in his campaign. He ran a vigorous campaign that was "progressive" on the core issue in the South—race relations. After losing the 1958 governor's race to John Patterson, Wallace searched to determine why he failed, ultimately confiding to his key supporters—including Seymore Trammell, who was his campaign treasurer and would later be his "main man" in many future state and national campaigns: "I got out-niggered by John Patterson. This is the first and last time I will ever be out-niggered by another candidate."

Wallace for Governor

In the spring of 1961, Jerona, aware of my great interest in politics, invited me to join her family for a day trip to nearby Eufaula, Alabama, for an old-fashioned picnic and political rally for George Wallace. The fighting judge—quickly rebounded from his 1958 defeat—was already running for governor again in 1961. I was anxious to see this southern liberal in action.

We drove west on the black asphalt roads, crowded in the Atom Smasher, toward Alabama. When we stopped outside of Eufaula for gas and a Coke, Mr. Trammell took out a couple of Confederate flags and draped them on the sides and rear of the van just to be sure that there was no doubt what this was all about. We went through Eufaula—the county seat—but saw very few people around as we drove through town and circled the courthouse. When we stopped to get directions to the Wallace rally, a fellow on the side of the road told us to simply go north of town and follow the rest of the traffic.

"Everybody's going to see George . . . he's a local boy."

Later, I would learn that Barbour County—like so many small counties in Georgia—was all about politics. Hamp used to tell folks in his small county that "politics is our major industry." Since six governors of Alabama were born in Barbour County, one might've said that politics was Barbour County's "major export."

We followed the traffic and turned down a dusty dirt road leading to the local high school. We got out of the Atom Smasher and walked toward the football stadium. Just as we approached, a group of men dressed in Confederate uniforms, who made up a ragtag band, were marching on the field playing Sousa's "The Stars and Stripes Forever." The crowd clapped politely. However, when the trumpet sounded the first ten familiar bars of "Dixie," the crowd stood up, yelled, and clapped wildly, a few attempting the shrill rebel yell. This was red meat for this crowd. For the next hour or so, no-name local country music singers, stock car drivers, and local politicians took turns preaching, singing, and pitching as folks milled around, some eating from packed lunches while others went through the food line for a couple of bucks, eating fresh barbecue and Brunswick stew—which soaked through the limp white paper plates—with plastic forks.

After lounging around for a while, I saw a man with a stocky build and wavy, strawberry hair surrounded by a crowd of folks. Recognizing his physical traits and facial features, I knew immediately that it must be Mr. Trammell's brother, Seymore. I went up to him, introduced myself, shook his hand, and told him that I was there with his younger brother's family. Once he figured out I was not an Alabama voter and had no family or kin here, he brushed me off, quickly turning his back to focus on some real Alabama voters.

In the middle of the afternoon, we heard sirens and soon spotted several police cars, lights flashing, streaking down the dirt road to the high school. When they got to the stadium, the motorcade drove around the track. In the middle of all the official vehicles was a shiny red convertible. As it slowed, a man, a woman, and a small boy climbed on the back of the seat, waving to the crowd with one hand and hanging on for dear life with the other. The convertible bumped and swayed around the track, circling the field a couple times before pulling directly onto the field. The band played "Dixie" over and over again while the Wallace caravan pulled up in front of the stage, and the crowd cheered loudly.

I finally got a good look at Wallace when he jumped from the back of the car. He was short and compact, an ordinary-looking man, dressed in dark slacks, a white short-sleeved shirt, and a thin black tie that matched his slick jet-black hair. He then did a 360-degree turn—waving heartily—and extended his hand to a plainly dressed lady seated on the back so she could rise and step down. Then he leaned over, plucked the small boy from the car, turning so that the two could wave together, in sync, to each side of the stadium audience. As the Wallaces climbed onto the stage, the band struck up "Dixie" once again, and the crowd worked itself up from loud applause to a feverish roar.

George Wallace worked the platform efficiently, gliding swiftly down the line of local dignitaries and politicians who waited to greet him. Shaking hands with one arm and pulling each person toward him for a brief embrace, Wallace moved from person to person fluidly and quickly, taking a little more time to kiss the local beauty queen. Some local official got up and started talking, but he quickly lost the crowd and only regained their attention when he said with a great flourish, "It is my great honor to present to you not only a son of Barbour County and the next governor of Alabama, but also the son of the next governor of Alabama, George Corley Wallace Jr."

With that the young boy—who looked to be eight or ten years old—got out of his chair next to his father and marched bravely to the podium, where somebody had placed a large wooden block. His proud daddy came up from behind and lifted him under him arms onto the box. The crowd went wild.

The young boy said in a loud and confident voice and in a thick drawl, "Thanks very much folks . . . my name is George Wallace Jr." It was hokey, but it sure worked. Young George delivered what was obviously a carefully prepared intro, inviting the crowd to "give a warm Eufaula welcome to my daddy and the next governor of the great state of Alabama . . . George Corley Wallace!" Wallace's compact body supported a rather large head, further exaggerated by that full head of black hair. Although he occasionally smiled when delivering a punch line, it seemed forced and unnatural. Wallace's smile looked more like a sneer, which seemed almost fitting as he denounced the federal government and the U.S. Supreme Court as being "out of control and trying to tell us down here in Alabama how to raise and educate our children."

"This George Corley Wallace sure is a bundle of emotion," I thought. Wallace spoke without notes, but his lines were carefully rehearsed, and his hands chopped the air with each catchy phrase.

But where was the southern liberal I had heard so much about from the 1958 campaign? His message was certainly not what I had expected based on his earlier race, which had earned the support of black Alabamians and progressive whites. George Wallace's message this time around was plain and unequivocal—aimed at rural white Democrats who hated Washington and feared blacks going to school with their children, taking their jobs, and marrying their daughters.

As we drove home that afternoon, I reflected on what I had seen and heard. George Wallace was certainly effective as a candidate. He obviously had had a convenient "change of heart" and was going after the redneck vote. Sure, every person I knew—except for my uncle Clarence Jordan—was a segregationist: Hamp, my parents, my neighbors, my schoolmates, and my friends. But there was something hard, mean, and raw about George Wallace. The reaction of the crowd to Wallace's message was unsettling. They came in happy and left angry, feeling threatened and wanting somebody to do something about it. Even though he had this crowd of Eufaula homefolks solidly behind him, I didn't think a candidate like George Wallace with just a straight racial appeal could be elected governor of Alabama—not in the 1960s!

One year later, George Wallace won the race for governor by a landslide.

Four years later, a man named Lester Maddox—claiming Wallace as his role model and leader—was elected governor of Georgia. I was surprised that these racial undercurrents were so powerful as to cause our citizens to totally ignore a candidate's intelligence, background, and experience when making a voting decision. It was a lesson I'd learn and relearn for years to come.

Chapter Eleven

■ ■ ■

WASHINGTON, THE FIRST TIME AROUND, 1963

Washington Intern

As the winter quarter of my freshman year at the University of Georgia was winding down, I started thinking about the summer. I had no interest in sticking around Albany, hanging out with my fuddy-duddy parents, and working another summer as a lifeguard.

I had Washington, D.C., on my mind.

It wasn't, however, just because of my decade-long interest in politics. It also had little to do with my passion for history, a subject that—despite my mediocre academic performance in most of my other classes—I had developed a keen interest in throughout my later years of high school.

It was because of a girl.

■ ■ ■

At the beginning of the quarter, I had fallen—"big-time," as we used to say—for a fast-talking, sassy blonde from Arlington, Virginia, named Karen. We had met at a stuffy social at the Kappa Alpha Theta house—where our sister sorority resided.

Socials were a time-honored tradition of fraternities and sororities at the University of Georgia in the 1960s—social gatherings to present the new members who had pledged during the fall rush. It was widely known among the brothers that socials were lame events, but they were required for pledges like me, and there would be push-ups to do and toilets to clean back at the Phi Delta Theta house if I didn't show up. The designation of the Thetas as our sister sorority meant absolutely nothing other than some imagined relationship from the past. As a group, the Thetas had a reputation as great students and great girls, but *not* as great-looking ladies.

I showed up to the 1962 winter social—held in the Theta's red-brick, antebellum house with large white columns that reached up to the second floor—with a few of my Phi Delt buddies, all of us clad in the standard uniform of khaki or gray slacks, blue blazers, dress shirts, and patterned neckties. As we milled about the dull party, drinking iced tea and Coke (no beer, of course) and eating squares of cake off of little glass plates, I found three or four of my best buddies surrounding a striking blonde who held their rapt attention. Just as I stepped in to check it out, she delivered a punch line (for what I would later learn was a very risqué joke) that cracked the group up. As the hearty laughs subsided, I awkwardly stepped into the circle of frat brothers surrounding her, blurting out, "What's so funny?"

Hardly looking at me, she glanced in my direction, smiled, and said, "Not you, buster!" She quickly turned and strutted to the punch bowl, obviously knowing—and relishing the fact—that five pairs of male eyes were following her beautiful pair of legs all the way there. My Phi Delt brothers howled with laughter at her embarrassing put-down. I felt like a fool at a complete loss of words, but I also felt like I had nothing left to lose, and so I followed the blonde like a puppy dog to the crystal punch bowl—which sat on an antique mahogany table—where I started to introduce myself.

"My name is Karen," she said, beating me to the punch as she extended her hand to shake mine with a strong grip.

"And my name is Hamilton Jordan," I said, trying to squeeze back harder. I was not about to let this babe put me down verbally *and* physically on the same night!

She melted me with a smile and a mock southern accent, saying, "With a name like that, Massa Hamilton, you must live on a plantation somewhere!"

"I do . . . and I'm here tonight looking for some kitchen help! That's what I want to talk to you about!" She laughed so hard that she almost dropped her punch.

And that was the start of it all.

■ ■ ■

Months later, my romance with Karen had easily become the most intense relationship of my life at that point, as well as the most fun I had ever had with a woman up to that point. I did not, however, have enough confidence in myself or our relationship to think I could hold onto her over the summer with mere postcards and occasional, carefully rationed long-distance calls. Mindful of our own whirlwind relationship—meeting at a fraternity social and then going out sixty or seventy nights in a row—I knew that Karen hardly seemed like the kind of woman who would sit home at night, loyal to a far-away boyfriend. I was pretty much convinced that Karen could be someone else's girl by the time fall quarter rolled around—and I did not want to take even the slightest chance of losing her.

One of my Phi Delt brothers told me about summer internships in Washington working for members of Congress, the most prized assignment being with our own Senator Richard Russell from Georgia, arguably the most powerful member of the U.S. Senate. My fraternity brother introduced me to a friend who had interned for Senator Russell and had indicated a willingness to call a member of the senator's permanent staff on my behalf.

Never mentioning Karen or the fact that she lived only a few minutes outside of Washington, I proposed to my parents that an internship with Senator Russell would look great on my résumé. With politics in her blood, my mother jumped at the idea of my working for Senator Russell. And, after all, wouldn't still-grieving Hamp get a kick out of the idea of my working for one of the most powerful senators—and a proud Georgian? The way I described the opportunity to my parents, I would likely spend my summer sitting at the right hand of the great man, discussing issues and occasionally whispering advice.

There was, of course, the small issue of my spring quarter grades. I learned growing up that it is not always easy being the child of a teacher. My mother's aunt—nicknamed Dudgy—was a doting and extroverted teacher who bubbled with life. She lived with my grandfather's family for a number of years and, having had no children of her own, Dudgy took it upon herself to teach my mother—the eldest of four children—to read, write, and count when she was only three years old. An anxious learner, my mother was an adult-pleasing sponge who soaked up of all the special attention and "learnings."

By the time she was ready to enter school, Mama was so far ahead of her first-grade classmates that she skipped several grades and was placed in the fourth grade when she was only six years old. As schools in those days only had eleven grades, my mother graduated from high school when she was thirteen and from Agnes Scott College in Atlanta at seventeen. Soon afterward, still a teenager herself, my mother was teaching high school math in Albany to students her own age and older.

Growing up in Albany, my siblings and I must have heard this story hundreds of times—never from my humble mother, but from scores of well-intentioned family members and friends she taught, all of whom seemed to think this anecdote would surely inspire Mama's own children to greater academic achievement. It didn't. Probably in some form of unconscious rebellion, I never excelled in high school and *particularly* hated math.

The first quarter I was at the University of Georgia, I explained away my fall quarter grades to my parents—an 81 average I described as a "solid B"—by pointing the finger at my loud, boisterous, fun-loving roommate, also a Phi Delt pledge. I shared with my parents the simple (if incomplete) truth: my roommate, a Mr. White Patton from Lookout Mountain, Tennessee, was a good guy—but he partied *all* the time and stayed up *all* night, which hardly created a good atmosphere for my dorm life and studies. What I failed to mention was that 95 percent of the time, I was out partying with White myself.

I told my parents that I missed them terribly (true) and that it was a "tremendous social adjustment" being away from home (not really). On top of that, I'd invested an enormous amount of time in fraternity rush, which had landed me a bid as a Phi Delta Theta, the beloved fraternity of both my father and my mother's father (making me—in the parlance of the Greeks—a double legacy. When I was formally initiated into the fraternity later as a brother, both my dear father and Hamp were in attendance, wiping away tears during the highly secretive initiation ceremony).

My pledge brothers elected me president of my Phi Delt pledge class, and, as I explained to my parents, this was not only a great honor and responsibility, but it took time—stretching the truth here a bit as, in fact, all I was ever asked to do was to call roll at our monthly pledge meetings.

My hard-working, intelligent parents—especially Mama—were not ones to let me off easy; they expected a lot from their children. However, they loved me, trusted me, and were willing to give me the benefit of the doubt in looking beyond my mediocre first-quarter performance in hopes that I would simply learn my lesson and do much better.

However, when it came to explaining away my sagging winter quarter grades—low Bs and a couple of Cs—I had a little more trouble, and my parents put me on notice: bring up my grades, or suffer dire consequences. I had heard the same words before all throughout high school: "You are not working to your potential." But this time, my mother seemed deadly serious. "We are not sending you to college just for you to get by or to be average." While I did not study or work to my potential that spring quarter of my freshman year—highlighted by great parties on the Phi Delta patio—I sure partied to my potential and had fallen head over heels in love with Karen.

In early May—largely as a result of the recommendations of the former Russell intern and obviously *not* based on academic performance—I was offered and accepted a summer internship with Senator Russell. My mother was as excited about it for me as I was. The only person more proud, as expected, was Hamp, who beamed with pride when I shared the good news. Still, I was holding my breath at the end of the school year, knowing my grades for the spring quarter were going to be disappointing—if not shocking—to my dear parents. While I did not lie outright to my mother and father, I did not share with them my worst fears—that my B to B− slide from fall to winter quarters had continued downhill. I knew that they would be disappointed, probably even mad, and might not let me go to Washington for the summer. At the same time, I was getting more and more excited about this summer opportunity in Washington that I had stumbled into. JFK was in his third year as president, Congress was debating far-reaching civil rights legislation, which was being stalled by southern senators—led by Senator Russell—and there I would be, smack dab in the middle of history in the making, working for Senator Richard Russell himself!

Furthermore, lovely Karen lived only minutes away, available to party every night and continue the fun and romance of the winter and spring!

I knew there was a good chance my grades for spring quarter would arrive home in Albany in early June, just before I was supposed to leave for Washington—and if my grades were as bad as I feared, I might never make it out of Georgia that summer. However, if I were already on the job in Washington when my grades arrived, it would be harder for my parents to bring me home.

You could set your watch by our mailman in Albany. Every day—rain, sleet, or snow—he showed up in the early afternoon in our little neighborhood wearing the blue uniform, lugging the big brown leather bag hanging over his shoulder. My first day home, I took a walk up to the corner house, which came before our house on the mail route, shook hands with the mailman, and exchanged pleasantries.

He asked if I was looking for something.

"Do you think . . . " I started, not sure how to pose my question, "Would it be possible . . ."

"Save your breath," he said with a slight smile; he'd heard it all before. "Looking for your grades?"

I was surprised. "How did you know?"

"Several kids every quarter try to intercept their grades before their parents get their hands on 'em. Nope, I can't give you your grades. The U.S. mail is federal property, and my job is to deliver it to your mailbox. What happens between the mailbox and your house is none of Uncle Sam's business." Baring my soul, I confessed I had had a bad quarter and was worried my once-in-a-lifetime opportunity in Washington to work for Senator Russell was at stake.

"Tell you what I can do—several kids on this route are UGA students. I'll let you know when the UGA grades start arriving, but you know what you should do?"

"Yeah," I replied. "Level with my parents."

"That is exactly right. Shoot straight with them . . . you won't be the first or last kid around here who goes off to college, has too much fun, and has a bad quarter."

I knew he was right, but I could never bring myself to tell my parents to expect disappointing grades for spring quarter. I had let them down and was not proud of it, but I was selfish and unwilling to take the chance of losing my summer opportunity—and probably Karen—to do the right thing.

For the next several days, I met the mailman every day on the corner until one afternoon, he told me that two of the UGA students on his route—with last names earlier in the alphabet than my own—had received their grades that day.

The day before I was scheduled to leave for Washington, the official-looking formal letter with red and black letters came from "The Dean of Students, University of Georgia." I took the stack of mail and walked it into the house, slipping the offending envelope into my pocket before laying the rest of the mail down in its usual place on the kitchen table. When I got to my room, I tried reading my grades by holding the envelope up to the light, but I could not see through the folded paper. After placing the letter under my mattress, I packed for Washington and planned for my escape early the next morning.

Getting up before sunrise while my parents were still sleeping, I went out to get the morning newspaper and slipped the letter from the University of Georgia back into the mailbox. It was barely light when both my parents took me to the dingy Trailways Bus Terminal in Albany—located on the edge of Harlem—for the long trip to Washington. The last thing I said to my parents as I boarded the bus was, "Be sure to call me when you get my grades!" The deed was done. I was not proud of my deceit, but I rationalized that it was my duty to go to Washington and work for Senator Russell rather than simply hang around Albany and be worthless all summer.

The bus ride from Atlanta to Washington was long and hardly "express," as advertised. We stopped in Columbia, South Carolina; Charlotte, North Carolina; and Richmond, Virginia en route to Washington. The bus was different from the city buses in Albany, which featured a front door for white passengers and a rear door for blacks. When you saw folks waiting at the bus stops in Albany, there would be two groups—a few whites in front at the bus stop sign and usually a large number of blacks waiting five to six yards back, about where the rear door would be.

But on this bus, there was only one entry door, right up front. The blacks entering the front would quickly move to the rear, always taking seats at least two or three rows behind the last white riders. Almost ten years after Rosa Parks's brave and defiant act, these buses were still stuck in strict segregation. I probably didn't even think of it at the time—it was simply the order of things. An odious tradition.

I read the newspaper, my *Time* magazine, and even started a couple of books that I had brought, but I still had a lot of time to think on the sixteen-hour trip. I was ashamed of the way I had left Albany. Trying to forget about my unseemly exit and my poor grades (which my parents could be reading at any moment), I thought about the exciting summer ahead. I thought about all of my goals for the summer—which I would later turn into a written list to be taped over the mirror in my bedroom in my Washington summer apartment.

At the top of that list would be one word—"Karen."

The winter and spring quarters at UGA had been great, and now, Karen and I would have the entire summer in Washington together—no dorm, no dorm mother, and no damn curfews! Sure, there would be some challenges. I had a day job, and Karen did, too: working as a salesperson in the women's department at Garfinckel's, a high-end retail store. But we would get together every night. Karen would introduce me to the nightlife of Washington and her favorite bars and eateries in Georgetown, and I would introduce her to national politics. Picking up where we had let off in Athens, it was going to be a hell of a summer!

Having been so preoccupied with getting out of town before my grades arrived, I had really only thought about my summer job with Senator Russell in the abstract. But, Karen aside, I was legitimately very excited about my internship, and I set many goals for myself in the political realm as well. One was to meet every single member of the U.S. Senate. After all, I was going to be there for almost a hundred days—certainly it was not unreasonable to think that I would see four or five senators a day and that I would have a decent shot of meeting all one hundred of them? I even thought about getting an autograph book for the senators to sign to document these encounters—something that Hamp, in particular, would enjoy seeing.

Another goal was to meet Vice President Johnson and President Kennedy. I realized that this was not going to be easy, but I was going to be associated with *the* Senator Richard Russell, and that was certainly going to open a lot of doors for me!

Finally, I wanted to visit the White House . . . but I figured that would be a piece of cake.

I was exhausted but excited when we pulled into the Washington bus terminal at close to eleven p.m. Although I had wanted Karen to meet me, my mother insisted that her younger sister, Sydney, who lived in suburban Washington, pick me up since I was staying at her house for a few nights before moving into an apartment with several other Russell interns. The first thing out of Aunt Sydney's mouth after a welcome hug was, "Your mother wants you to call home as soon as we get back to the house . . . no matter how late it is."

My grades, I thought. They aren't happy. I dreaded making that call. My mother answered the phone—my father was already asleep. There was no pleasantries, not even a "how was your trip?" The first words out of Mama's mouth were, "If we had gotten your grades yesterday, you would be sitting at home right now, preparing to go to summer school and looking for a job."

I said nothing.

Mama went over my grades. Reading them, one by one, I could hear the irritation in her voice as she seemed almost to spit them out: "You made a C in English. You made a C– in History 101, your *major*," almost shouting that for emphasis. Then finally, "You made a D, a *D* in *algebra*!" again raising her voice.

Oh my God, I thought. These were even worse than I had expected! I tried to feign surprise, but Mama, unable to contain her exasperation, cut me off. "I cannot even imagine a child of mine almost flunking a math course!" She told me that she wanted me to come home immediately and hung up the phone. Mama had never talked to me like that before in her life. I truly felt miserable for disappointing Mama. I was correct in assuming that she would be angry, though; if I hadn't pulled my mailbox trick, I would clearly have never made it to Washington.

Early the next morning, my father called from his office. He was not a happy camper either, but he was already playing peacemaker. He told me to stand by for the day, not to start back to Georgia yet, and to call home that evening. By the time I called that night, my mother had calmed down a little bit, and it was obvious to me that Daddy had been working on her. She realized that it would not be good to have won an internship with Senator Russell and then not show up for work. On the other hand, Mama worried that I would be using an internship that could have gone to—as she relished saying—to a "more deserving student."

"What are we going to do about your grades, son?" Mama asked.

I leveled with them. "I screwed up bad. I know you are disappointed in me. *I* am disappointed in me, too." I admitted that I did not study enough, that I got distracted at the fraternity house, and that I spent too much time socializing. I promised them and myself that it would not happen again, and I meant it.

"Son, you have to make a decision. You come home right away for summer school, or stay in Washington for the summer but miss fall quarter at UGA and get a job in Albany!"

At least Mama was giving me a choice, but it was not an easy one to make, especially in regards to Karen. This was my worst nightmare—if I stayed in Washington for the summer to be with Karen, I wouldn't be with her in Athens for the fall quarter, and I would miss the Georgia Bulldog football games, frat parties, rush, and living with my buddies at the Phi Delt House! It was a lose-lose situation if I ever knew one. Faced with this lousy set of options, I went for immediate gratification and decided that I might as well stay to enjoy Karen, Washington, and my internship. It would be better, I thought, to miss fall quarter than to go back to attend summer school, miss Karen, and probably lose her. Maybe I could convince her to fall so madly in love with me over the summer that she'd be willing to stay with me during our quarter apart, with her at school in Athens and me working in Albany?

"I'll stay," I told my folks, guaranteeing them a much better academic performance going forward.

Mama had the last word—as she usually did—attributing my "downfall" to falling head over heels for Karen. "She may be a lovely girl, but she was *not* good for your grades!"

I didn't respond to affirm this assertion, so Mama never knew how accurate she was—or perhaps she did!

■ ■ ■

I was both excited and nervous on the first day I ventured to the Old Senate Office Building to start my internship. All dressed up in my brand-new blue blazer, gray pants, blue shirt, and a distinctive red-and-black Georgia Bulldog tie, the fact was not lost on me that the University of Georgia was very important in Senator Russell's own life!

Walking the halls of the cavernous Senate Office Building was surreal. Other than the occasional individual dashing from one office to another, there was very little traffic, and my every step echoed down the huge, dimly lit corridor. The click-click-click of my new shoes on the shiny marble floors finally stopped when I came to the large wooden door for room 205, emblazoned with a small wooden sign that read, "Russell of Georgia." After being welcomed by a receptionist with a familiar drawl, I sat in the waiting room for a few minutes until a young man—not much older than I was—opened the heavy wooden door and walked me to the back to meet Bill Jordan, whom he described as "the boss."

A lanky man in his late thirties wearing a suit that seemed too big for him, the gentleman rose from his desk, flashed a friendly smile, and said, "Howdy Cousin, I am Bill Jordan. Two Jordans from Georgia? We gotta be kin!"

He told me that he was from Milledgeville and mentioned several of his Jordan relatives, none of whom were familiar to me. I told him that my Jordan family was from Macon and Talbotton. He said he did not know the Macon Jordans but did know the Talbotton Jordans. "Peach farmers, right?"

"Yes sir, and one or two lawyers."

After a minute or so of small talk, Bill rose and led me by the arm toward a huge wooden door. He cracked the door just a bit, paused, and stuck his head in. I could hear him ask, "Senator, do you have a minute to meet our new intern?"

"Yes, yes, yes," came the voice behind the door.

Bill Jordan tugged on my arm, and we quickly walked into a huge office, where I caught my first up-close and personal glimpse of the great man. Sitting behind an enormous wooden desk—flanked by the American and Georgia flags and stacked high with books, files, and papers—Senator Russell sat hunched over a stack of letters, signing them quickly, while a lady stood to the side, removing each sheet of signed paper one by one.

Looking around the office, I couldn't help being impressed by the wall, filled with citations, memorabilia, and photographs, most of which looked old and weathered as if they had been developed long ago. I would simply have to come back many times just to study these walls! Giving the correspondence on this desk his complete attention, Senator Russell finally paused, giving the lady a set of instructions to change a greeting or to "do this one over." At last, he looked up and stood up from his desk, asking, "Who do we have here?"

I had expected and assumed that this man the press called "the Georgia giant" would be physically large, but Senator Russell was not—possibly five foot eleven, maybe a bit taller, and balding, with a prominent nose and a bit of a paunch. He wore a handsome, dark blue, double-breasted suit not far off from the type I'd seen Edward G. Robinson wear in gangster movies. On his long lapel, Senator Russell wore a Masonic pin—just like Hamp.

"Senator Russell, this is William Hamilton Jordan from Aw-ben-ny, Georgia," Bill said, seeming to enjoy knowing and displaying his knowledge of how the "locals" pronounced my hometown. "He is a Russell intern this summer and is going to be a vertical engineer for the American people," said Bill. "Vertical engineer?" I thought.

Senator Russell chuckled and peered over his horn-rimmed glasses, giving me the once-over. He stepped from behind his desk and extended his hand for a firm handshake.

"A cousin, Bill?"

"No sir, just a coincidence."

"Sir, Bill's got my name right," I offered, "but there's more to it. My full name is William Hamilton McWhorter Jordan," I said as I took the great man's hand.

"My, my, my. You must be Hamilton McWhorter's grandson or his nephew?"

"Grandson," I said proudly.

"What do you call your granddaddy?"

"We call him Hamp, sir!"

"Well, son, that is what his many friends call him. So, I am going to call you Little Hamp, because your granddaddy is an old and dear friend I don't see much anymore. I don't get home much with all my duties here. I haven't seen Hamp McWhorter in ten years."

After inquiring about Hamp's health, the senator asked, "Do you know how far back your grandfather and I go?"

It was one of those questions people ask but really want to answer themselves, so I just stood quietly. I did know but was anxious to hear him talk about their friendship.

"We grew up just down the road from each other. Lexington is about forty miles from Winder, where I lived. We both attended the University of Georgia and graduated from the law school there. We both served in the legislature together. In fact, Hamp was president of the senate when I was governor and when I was elected to this job."

I told Senator Russell about watching the 1952 Democratic Convention with Hamp on television in Lexington and recording the Russell delegates on Hamp's yellow legal pad. I remembered that every single one of his delegates was from the Deep South.

"Hamp always thought you should be president, Senator Russell," I said.

The senator almost looked embarrassed by that comment, dodging the notion and changing the subject, asking, "What is your mother's name?"

"Adelaide McWhorter. She is the oldest of Hamp's four children."

Senator Russell sat back down in his large leather chair. Leaning back, sighing, and, seeming to relax, he said, "I can remember visiting your grandparents in Lexington when your mother and her siblings were all toddlers. They were pages for me in the Georgia legislature when I was Speaker of the Georgia House."

Senator Russell had a rich, melodious voice, and his words and tone conveyed enormous self-confidence. There was a patrician air about the great man that invited admiration—but not intimacy. He asked me about the prospects for his beloved Georgia Bulldog football team, and then, as quickly as it had begun, my visit with the senator—lasting little more than two or three minutes—was over. "Well, Little Hamp, have a great summer. I will tell you the same thing that I tell all the interns: there is much to learn here and much to do. You are a long way from home, but—"

Three short bursts of a loud buzzer blared as a light mounted on the wall behind his desk flashed off and on.

"Time to go, sir," said Bill Jordan, who then explained to me that a roll call vote was underway on the Senate floor. Senator Russell grabbed several folders on his desk and walked quickly toward a side door opening directly onto the Senate corridor.

"Got to go, young Hamp . . . your granddaddy would understand. We spend as much time here trying to stop bad legislation as we do passing good laws. All of us here are your family for the summer, so you let us know when and if you need anything, you hear?"

And he was gone.

After my meeting with the senator, Bill sat me down in his office for about five minutes to show me the ropes. He told me that my job was easy but important: be on time, look neat, keep my mouth shut about what I saw and heard, spend as much time as possible in the office helping out, and understand that I was representing Senator Russell and his staff in everything that I did. Bill said that the young men who did this (there were zero female interns on Russell's staff or anyone else's, for that matter) made a real contribution, but also learned a lot about Georgia, national issues, and politics. His quick admonition ended with a suggestion to have fun but to "Never, ever embarrass yourself or the senator. It is a great privilege to work for Richard Russell."

Although I had not spent much time with this great man, I believed that this was merely the first step in building a wonderful personal relationship with him. I was overwhelmed by the attention shown me by "Russell from Georgia" and remained awestruck the rest of the day. Little did I know that this would be the first and *last* time I would see Senator Russell alone for the entire summer other than seeing him from a distance getting on and off the elevator at the Capitol. It would also be the only time I would ever be in his private office, where I had hoped to more leisurely study the pictures and memorabilia adorning his walls.

Actually, once, Senator Russell *did* yell out to me "Little Hamp!" as he entered the Senators Only elevator. I waved back, proud to be publicly acknowledged by the great man! But it was hardly the extent of interaction—and friendship—I had hoped for.

Chapter Twelve

■ ■ ■

VERTICAL ENGINEER

After I finished meeting with Bill Jordan, he sent me to see the intern coordinator for the Senate. There were two job options for young Senate interns, depending on their age. If one was twenty-one or more years of age and willing to undergo a day-long training session and a simple written test, an intern could become a Capitol Policeman overnight, which meant wearing a uniform, carrying a gun (with no bullets), and creating a "presence" around the Capitol. As a practical matter, it meant you would be stationed in areas of maximum traffic, providing directions to tourists. You were, in short, a glorified Capitol tour guide. But the shiny badge, the gun, and a good swagger put you in a darn good position to meet one of the many pretty women who swarmed the Capitol on summer tours.

Or, like me at the age of nineteen, you could be a "vertical engineer," positioned at one of the elevators in the Senate or the Senate Office Buildings.

"Driving" an automatic elevator required a person not only to be able to count all the way to three—the number of levels in the Capitol—but also to be able to move at least one finger from button to button, understanding how to push the right button with the right number on it.

No written tests required.

The interns who were cops strutted around the Capitol and made fun of the elevator operators, always bragging about girls met and telephone numbers acquired during the course of handing out tourist tips.

One favorite story making the rounds of the elevator operators in the summer of 1963 was of a Capitol cop the previous summer who—after giving bad directions to an impatient tourist—got yelled at by the tourist, resulting in the young cop wetting his pants on the spot. This profile in courage was often cited when the Capitol cops got too full of themselves.

■ ■ ■

I went directly from my meeting with Bill Jordan to the cramped office of the crusty old man who supervised the Senate Intern Program. He handed me a book with the pictures of all one hundred senators and told me in no uncertain terms, "Learn it. We'll give you three days to learn every senator. But don't come back until you know 'em, every one!" Over and over, he told us the same stories of interns who had been fired on the spot for failing to recognize senators.

"The senators run this place. If you kids screw up, you might lose a summer job—but my *career* is on the line. I have two years left before I get my retirement, and it is *not* an option for me to get screwed over because you interns make a mistake!"

I lived with that Senate photo book for several days, trying to match each face with its name and corresponding state. I got an extra copy of the little book, cut it up, and put the faces and names on the table in my little apartment and—like doing a puzzle—struggled mightily to match up the name with the face.

I was assigned to a four-hour shift each day at the bank of elevators on the Senate side of the Capitol, where the underground railway car whisked the senators—and crowds of tourists—to and from the Old and New Senate Office Buildings. One of those elevators was marked for "Senators Only"; not even the boldest and most senior Senate staffer would step on that elevator and risk alienating a powerful U.S. Senator in a hurry.

When it was time to vote, the bells in the senators' private offices rang and calls went out from the sergeant-at-arms and cloakroom staff to each office. The quiet, dark halls of the Senate Office Buildings were suddenly streaming with senators rushing to vote with aides following along at all sides, giving them messages, reviewing schedules and requests, and even reviewing correspondence. The underground railway dumped them off in the basement of the Senate, right at the bank of elevators where I worked. These elevators took them to the second floor, where they rushed off, dashed into the cloakroom or onto the Senate floor, and cast their vote.

I thought I was pretty proficient at identifying senators from studying my little photo book, but I was shocked to learn otherwise when I actually started working, straining to connect each distinguished-looking face I saw with one of the one hundred scattered photographs. Without exception, the pictures were all very flattering, most taken years or even decades before the summer of 1963. They reminded me of promotional headshots I had seen of famous old movie stars—ten or twenty years removed from present-day reality. A few, like Senator Harry Byrd—who wore white plantation suits—or Senator Mike Mansfield of Montana, Everett Dirksen of Illinois, and Leverett Saltonstall of Massachusetts, had distinct, craggy faces that were often in the news media, and thus easy to recognize. But then there was everybody else: the fifty or sixty senators like Milton Young of North Dakota or Roman Hruska of Nebraska whom I had never heard of or seen before. Most of these senators were not famous nor physically impressive nor imposing nor memorable in any way. These men may have been VIPs in their home states, but in Washington, D.C., they looked like normal people—most of them appearing nothing like the faces of the outdated photos in my little Senate picture book.

I finally figured that the best strategy was simply to treat *anyone* coming at me as a potential senator. Whenever I saw a dignified-looking man in a hurry, who was well dressed, carrying a briefcase, and had others following him, I would step forward and say, with the air of respect that one might accord a U.S. Senator: "May I offer you a ride?" The other "drivers" went crazy with my tactic, kidding me that I was merely extending senatorial courtesy to lobbyists and well-dressed tourists and giving them express rides, but I didn't care. I just wanted to keep my job and had no intention of screwing up. After a couple of weeks, I had gotten a look at most of the senators, eventually cutting back on offering rides to just anyone who *might* be a U.S. Senator.

Senator Mac

The Senators Only elevator had been run for many years by a colorful and crusty old character named Mac. I never knew Mac's last name—the old-timers around the Senate just called him "Senator Mac." With his slicked-back gray hair, old-fashioned double-breasted suits, loud ties, and spats (on special occasions), Mac looked like he was straight out of a 1930s gangster movie. It didn't take me long to learn that Mac's favorite pastime was horse racing—or, more specifically, reading the racing form, giving and receiving tips on horses, and betting on races at nearby Pimlico.

Mac was also a walking encyclopedia of Senate history, facts, precedents, and scuttlebutt, but he would be the first to tell you that gossip was his most important asset. "Anybody can collect and remember goddamn facts. But if you want to get really good shit on these politicians, you keep your ear to the ground, and you gotta be trusted!" Mac knew which senators expected a greeting, appreciated a good joke, desired a tip on the horses, or would be titillated by the latest gossip. He also knew which senators simply wanted to be left alone on the quick rides up and down, to and from the Senate. Mac specialized in knowledge of who was sleeping with whom—not just the senators, but key staff people as well. I learned over the summer—as I gained Mac's confidence—that he quietly passed along his hottest gossip to his favorite senators, and many of them reciprocated with their own best stories. Mac could give you a short profile (more like an editorial) on almost any senator, and he usually felt obliged to do so right after giving them a ride—if he thought he could trust you to keep your mouth shut.

"Hubert Humphrey is a nice man, but he needs to shut up and listen more . . . LBJ is a shrewd, conniving son-of-a-bitch. He'll use the hell out of you and cut your throat if you get in his way. That's why he was so successful in the Senate and so miserable today being vice president, playing second fiddle to the Kennedys . . . Your man [talking about Senator Russell] is a southern gentlemen, but he's a loner. He is *the* most powerful member of Congress. There is not a Republican or Democrat in the Senate who does not go to him for advice and help—and he gives it. But Senator Russell doesn't let anybody get too close. He has very, very few real friends . . . Teddy Kennedy is hard working and may be the smartest of the Kennedys. He'll go places if he keeps his pecker in his pants. He wasn't here two months before he was bedding down two or three of the best-looking secretaries. The shit's going to hit the fan when Teddy gets caught screwing another senator's wife . . . or even worse, another senator's girlfriend!"

I soaked all of this up and could tell that Mac enjoyed having a new audience for his gossip and opinion. These little nuggets of information largely formed my emerging view of these important men. (There was only one woman in the U.S. Senate at the time, an elegant lady, Margaret Chase Smith of Maine, whom Senator Russell affectionately called "Sis.") I had heard from more than one senior intern that Mac—a divorced bachelor with no kids—often took one or two summer interns under his wing during their tour of duty. When Mac started calling me "Jaw-ja Boy" after a couple of weeks on the job, the other interns said that I had become one of "Mac's boys." I learned a lot more from Mac about Senate rules, senators, and politics than I learned from any of my other bosses that summer.

When the Senators Only elevators were in use, the senators could ring one of the regular elevators we drove by simply buzzing three times. When we heard that buzzer, it meant that Mac had a senator or senators already in his elevator and might not quickly reach the call from another waiting senator. *All* of the amateur operators (interns) were supposed to empty their elevators, override the direction of the elevator, and race to be the first to pick up the waiting senator. In fact, because the elevators we operated were totally automatic, the only reason my job existed was for that rare occasion when a senator needed an elevator. When senators were running late and risked having a vote concluded without their vote being cast or recorded, a friendly senator who shared the missing senators' position on the issue would rise on a point of order and make some delaying motion or even a brief speech to give the senators enough time to rush over on the subway cars, ride up to the second floor in Mac's elevator, and rush in just in time to cast their votes.

Russell of Georgia

I remembered something Hamp told me before I left for Washington: "A prophet is not without honor, save in his own land," he said, quoting a favorite Bible verse. Hamp said that the Georgia people took Senator Russell for granted and did not grasp his role in the Senate and Washington. "Dick Russell may look ten feet tall here in Georgia, but wait till you get to Washington! Dick Russell is a giant."

Hamp was exactly right. Every day I would learn more about Senator Russell's history and style. For example, I learned:

- The way he presided over General MacArthur's triumphant return to the United States after President Truman fired MacArthur defused the politically charged atmosphere.
- Russell had a penchant for reaching out and quietly helping freshman senators, regardless of party or political persuasion, on issues of merit.
- He had a staunch, old-fashioned patriotism and loyalty to the institution of the presidency.

I quickly realized that everything I knew and had learned about Senator Russell was in the present tense. I knew very little about his life before coming to the Senate other than the superficial understanding gained from reading the *Albany Herald* and hearing Hamp's remembrances, which were very personal but also twenty-five years old.

While Senator Russell was a huge presence in Georgia politics, most people—like me before coming to Washington—had never laid eyes on him. Other politicians rode in Fourth of July parades, were available for Kiwanis Club and PTA meetings, and delivered graduation speeches. However, Senator Russell was seen by most of us back home as being almost *above* politics, even beyond campaigning. He was not just our senator—he was the *nation's* senator in Washington, protecting us from Communism and keeping our military strong from his powerful position as chairman of the Armed Services Committee. And, as many white folks in the South would add, he was also protecting "our way of life."

It was a big deal for Senator Russell to come home to Georgia. With no wife or children of his own, Senator Russell seldom returned to the South; such visits were usually personal and very rarely political, most likely to spend Christmas or Thanksgiving with his extended family. While there had been some talk that Georgia's popular young governor—Carl Sanders, elected in 1962—might consider challenging Senator Russell for his seat in the 1966 election, no one really thought that Sanders (or anyone else, for that matter) had any chance against Senator Russell. However, some pundits wrote columns handicapping such a race. While predicting that Russell was "probably unbeatable," they could not help but note that it had been more than thirty years since Russell had conducted a vigorous campaign when he challenged a powerful and popular incumbent who was considered "unbeatable" on the very issue of his being "out of touch" with the people of Georgia. Since then, a whole new generation of young Georgians had come along who only knew about Senator Russell in the abstract.

Senator Russell and his team, however, took note of Sanders's ambitions and these rumors. Many speculated that this drove the senator and his staff to recruit some talented young Georgians—like recent UGA graduate Earl Leonard, who was his press secretary. Leonard and a few others like him were much more in touch with Georgia politically and had their own networks of friends and acquaintances throughout the state. Even Russell's use of summer interns was a new practice, only having begun a few years before my own stint as a vertical engineer.

I was disappointed that there were no great or even good biographies about Senator Russell, and so I figured that I could at least learn something about the Senate. A novel, *Advise and Consent*, sent to me by Hamp for Christmas, told the story of the institution of the Senate around the issue of the confirmation fight over the president's controversial appointment of a secretary of state. The best information I could find about Senator Russell was contained in a number of profiles and feature stories about him in the *Washington Post* and *New York Times* and in a couple of cover stories on Russell in *Time* magazine, one from 1952, when his candidacy for the presidency was treated very seriously by the news media and the political elites, and another in 1957, which focused on Russell's role in the Senate and the power that he had accumulated to make or break legislation.

Richard B. Russell Jr. was the first son of an old, proud, and prosperous Georgia family who lost much of their wealth in the hard days of Reconstruction following the Civil War. His father—Judge Richard Russell Sr., for whom Richard was named—was a successful lawyer and judge who went back and forth between the bench and the practice of law in order to raise his large family—thirteen children—in the style of a well-to-do landowner. The old judge, however, seemed unable to keep his hands out of elective politics and made regular and failed attempts at major statewide office—running several times for governor and U.S. Senator—before finally being elected chief justice of the Georgia Supreme Court in 1922.

Young Richard Russell idolized his father and was often at his side during his regular and unsuccessful campaigns for high office. Richard

Russell Jr. was a fast study. The son soon developed his own personal interest in politics and was elected to the Georgia legislature at the age of twenty-three. He demonstrated a natural intellect, a commitment to work, and a self-effacing honesty in dealing with his colleagues—all traits that immediately catapulted him into positions of responsibility and authority. By only his second term in the Georgia House, word among the political leaders and the press was that "young Russell is going places."

And going places very fast. Russell was elected Speaker of the House at the age of thirty, then became the "boy governor" of Georgia at the age of thirty-four when he introduced and passed legislation reorganizing and streamlining state government. The significant savings and efficiencies that resulted from Russell's reorganization of Georgia's government were acclaimed and imitated by many other states.

Halfway through Russell's highly successful term as governor, Georgia's senior U.S. Senator, William Harris, dropped dead of a heart attack. Much to the surprise of the Georgia electorate, young Governor Russell called a special election and announced that he would be a candidate against the dean of the Georgia Congressional delegation, the very popular and experienced Charles Crisp. Russell was considered an underdog throughout the campaign; many of his staunchest supporters believed that young Russell should have completed at least one if not two terms as governor before offering for the U.S. Senate. Most of the newspapers in the state and the political establishment supported Congressman Crisp. Governor Russell ran an aggressive, populist campaign, employing radio ads, mailings, and advertisements in a way never before seen in Georgia. Russell kept Crisp on the defensive and made big news the final weeks of the campaign when the Georgia governor/senatorial candidate was asked to speak at the Democratic National Convention in 1932, the year Governor Franklin Delano Roosevelt was nominated for president. Young Russell made a good speech, wrapping himself in Roosevelt's popularity and New Deal, designed to address an economic depression that was particularly severe in the rural South.

Defying all the pundits, Richard Russell defeated Crisp in a landslide. It was his biggest victory and his last real campaign, because he was never seriously challenged again.

Richard Russell: Senate Years

When I arrived in Washington in the summer of 1963, Senator Russell had been in the U.S. Senate for three decades. Richard Russell's natural skills, talents, and work habits—honed in Georgia and applied for thirty years in the U.S. Senate—made him, without question, the most powerful member of the Senate, indeed the entire Congress. His work ethic was unrivaled, and his capacity for reading was legend. His formal roles—chairman of the Armed Services Committee, ranking Democrat on the Senate Appropriations Committee, and chairman of the Southern Caucus—gave him real power in the Senate. But students of the Senate would be quick to tell anyone that Russell's real power lay in his expertise of the Senate rules, procedures, and precedents, and the enormous respect of his colleagues.

Although he had dated throughout his life and had a series of girlfriends, Russell had never married. When questioned about his bachelorhood, Russell's canned response was that he was "married to the Senate," and no one ever doubted this man's total commitment and devotion to the institution.

According to Russell's biographer Gilbert Fite, there was one girlfriend whom he dated for years and almost married, but he changed his mind at the last minute, ostensibly due to the fact that she was Catholic in a state that was overwhelmingly Protestant in the heart of the intolerant Bible Belt. Apparently, Senator Russell called the editor of the *Atlanta Constitution* after the wedding announcement of his engagement to Miss Patricia Collins of Atlanta had already been typeset. He informed the newspaper that the wedding was off and insisted that the announcement not be run; the paper complied. Senator Russell continued to see Collins for several years, until she finally married someone else.

There was no doubt that Richard Russell had made a calculated political decision—clearly Catholics were an enormous liability in southern politics. When I learned this fact about Senator Russell and his Catholic girlfriend, I could not help but think about the very different decision that Hamp had made when he married a beautiful, young Jewish girl and never ran for statewide office.

Even the senator's closest friends and colleagues would say that Richard Russell was a man easy to work with but not an easy man to know. While always open to legislative relationships and collaborations with

Democrats and Republicans, he was not open to intimacies. Russell's formal, patrician bearing never allowed his colleagues to feel too familiar or comfortable with the great man. How like a southern man.

At the time I came to Washington in 1963, Russell's power in the U.S. Senate was at its zenith. He was still keeping our military strong and protecting our country around the world, but most of his time, effort, and thought was focused on protecting—as his supporters would put it—"our way of life" in his beloved South. Through his legislative leadership and his unique tactical knowledge of the Senate rules, procedures, and precedents, Richard Russell and a small minority of the Senate—twenty-two senators from the old Confederate states that comprised the "Southern Caucus" that he chaired—wielded disproportionate power in the body.

Washington

I had first visited Washington with my family when I was seven or eight years old, and by the time of my internship my memories were somewhat vague and of the tourist variety: monuments, the Capitol, Arlington, and places like the Smithsonian, where I discovered that embarrassing bit of history about the McWhorter who had won a Congressional Medal of Honor—fighting for the Union!

As I moved around town that first week that I was there for my internship, I was pleasantly surprised at the pace and sounds of Washington: it truly did seem more like a southern city than a northern city. It was hot as hell and sure humid enough, and everywhere I turned, I found myself meeting and talking with people from small towns with thick southern accents. Hearing those "ma'am's" and "y'all's" so far from home was certainly music to my South Georgia ears.

And if Washington was a southern city, the U.S. Senate was the Deep South. I was struck by how many of the Senate employees were not only from the Deep South but also from small towns in the rural Deep South. It was not long before I realized the dominant role that the South had in the Congress. One of the old-timers who worked in the Senate cloakroom put it this way: "Son, anybody 'round the Senate worth a shit is either a southerner or an old codger—and usually both!" And, from my experience, he was right.

Seniority and the South

The first few days at work in the Senate were confusing as I found myself lost in the maze of halls and rooms in the massive building, asking
lots of questions about the people I met and the things I observed. So
many of my questions about the Senate were answered in a single word:
"seniority." Why was one senator—who seemed so much smarter, more
able and articulate than this other senator—not the committee chair?
Seniority. How did Senator Hayden—who was very old and seemed out
of it—get to be president pro tempore of the Senate? Seniority. How are
committee assignments made? Seniority. Why does this senator get such
a remote office? Seniority. From matters large (Why does this senator
have such weak committee assignments?) to small (How does Senator
Russell get twice as many interns as most senators?), the answer was
usually one word: seniority.

When I came to understand how little I really did know, I began to go
to the Library of Congress to read about seniority. I had always thought
that seniority was something that happened in reaction to Reconstruction, but I learned that seniority had its roots in the period before the
Civil War. As early as 1845, Senate rules had been passed that said that
party caucuses will determine the membership of the committees; that
within each committee, the chairmanship would be determined by the
majority party; that the chairman of each committee would be determined by "length of service"; and that committee membership would
pass over from Congress to Congress to Congress.

Historian William White, in his landmark book on the U.S. Senate,
Citadel, wrote that "once a chairmanship is attained, it is not in practice
lost by any man . . . the [seniority] perquisite may be considered to be
for the political life of the holder; it is in this sense hardly less than an
old-fashioned kingship." By the 1960s, thirteen of the fifteen standing
committee chairs were headed by senators from the old Confederacy
or sympathetic senators from border states or Republicans who shared
the southern view on the social and racial issues that had come to the
forefront during the civil rights movement.

Even these lopsided margins understated the real clout of the South,
because if one closely examined the membership of the key committees—Rules, Appropriations, Armed Services, Foreign Affairs—the
southerners were disproportionately represented on these commit-

tees. In addition, because the South was so totally dominated by one party—the Democrats—southern senators had only to worry about being challenged in their own party, rarely had serious opposition, and occasionally had token opposition for almost one hundred years. It was a great irony that the system also provided the national Democratic Party its loyal support. So, Georgia, which gave President Kennedy his greatest majority outside of Massachusetts in his 1960 presidential campaign—62 percent—also provided the political leadership in the Senate to thwart, delay, and ultimately block his greatest domestic initiative—the 1963 Civil Rights Bill.

LBJ

One day in July, I was "driving" a group of tourists from the basement subway to the main floor, where they could stand in line to briefly view the Senate chamber when it was not in session. The instant the door opened, a tall man, neatly dressed with a crew cut and military bearing, started barking, "Please exit quickly. We need this elevator. Please exit."

When I started to object, another man stepped forward and said sternly, "I am head of the vice president's Secret Service detail. The vice president is coming—we need this elevator!"

I looked down the hall and saw an enormous head bobbing over a moving crowd of people. A large man—his long arms swinging forcefully back and forth—took quick and purposeful strides toward us, with several people clustered around him scurrying to keep up.

A couple of tourists clapped and a few tourists yelled out, "Mr. Vice President!" Another one just yelled out, "LBJ, LBJ!" Johnson's smile looked forced as he waved blindly in the direction of the tourists now completely cordoned off by the security guards. Thinking fast, ever mindful of my goals taped to the mirror at my apartment, I stepped back inside the elevator and stood in the back corner just as the group approached. The Secret Service agent glared at me for a second but must have decided that removing me would take more time than it was worth. The vice president and his entourage piled into the elevator with me.

My mind was racing now, trying to think of what I would say to LBJ. I was thinking that "Mr. Vice President, I work for Senator Russell" would probably be best. But my thoughts were broken when the elevator door closed on the excited crowd of tourists, and I heard this booming voice almost yell, "Cocksuckers!"

I peeked around the shoulder of the agent in front of me and saw the vice president towering over a young man with a briefcase who shrunk visibly under the vice president's glare. Johnson said it again, this time drawing it out in a singsong voice, "Cocksuckers." LBJ was huge, and his large head with big floppy ears was bent down in the face of this poor aide. "Those cocksuckers at the White House," pausing as if searching for the right insult, "they don't know their heads from their assholes."

The elevator jerked upward.

"Goddammit, we are going up!" LBJ shouted. "I want to go down to the subway—can't we find someone who can drive this damn elevator?" The elevator was headed up before being commandeered by the Secret Service, and the man now driving did not know how to override the earlier command to go up. I found myself—just like his poor aide—shrinking down in the other corner. I was no longer anxious to meet LBJ and just wanted the man to get wherever he wanted to go. After the doors opened and shut on the third floor, I was relieved to hear the vice president talking in a normal voice. "Now you get on the phone and tell Larry O'Brien [head of Congressional Relations for the Kennedy White House] and the fellas at the White House not to ever, do you hear me, ever, send me down here to do their dirty work *after* they have screwed legislation up. If they want me in on the crash landing, I expect to be on board for the take off!"

"Yes, Mr. Vice President, but—" the aide started

"Shut up!" LBJ roared.

The door opened on the floor where we began our journey. A startled group of tourists waiting for an elevator quickly recognized the large man as their vice president and starting waving and whispering to one another, "It's him! It's LBJ!" Johnson smiled briefly, waved lamely, and, the instant the elevator door shut, started back on the poor aide, who by now had stooped so low that I figured he would be flat on the floor by the time we reached the basement. In an almost gentle tone, the volatile LBJ calmly said, "Do you know that when President Kennedy was a junior senator down here only a few years ago and I was majority leader that he could not even wipe his ass without asking my permission?"

The aide said nothing but shook his head up and down. I had forgotten about getting LBJ's autograph and was simply relieved to be getting close to the basement. Just as the elevator reached the basement floor, LBJ looked around and found me crouched down in the corner. I must have looked like a frightened puppy, as he softly asked, "What do you do, son?"

I stood up tall and tried to speak. "Er . . . sir . . . I . . .er . . ." I wanted to tell him that I worked for Senator Russell, but the words would not come. Johnson turned to exit the elevator and in a loud aside to his aide said, "That fella doesn't even know what he's doing. He oughta be working at the White House!"

And he was gone.

I learned later that the vice president had been in the Senate that day lobbying key senators and trying to salvage support for the civil rights legislation that was in deep trouble in the Senate, largely due to the delaying tactics and strategy of the Southern Caucus, led by the man I worked for: Senator Richard Russell. Maybe it was a good thing that I couldn't bring myself to speak to the vice president after all.

Afterhours

It didn't take long for me to recognize that Senator Russell's office operation was highly organized and effective—and it needed to be. Not only did the senator receive heavy constituent mail from Georgia, consisting of routine complaints about Social Security, the draft, farm policy, and so on, but Russell also received mail from all over the country, sent to the senator in his capacity as chairman of the Armed Services Committee. There were also letters from lots of folks, mostly from the South, who were encouraging him to run for president.

I learned that the seniority system even applied to me and, as the newest intern, I started out on the very bottom of the workforce—filing Georgia correspondence to and from Senator Russell. Most of the letters in the summer of 1963 from Georgia to Senator Russell were focused on the civil rights legislation before the Congress, almost always supporting Russell's position and leadership on this issue. There were a few—very, very few—letters from Georgia that expressed support for the civil rights bill.

In filing this correspondence, we had several assignments. First, I did a final check to be sure that the inside address and salutation matched up with the address on the envelope and to ensure that the response seemed appropriate for the letter. It almost always did, but sometimes we would find an error or mismatch. While not instructed to do so, I usually looked over the original letter and then examined the response. Some of the incoming letters looked like they were written on lined notebook paper that we used in grammar school. Often the handwriting looked tortured and represented the ranting and raving of someone writing about "the niggers" and "communists and race mixers," invoking the Bible, God's law, and so on. Occasionally, Russell would receive a serious typewritten letter from an educated source—an attorney or businessman or teacher, perhaps—that was tempered and reasoned, written in support of the senator's position, parroting Russell's constitutional states' rights argument. But whether the correspondence came from a barely literate farmer or a more sophisticated voter, Senator Russell's response always took the high road, making the arguments on behalf of the Constitution and the private property rights of citizens to welcome or deny whomever they wished in their businesses—it was the core argument against forced racial integration, because it was the only argument that held *any* debatable legal merit.

While these letters were obviously politically responsive to 98 percent of the writers, there was never a doubt in my own mind that they were the deeply held and deeply felt beliefs of Richard Russell. Like my dear Hamp, Russell's own life and background could never allow him to contemplate that he might be wrong. However raw or racially offensive some of the letters he received might be, Russell's response would simply ignore often outrageous claims and charges and accept the writer's argument as being for states' rights and the constitutional guarantees that should allow for these questions of public accommodations and education to be resolved state by state.

The Senate

It was surprising and disappointing to see how little business was actually conducted on the floor of the Senate. Only rarely would Vice President Johnson—who, as president of the Senate, had an ornate suite of offices in the Senate building—make an appearance. His duty as vice president was to preside over the Senate on votes close enough that he might be required to cast the deciding vote.

I was in the gallery on a couple of occasions when votes were held on the Great Society legislation, which Russell and the Southern bloc opposed on both budgetary and philosophical grounds. One by one, most of the Democratic senators walked up to the rostrum where LBJ sat to shake the hand of their former colleague and to exchange small talk. Senator Russell just sat there in his seat, reading a document and occasionally welcoming senators who stopped by to shake hands or stoop down by his desk and make some comment or ask a question.

Finally, I saw the vice president summon a Senate page, scratch a note on a piece of paper, and point him to Senator Russell. Russell opened the note, smiled slightly, stood up, and went to the cloakroom on the side of the Senate, with the vice president following him out. I wondered what they talked about—the former mentor and student—now that their roles had changed?

Mac told me told that LBJ was a "bigmouthed know-it-all" and that "the only time you ever saw Lyndon Johnson shut up during his Senate days was when he was in the presence of Senator Russell." He continued, "Johnson would talk your ears off, but he was a different person when Senator Russell was around. He would be deferential to Senator Russell, even quiet and would listen. LBJ simply knew that Russell knew more about the Senate than he could ever learn."

■ ■ ■

There was one other brief encounter in July when one of the senator's secretaries asked me if I would fetch some barbecue for the senator. The great man briefly stepped out of his office, handed me a ten-dollar bill for the taxi fare and the food, gave me the address, and—confirming Russell's reputation as a penny-pincher—told me exactly what it should cost, asking that I bring back a receipt.

I was surprised when the taxi made its way west of the Capitol into what was obviously an all-black section of Washington, stopping at a little weathered shack with a rusty Coca-Cola sign hanging over the door that read "Mamie's Bar-B-Q." Another Mamie's sign featured a colorful pig painted on the side and the words "Take Out Orders." As I stepped into the restaurant, which must have seated only fifteen or twenty people in a handful of booths, my eyes were drawn to the large black lady behind the counter, who looked up and smiled broadly when I walked in, saying, "Betcha coming to pick up Senator Russell's carry-out order?"

"Yes ma'am, I am."

She handed me two large grease-stained paper bags and rattled off its contents—one barbecue chicken, an order of pork, side order of Brunswick stew, side order of baked beans, buttered rolls, hot sauce, and a jug of sweet ice tea. She took the ten-dollar bill, handed back the exact change the senator calculated, adding, "Senator Russell always wants that receipt!" which she slipped into the bag. "We awfully proud to have Senator Russell as one of our customers," she said with a smile.

As I sat in the taxi on my way back to the Capitol, I thought about the irony of Senator Russell—leading the forces against civil rights on Capitol Hill, and certainly *not* championing this lady's best interests— ordering barbecue from Mamie's. Nevertheless, she was proud as punch to have the important senator as one of her regulars.

I had hoped to be able to deliver the food personally to Senator Russell in his office, finally get a chance to chat briefly with him, and possibly even take a longer look at some of the memorabilia on his wall. Unfortunately, however, I was intercepted by one of his secretaries, who thanked me, took the food, the change, and the receipt, and carried the whole package into his private office.

White House Visit, August 1963

With only a few weeks left in my internship, most of my personal goals for the summer—taped on the mirror in my bedroom—were still not realized.

First was my failure to conquer the first and highest item on my goal list—Karen. Although she was still my girlfriend for the summer and our relationship remained steady and intense, I failed to sweep Karen off her feet and give her the romantic summer of a lifetime that I had anticipated.

Karen and I had to make modifications to our relationship that I hadn't anticipated; not only did we both work full-time day jobs in different parts of town, but Karen lived with her parents—an older couple who were very conservative and very protective of their youngest daughter. We were left to deal with strict curfews and rules that might have been imposed on a high school student—restrictions the likes of which we hadn't experienced falling for each other at UGA. We still had a fun summer, but I hardly felt like I would emerge from Washington with Karen's heart safely in my hand, to keep secure during the long fall quarter we were going to spend apart!

And while I had hoped to meet all one hundred senators, I had come to realize that that would never happen, as a number were very old and one or two—like Carl Hayden—were in such poor health they rarely even came to their Senate office or to the Senate chamber. Still, I had probably "met" (or, more literally, seen up-close) fifty or sixty senators, including most of the key ones in my estimation—the energetic Humphrey, young Ted Kennedy (who looked like a movie star), the stoic Robert Byrd from West Virginia (who made long and boring speeches), and others. Not a bad result—but that goal could *not* be checked off!

Despite being tongue-tied and failing to achieve an official introduction, I felt justified in crossing off "meet the vice president" as a result of our ride together when he hijacked my elevator. There was no need to be technical! I had made zero progress, however, in getting to the White House *or* meeting President Kennedy. I realized now that the latter was a very long shot, but I had not given up!

In early July, a friend from Maryland, who went to private school with Sargent Shriver's children, promised to get me into a Peace Corps ceremony at the White House, where President Kennedy would celebrate the send-off of a new crop of volunteers to their foreign assignments. I made it all the way to the West Gate of the White House and was in the process of being cleared by the security guards, but for some reason, my name had not made it on the approved list of invitees, and I was left stranded at the gate. I even showed the White House guards my engraved United States Senate ID card, which seemed to make no difference. Although I have never been a name dropper and was never inclined to be one, once I realized that they were not going to let me in, I decided to drop the bomb and told the security guard in a quiet voice, "I work for Senator Russell of Georgia." I confidently waited for a reaction, an opening to the event, and probably even an apology from the guard but found that this fact—so powerful on Capitol Hill—had absolutely no impact with the White House security guards.

"Sorry, son," the security guard said. "You are either on this cleared list or not—and you aren't!" Dejected, I took the long walk back down Pennsylvania Avenue toward the Capitol, doubting I would ever have another chance to meet President Kennedy or really see the inside of the White House.

■ ■ ■

I did end up getting to the White House to meet President Kennedy, even though it was not *quite* what I had imagined at the beginning of the summer—JFK and I chatting it up in the Oval Office, followed by a personal photo of us shaking hands to show all my friends and my parents—and most important, Hamp.

I learned through several interns in other Senate offices that there was going to be an end of the summer function on the South Lawn of the White House for all the young people working as interns in Washington that summer of 1963. I checked with one of the purple-haired ladies in Senator Russell's office, who admitted to having seen such an invitation but explained that she had probably thrown it away.

"Why in the world," she asked, "would you want to go to a White House function when President Kennedy, Bobby Kennedy in the Justice Department, and Teddy Kennedy in the Senate have been fighting us for the past six months on every single issue Senator Russell cares about?" Surprised by her attitude and lightly veiled insinuation of disloyalty, I told her that, as a history major, I simply needed and wanted to see the White House.

"Why don't you go on a White House tour? We have VIP passes; the tour guides are excellent and know the history of each room, the paintings, and the furnishings."

"That's a great idea," I said, feigning interest.

August 27, 1963, JFK and Me at the White House

By asking around, I was finally able to wrangle an invitation to the White House event through an intern in Michigan's Senator Hart's office. This time, there was no trouble at the check-in, my name was on the approved list, and I soon found myself standing on the South Lawn of the White House, one of only five thousand student interns at this "exclusive" event. The South Lawn was chock full of young student politicians—indeed, I doubt if there had ever been or ever would be more raw political ambition per square inch than was assembled there that day on the South Lawn. But I didn't care and was enthralled just to be there. Here I was, standing on the South Lawn of the White House on a summer afternoon, the West Wing to one side, the Residence behind me, and the Washington Monument—circled by American flags—at the bottom of the green expanse before me. All the while, the U.S. Marine Corps band was playing Sousa marches in the background.

How could it get much better for someone who loved history and politics? I must have looked like a spinning top—constantly turning to stare at the West Wing, trying to imagine the Oval Office and what was going on inside, and then facing the Residence and the Truman Balcony. I could easily imagine the president and Mrs. Kennedy standing there with Caroline and little John-John waving down to us, just as I had seen them do in newsreels countless times. My first trip to the White House was a magic moment that I would never forget, and I was happy that I did not know a lot of the interns—most of whom worked in agencies of the federal government and not on Capitol Hill—who were likely to waste my magic moment with self-promoting small talk and gossip.

There was a ripple in the crowd, and applause suddenly broke out from the direction of the West Wing. My guess that President Kennedy had emerged from the Oval Office was shortly confirmed when the Marine Band abruptly stopped in the middle of a song and started playing "Hail to the Chief."

I could feel my heart pounding.

JFK was indeed outside and slowly making his way to the speaking platform, reaching out right and left as he walked on the grass through a mass of interns, with Secret Service agents walking ahead of him and pushing people back. I was thrilled, gawking as the handsome young president bounced up the stairs onto the makeshift stage on the South Lawn. The students that had been scattered all over, drinking punch and eating cookies, surged en masse to the area in the very front of the stage. Trim, fit, and tan, JFK flashed his famous smile and, standing in front of a microphone, took off his coat and rolled up his sleeves. I found myself cheering wildly. The president welcomed us to "the people's house," as he called it, talked a bit about public service, and then spoke about arms control and civil rights to the large throng of teenagers—overwhelmingly boys—as if we were adults. When his speech was over, the Marine Band broke into "The Stars and Stripes Forever." The festive Sousa march started the crowd clapping. Interns up front surged toward the side of the stage where JFK was exiting. Ever so often, the president paused to shake or just touch a few in the ocean of outstretched hands. When he reached the porch on the side of the Oval Office, he turned and, smiling broadly, waved to the mass of young people clapping wildly, all eyes still glued on him. After receiving a rousing roar of approval, the youthful president quickly ducked back into the Oval Office.

I was drawn like a magnet to the president; even though I didn't get closer than twenty yards from him, it was still exhilarating. Surprised and almost embarrassed by my emotional attraction to the president, I tried to gather and understand my feelings as I made the trek back to the Senate. Senator Russell might still have my head, but after I left the White House that day, John Kennedy had my heart. Was it his youth? Or his charisma? Or the fact that he had talked to us—and to me—as adults about our country's challenges?

Exiting the South Gate of the White House, I realized this was the first and probably last time I would ever be there. Sure, I wanted to come back to this great place someday, like every single one of the five thousand other interns, but that didn't seem very likely. While my White House visit was certainly not what I had imagined or hoped for at the beginning of the summer, I was able to cross off my remaining goals: "Visit White House," and I even rationalized crossing off "Meet the president." I got to the White House and saw this great man in person. Anyone would have to admit that was quite an accomplishment, even though I had no handshake or photo to prove it.

Years later, I would go back and retrieve President Kennedy's remarks from that day. The words he spoke were special, not only because they were the first and only time that I would hear him speak in person, but because the words and example of JFK made government service appear noble, exciting, and important. On that late summer afternoon, I felt some instant, unexplainable connection to President Kennedy and began to believe that my personal hopes and beliefs for our country were projected onto this man.

It had been a wonderful—close to perfect—summer. The seeds of interest in politics and government planted by Hamp many years before certainly sprouted for me in Washington in the summer of 1963—but not always in ways that Hamp would have approved . . . or even fully understood. That summer would mark the second time that Martin Luther King Jr. directly touched my life—and changed me—forever. In later years I would realize that the March on Washington would turn out to be my most important experience in those months.

Going Home, September 2, 1963

The day before I left for Albany, I made the rounds, stopping first at Senator Russell's office, where I thanked all the staff that had been so kind to me. I didn't feel particularly close to any of them, except for Senator Russell's shrewd and gregarious press secretary, Earl Leonard, who was closer to my age and had been particularly kind. Senator Russell's staff was composed of deeply committed professionals who were intensely loyal to him, but they seemed so loyal that they would accept the great man's judgment on almost any subject without question or reflection.

I had only really seen Senator Russell the first day I came to work at the Senate, and so it made sense that I might be able to see him on the last. After all, I simply wanted to express my appreciation for the opportunity. However, one of the old battle-axes was standing guard that morning over the senator's schedule. With a big fat phony smile, she said that she knew that the senator would love to see me but that he was presiding over a committee meeting that could last all morning. I thought for a moment that I was paying the price for not taking her to dinner a few times like several of the other ass-kissing interns, but, upon reflection, that would have been too much of a price to pay for a thirty-second good-bye from the great man.

The hardest part of my last day in the Old Senate Building was saying good-bye to Mac, the closest friend I had made that summer. Standing in front of his Senators Only elevator, I tried to express my thanks but found myself tongue-tied and a bit emotional. Mac mumbled that he wasn't much for good-byes, gave me a slap on the shoulder, and seemed almost happy to get a buzz on his elevator from a waiting senator.

"Gotta go," he said, forcing a smile. "Wonder which asshole it will be this time?" He gave me a salute and said, "See ya, Jaw-Ja Boy!" as the doors to his elevator shut tight. I wiped at my eyes as I walked away from the familiar bank of elevators and this man who had been the focus of so much of my summer education and fun.

When I walked out of the Senate Office Building that day, I also felt that I was saying farewell to some part of myself and my past. Three months prior, I had arrived in Washington as a self-assured, gregarious, and rather clueless nineteen-year-old intent on learning a great deal during my summer in the nation's capital. However, I ended up leaving Washington, D.C., with many more questions than I had gained answers.

A talkative taxi driver took me to the bus station where I would begin the long trek back home to Albany.

"Here on vacation?" he asked.

"Nope . . . worked on Capitol Hill for the summer."

"Work for some big shot?" he probed.

I was almost surprised at my instinctive reaction and heard myself saying, "Nobody you heard of."

As those words tumbled out of my mouth, I realized for the first time that I was no longer so proud of my modest connection with Senator Richard Russell. If I had received that question two months—or even two weeks—prior, I would have bragged about working for Senator Russell, which was sure to have impressed the listener. Maybe it was the cumulative effect . . . what I had seen in Albany, hearing Kennedy at the White House, and, as I recount in the following chapter, witnessing the incredible March on Washington. I realized that I was increasingly uncomfortable with the side of this argument I seemed to have landed on.

I finally boarded the so-called "Express" Trailways bus to Atlanta. I was glad to have the long ride and time to think and to try to clear my head. After all of the debates in the Senate, the new legislation introduced, the grand rhetoric from the White House, the Supreme . Court decisions, and the countless editorials in the *New York Times*, the truth was that nothing had really changed over the summer. There was still the two-row gap at the back of the bus, separating the whites and the blacks. When we stopped, the whites filed out first and went inside to the "white only" restaurant. At one stop, a black man asked me to buy some crackers for him inside, which I was glad to do. And at every stop, one or two black people would get off and on, watched carefully by the bus driver in his rearview mirror as they made the long walk to the very back of the bus.

The signs that had been so much a part of my growing up—"White Only" and "Colored Only"—no longer seemed just part of the southern landscape, instead screaming out to me on this trip as *proof* that notions of civil rights and states' rights were *not* just part of some abstract political debate but a sociopolitical conflict so crucial that it would singly shape our country's meaning and future, its repercussions resonating powerfully into the future for as far as any American could imagine.

There was no doubt in my mind from that day on that real change was coming to America and to the South, whether the white people of Albany liked it or not. What was much less clear, however, was *how* that would happen and, of most concern to me, if my beloved South would erupt in a new cycle of violence as we would be forced to abandon a way of life that was several hundred years old—but now had to end.

Chapter Thirteen

■ ■ ■

THE MARCH ON WASHINGTON, AUGUST 1963

The very day after my visit to the White House to "meet President Kennedy" while I was working for Senator Russell, the March on Washington came to town.

Over the spring and early summer of 1963, the leaders of the civil rights movement—frustrated with the lack of progress in the Congress on President Kennedy's civil rights legislation and blocked by the Southern Caucus of the Senate led by Senator Russell—began to discuss ways to dramatize their plight, including a massive March on Washington.

It had been nine years since *Brown v. Board of Education*, and the real steps toward an integrated, color-blind society were, at best, baby steps. Using myself as an example, graduating from high school in 1962 and college in 1967, I never once attended a single class with a black student. The civil rights leadership felt that black voters had elected John Kennedy president and could point to a handful of critical states where increased black turnout was at least one of—if not *the*—deciding factor in JFK's razor-thin victory over Richard Nixon in 1960. While there were no public statements made criticizing the Kennedy Administration, there were growing doubts among the black leadership about the president personally, the entire administration, the depth of their commitment to civil rights, and their willingness in this election year to go all out.

In early June 1963, President Kennedy made what was billed as a major civil rights speech. While the reaction from the civil rights leadership was positive, there were stories the following week that Kennedy's popularity in a national Louis Harris survey had dropped for the first time below 50 percent, due in part to the loss of white Democrats in the South.

While the Kennedy rhetoric and intentions on civil rights had been good, his results in getting tough, enforceable legislation were modest at best. There were nagging doubts among Roy Wilkins, King, and others that the president and his brother Bobby had calibrated the reaction of many whites to civil rights and simply wanted to get beyond the 1964 presidential election, maintaining at least the possibility of carrying the traditionally Democratic South.

On June 12, civil rights leaders announced a massive march on Washington to be held in late August led by Roy Wilkins, Bayard Rustin, Martin Luther King Jr., and other leadership of the movement. After their announcement, the president met with the black leadership to actively discourage such a contentious public act.

"We want success in Congress, not just a big show at the Capitol," President Kennedy argued. "Some of these people in Congress are looking for an excuse to be against us. I don't want to give any of them a chance to say, 'I'll be damned if I will vote for it at the point of the gun.'"

While the other leaders listened respectfully to the president, the young preacher Martin Luther King Jr. told Kennedy, "Mr. President, there is never a perfect time to practice civil disobedience against such an obvious wrong!" Even the strongest civil rights supporters in the Congress—largely Democrats but even a handful of progressive Republicans like Jacob Javits of New York—publicly warned that a demonstration aimed at pressuring the Congress would most likely backfire and cost the movement support.

King confided to his young aide Andrew Young: "We have created this huge army of young, idealistic volunteers. We cannot ask them now to just sit on the sidelines . . . They want to be involved. They have to be used. A march could be constructive."

The whole idea of a march on Washington had its roots in an earlier effort that was planned in 1941 by A. Philip Randolph, who organized and led the black railway porters union. Randolph traveled the country speaking out against the blatant discrimination against blacks that were fighting and dying for their country around the world but blocked from getting jobs in the defense industries, which were totally dependent on U.S. government contracts. Randolph began to talk publicly about a national march on Washington. Remembering the march of disgruntled veterans following the Spanish-American War, which ended in riots in Washington, FDR finally signed Executive Order 8803 in 1941, which ended this practice.

Growing up in Georgia, heavily influenced by Hamp's opinions, now working for Senator Russell, and surrounded by other interns from Georgia, I knew that I had been receiving a heavy dose of only one side of the story in room 205 of the Old Senate Office Building. I swapped elevator shifts so that I could watch Roy Wilkins, head of the NAACP and considered the grand old man of the movement, testify before the Senate Commerce Committee. Prior to being peppered with comments and questions from senators on both sides of the issue, the dignified and somewhat aloof Wilkins read an elegant statement describing the plight of black families vacationing that summer: "For millions of Americans, this is vacation time. Families load their cars and trek across the country. I invite the members of this committee to imagine themselves a darker color and to plan an auto trip from Norfolk, Virginia, to the Gulf Coast of Mississippi."

The elegant Wilkins then posed to the senators the following questions: "How far would you drive each day? Where and under what conditions can you and your family eat? Where can they use a restroom? Can you stop after a reasonable day behind the wheel or must you drive until you reach a city where there will be relatives or friends who will accommodate you for the night? Will your children be denied a soft drink or an ice cream cone because they are not white?" Wilkins concluded, "The Negro American has been waiting upon voluntary action since 1876 [the year following the passing of the first Civil Rights Act, guaranteeing African Americans equal rights in transportation, restaurants, inns, theaters, and on juries]. He has found what other Americans have discovered: voluntary action has to be sparked by something stronger than prayers, patience, and lamentations."

Roy Wilkins painted for those in that Senate hearing a vivid human picture of the impact of segregation on black citizens, something I never consciously recognized nor completely understood, even while living with Old Black George, Annie, and Hattie. His testimony was not about political philosophy or states' rights; it was human narrative, and I was both moved and troubled to hear these stories of the real and practical implications of segregation. Wilkins's stories allowed me to imagine what it might be like to be black and live and travel in this country, particularly in my beloved South. When I heard Wilkins testify and had a chance to reflect on it, I knew that I had to question the judgment of the two greatest men in my life—Hamp and Senator Russell. It was not that they were bad—they were simply wrong.

But I didn't know what to think or do about it.

■ ■ ■

Leading up to the march, a disinterested observer reading the Washington press or listening to the hysterical speeches in the Congress would have thought that the rape and pillage of Washington was at hand. As the date drew near and the estimates of "marchers" soared from tens of thousands to hundreds of thousands to possibly even millions, so did the predictions of dire consequences. Stories quoting anonymous "FBI sources" expressed concerns about the Communist infiltration of the march, the prospects of riots, and the risk of militants torching the Capitol. The Washington City Council closed all the bars and liquor stores, making it illegal to sell any kind of alcoholic beverages the day of the march. It was bad enough to have this rabble of troublemakers descend on the nation's capital—what would happen if they had access to alcohol?

In the middle of all of this, I was not surprised to get a call from Mama—fresh from reading the *Albany Herald*—who suggested that I come home before the march, scheduled only days before I had planned to return to Georgia. I told her I could not just quit Senator Russell without notice. She admonished me to be careful and at least take the day off and not get involved in "that mess." She mentioned that the *Herald* had predicted likely race riots, burning, and looting. When hearing all of this, I was reminded of those demonstrations that King had led in my hometown in 1960 and 1961 and the rumors that had preceded and followed them, the most common being that these were not local folks but "Communists" and "professional agitators." All we saw on the streets of Albany were brave students from Albany State College, women like our own maid, Hattie, and other serious and committed people like her.

I was curious as to how the March on Washington was being perceived around the country and particularly how it was being played in the Deep South. For several days before the march, I went to the reading room in Senator Russell's office and thumbed through recent newspapers.

The *Atlanta Constitution* was the only major paper in the South that had taken a "moderate" position on race issues and seemed to be reporting the news leading up to the march right down the middle. My hometown paper, the *Albany Herald*, made no attempt to be balanced or fair. Sometimes, you couldn't tell the difference in the front page of the paper and the editorial page. On August 15, a column by David Lawrence that normally appeared on the editorial page was featured as the major front-page story in the *Albany Herald* and read: "Capitol March Leader Was Young Communist," amplified by the subtitle, "War Dodger Has Lengthy Jail Record." Lawrence charged—and it was reported by the *Herald* as fact—that March on Washington staff director Bayard Rustin was an "avowed member of the Communist Party" and had been convicted in 1953 of a "lewd act." This article and an editorial penned by *Herald* publisher James H. Gray insinuated that Rustin was a "sexual pervert who preferred boys." The source of this story was Senator Strom Thurmond, who would later reveal he had personally obtained this combination of information and slander from J. Edgar Hoover and the FBI. Tying this altogether, Gray predicted that "the public will react with strong revulsion to the revelation of the Rustin record. The president will pay a heavy price politically that will outweigh the Negro bloc vote he has confidently pocketed as a result of his total commitment to a minority that itself has been damaged by fuzzy-minded leadership."

In the August 18 edition, the *Albany Herald* declared in another headline story: "Capital in Uproar over Big March." This analysis predicted traffic jams, food and water shortages, and significant losses for downtown retail merchants and Washington's important tourism industry. The newspaper was also basically projecting an *assumption* that violence, rioting, and looting would occur. This was followed the next day in the *Albany Herald* with a headline reading "March Jitters Hit Washington" with a subtitle "Congress Backers Now Fear Violence." And if its white South Georgia readership was not already offended by the march, the *Herald* on August 25 had a front-page column titled, "Question: Who'll Pay Millions in Business Loss to Capital's People? Answer: Taxpayers All over U.S. to Suffer Penalty."

The day before the march, August 27, the *Albany Herald* proclaimed,

"Capitol Braces for Negro March that Threatens Nation, Sparks Could Set Off Mass Violence." Another lead article with a local twist told the readers that "Local Negroes Slap Albany in Washington March as Kennedy Welcomes Thousands." The story reported that several buses from Albany, loaded with members of several AME churches and student activists from Albany State College, were making the trip to D.C. with the purpose of "telling the story" of the continued abuse suffered by blacks in my hometown. It reported that the Albany group was scheduled to picket the Justice Department and the FBI had demanded meetings with Attorney General Robert Kennedy to demand an investigation of Albany "police brutality."

Going to the March

By the end of the summer—helped immensely by daily mentoring from Mac—I had learned my way around the Senate and developed enough street smarts to know how to get things done. Working for Senator Russell certainly had its advantages, and the coincidence of having the same last name as Senator Russell's right arm, Bill Jordan, often led people to mistake me for his son or nephew. Combined with my natural curiosity to see things close up and be a part of important events, this created some unique opportunities.

One day in late August, while filing constituent mail in Senator Russell's office, I answered the phone on the nearby desk. The person on the other end asked if this was "Mr. Jordan," and I responded that it was he. The caller identified himself as being from the Capitol Security Taskforce that had been organized for the march and said he would like to briefly describe security arrangements for the Capitol and the Senate for the upcoming march. He said he wanted to advise our office of the security plan for that day and wanted to see if the senator had any special needs or requests. He also indicated that several senators had expressed an interest in sending an observer to the march to view "this mess" in person and report back to their senator with their direct, firsthand account. He asked if Senator Russell's office had any interest in sending an observer.

It only took me a few seconds to realize that this was a call intended for Bill Jordan that had been referred to me by accident. But I saw an opportunity in that mistake.

I responded that he should send a written document summarizing his recommendations that could be circulated to the staff. On the possibility of sending an observer to the march, I said that I would get back to him. I hung up the phone and thought about the call. I only had ten more days in Washington. I had been served up an opportunity that would require me to tell what my mother called a "white lie"—a lie that doesn't really hurt anyone.

It was an easy decision. I called him back and told him what Bill Jordan had already announced—that Senator Russell did not want to officially close our offices and appear that we had been intimidated by the demonstrators, nor did we want to expose our staff to possible disruptions and acts of violence. Senator Russell had made a statement on the floor of the Senate that while he respected the right of any "citizen or group of citizens to petition their government," he would not be "intimidated" by a mob that had come "not to petition their government, but to threaten it." So, I informed the gentleman on the phone that our office would be operating with only a skeleton crew the day of the march but would officially be open for business. I also told the security officer that "we" did want to send an observer to provide a report on the march and indicated that "my namesake," William H. Jordan, would represent Russell's office. I forewarned the officer that his men would be very surprised at Jordan's youth but said that he was "smart as a whip" and would be writing a good report for the senator.

I held my breath for the next several days, half expecting my deceit to be discovered. I had second thoughts about what I had done; I could rationalize it in my own mind as being a "college prank," not harmful to anyone, but I knew that Bill Jordan, in particular, would not like what I had done. A lowly intern on the great senator's staff taking advantage of an operator's mistake to go see a march that Senator Russell vehemently opposed? Not anything to smile upon.

That was just one more reason for my wanting to do it.

But I was not found out. I got up early on the morning of August 28, 1963, and read the *Washington Post* and *New York Times*. The *Post* reported in a second-page story that a group was coming from my hometown not only to attend the march but also to protest the Justice Department's failure to prosecute persons who had allegedly abused protestors who had been sent to jails in nearby towns after the jails in Albany had overflowed with arrested marchers.

Trying to look "old" by wearing a dark gray suit, a white shirt, and a conservative tie, I met the security detail at the appointed hour in the underground Senate parking garage. There were two plainclothesmen wearing dark suits and stern expressions. I could tell that they were taken aback by my youth. I held out my hand, introduced myself as William Jordan, and quickly flashed my ID. They did not even look at it.

The two detectives automatically hopped into the front seat of the car, leaving me to sit in the back by myself. It was a white, unmarked vehicle with tinted windows and an internal siren, which sat on top of the dashboard. While not obvious, anyone taking a hard look at our car would probably figure out it was some kind of law enforcement vehicle. Even with the tinted windows, I sunk down in the seat as we peeled out of the Senate garage and onto the street. I was terrified that I could still run into Bill Jordan and be discovered.

Downtown Washington was closed down with yellow roadblocks and barriers blocking most of the main streets. An eerie quiet settled over the city. I remembered reading a column the day before from the *Atlanta Constitution* by Reg Murphy that stated the nation was "holding its breath" over the march. I could feel that very tension and sense of anticipation as we rode around, observing the solemn faces of both the policemen and the initial wave of protesters who had arrived early. The police looked like they were prepared for—and expecting—the worst.

I learned from a *Washington Post* story that, because there were so few places where blacks could stay, and because rooming for blacks was expensive in addition to being scarce, most of the buses had driven directly into Washington, possibly stopping at campsites or at black churches in nearby Virginia or Maryland.

Newspaper reports indicated that more than ten thousand law enforcement officers were on duty that day and that a significant number of National Guard units had been activated—armed and nearby, ready to deal with any major disorders or emergencies.

Most of the major stores in and around the area of the Capitol and the White House were closed. Many with large plate-glass windows were boarded up as if they were anticipating a hurricane or ice storm. These downtown merchants had read these same stories and reports and viewed the march as an unnecessary disturbance that would cost them business, adversely impact tourism, and possibly damage their stores. As if there were a need for a reminder of what might happen, there were also makeshift emergency first aid stations—white tents adorned with the bright Red Cross, with medical personnel in white scurrying in and out—on every block and a long string of them along the Mall between the Capitol and the Lincoln Memorial.

Once we got beyond the immediate area of the Capitol, cordoned off by the police standing behind wooden barricades, there were people everywhere, all walking in the direction of the Lincoln Memorial and the Mall. There were a few individuals and some small groups of four, five, and ten people, but most were large bodies of people, carrying homemade signs: "Charlotte A.M.E. Church" or "Montgomery Baptist Church," for example. Most of the church groups were older black men and women, dressed in their Sunday best; many of the men wore hats. There were younger groups of black people—sometimes sprinkled with a white priest or white students—wearing jeans and shorts and carrying school signs like "Clark" or "Tuskegee," and some carrying unfamiliar fraternity and sorority signs like "Delta Sigma Theta" and "Alpha Phi Alpha."

The marchers were a happy group, but a subtle tension had settled over the day, and many of the older black folks were looking around nervously, taking it all in. It made me think that they had never visited their nation's Capitol before and were wondering—and worrying—if they were going to be the targets of police dogs, fire hoses, and beatings that had been the hallmark of marches in Montgomery and Birmingham. Most of all, I noted the black women, dressed up, wearing hats and heels, moving with a particular pride. Some carried their Bibles in their hands, walking in quiet dignity. Occasionally, there would be a shout or some group would break into a favorite spiritual like "Lift Every Voice and Sing" or "Oh, Freedom" and most often "We Shall Overcome," the unofficial anthem of the civil rights movement. Other than the singing, there was not a lot of noise, just quiet determination to get to the front of the Lincoln Memorial in time for the speech making, which was scheduled to start at eleven a.m.

In front of one Capitol Hill diner frequented by congressional staffers, policemen, and locals, the owner had placed a huge homemade sign inside the window—obviously to flaunt in the faces of the marchers— which proclaimed, "Whites Only . . . FOREVER." A few young blacks were hard at work on the sidewalk, preparing an instant response, crafting hand-painted slogans on the back of their printed signs, which read, "Khrushchev can eat here, but I can't!" and "Negroes fight and die for USA but are not allowed to eat HERE!" and taped them all over the restaurant window, quickly covering up the offensive "Whites Only" sign.

While there seemed to be a steady dribble of folks on the side streets, there were not the masses of people that I expected to see. Was the highly publicized "big march" only a small to medium-sized march? Would it be a flop? As we turned up Pennsylvania Avenue, however, and headed in the direction of the White House, the groups of five and ten converged into groups of twenty and thirty, which in turn converged into groups of hundreds and finally thousands, happily marching, trudging, laughing, and singing—all headed toward the Lincoln Memorial. I wondered what the spectacle must look like from an airplane or atop the Washington Monument: thousands and thousands of people, coming from all directions, swarming toward the Lincoln Memorial. I smiled as I thought about the tiny black specks moving toward the giant, rectangular white building named for Lincoln; it must have looked like black ants converging on a big lump of white sugar.

The detectives driving me around could barely disguise their disdain for the events around us, and although they were careful with their words, their body language indicated that this was the last place in the world they wanted to be. They were probably accustomed to driving VIPs around—not a kid like me—and were not very talkative, other than an occasional mumbled comment insinuating, not so subtly, their feelings.

"Look at that one!" one man would say derisively to the other.

As we drove up Pennsylvania Avenue and turned to ride around the backside of the Lincoln Memorial, one questioned, "Where would you like to go, Mr. Jordan?"

I made a feeble attempt to break the ice and put them at ease about me. I asked them to please call me Hamilton and said that I was just watching this to write a report on the day for the senator. I told them that I would just leave it to them to give me a good look at the events of the day.

The bigger guy turned and smiled and said, "So you are just a regular guy, huh? Not even twenty and getting VIP treatment?" I told him that there was a reason for it: that Bill Jordan, who worked for Senator Russell, was my cousin. Another white lie. It seemed to work, and while deferring to me on where we went and what we did, they began to get comfortable with the idea of driving around with a kid in the backseat. Later on, the detective driving said, almost apologetically, that he hoped that I realized that they saw a "bunch of brats" in the course of doing their jobs. "We are always getting weird calls to get senators' kids out of jail or jams with the law, to pick up wives (and sometimes girlfriends) from the airport. I guarantee you, we've seen it all."

Whenever we approached a barricade, the detective riding shotgun would reach under the dashboard, the light mounted on the dashboard would flash red a few times, and then the D.C. police would wave us around the barricade. By eleven o'clock, a crowd gathered in front of the Lincoln Memorial. By noon, only about a third of the huge space in front of the memorial—which stretched around the Reflecting Pool, running almost all the way to the Washington Monument—was filled with marchers. We parked the car at the other end of the Reflecting Pool and just sat for a while, listening to the series of speeches blasted from giant speakers, which we could hardly decode as waves of powerful noise reverberated over the Reflecting Pool and Mall, seemingly flowing out into the streets. The big names of all of the significant speakers were memorable, but their remarks—barely audible where we were standing—were not.

My detective friends brought box lunches for us, and we eventually got out of the air-conditioned car. The hot, humid summer day felt like we were stepping into a sauna. We took off our jackets, loosened our ties, and leaned against the warm trunk of the car as we ate our sandwiches, munched chips, sipped Cokes, and sweated. The event went on and on as one speech melted into another, staggered by occasional songs from the likes of Joan Baez and Bob Dylan. But the songs that moved the crowd most were the familiar spirituals by Metropolitan Opera star Marian Anderson and Mahalia Jackson . . . songs that had also been so much a part of my own Baptist upbringing.

I remembered my uncle Clarence Jordan's comments on the role of music in religion when discussing the hypocrisy of the white Baptist Church. Wearing heavy-duty khaki work pants so popular with the local farmers and sitting in his favorite rocking chair in his tiny writing shack, Clarence once offered this thought: "Think about it—blacks and whites go to different churches, but we claim we are all Baptists or Methodists. We worship the same God. We believe that Jesus was the Son of God and sent here to die for our sins. We read the same Good Book. We subscribe to the same Ten Commandments as a guide to leading a good life. And we even sing the same songs from the same Baptist hymnal.

"Now," Clarence said, leaning forward in his chair with a twinkle in his eye, "even I would have to admit that I do believe *selectively* in some forms of racial superiority." He paused to let this shocking statement from him sink in, before continuing, "'Cause if you ever attended the biggest white Baptist church in Atlanta and then went to the smallest black Baptist church in Atlanta, you would find the black Baptist choir would win hands down every time over the white choir. Our black brothers and sisters have been given a special gift of music by the Lord, maybe so they can sing so beautifully and powerfully about their suffering at our hands."

■ ■ ■

The day was wearing on. The hot summer sun bore down, and temperatures rose to the high nineties. Many of the marchers around the Reflecting Pool kicked off their shoes and splashed their feet in the water in an effort to cool off. A few pulled up their dresses or rolled up their pants legs and walked knee-deep in water around the pool. It was late afternoon—close to four p.m. The crowd was just starting to melt away when the strong, perfect voice of Mahalia Jackson froze the crowd with her mournful rendition of "I've Been 'Buked, and I've Been Scorned."

> I've been 'buked, Lord, and I've been scorned.
> I'm gonna tell my Lordy when I get home
> Just how long they been treating me wrong.

It was followed by a powerful rendition of "We Shall Overcome," which soon had the mass of people standing up, either holding hands or draping arms around the shoulders of friends and strangers standing nearby, swaying like a wave washing back and forth to this soulful and familiar anthem of their movement.

When King came forward, he was given the same polite applause as the other key speakers, such as Roy Wilkins of the NAACP; A. Philip Randolph, the wise elder statesman of the movement; and the fiery young John Lewis of the Student Nonviolent Coordinating Committee (SNCC), who had reportedly toned down his speech after pressures from other black leaders who considered it too radical. Although King was well known and popular, his role was not yet firmly established in the movement. Many thought that King's reputation had been built largely on the good fortune of being the preacher of an elite church in Montgomery—which just happened to be the place where a brave woman, Rosa Parks, refused to get up and out of the "white only" section of a local city bus.

Some of the older leaders, particularly Wilkins, could barely contain their jealousy of King and were quick to bring up King's foray in Albany, Georgia, over the past two years, where King had invested his time and prestige with little or nothing to show for it. There was some speculation that the elders of the movement and march organizers had scheduled King to speak last *not* because it was a prime spot but because they thought it would be too late for the television cameras to take and edit their film in time for the evening news shows.

One of the detectives brought binoculars that allowed us to see the podium and the speakers. I saw King clearly as he came to the podium and started to speak slowly. The thirty-four-year-old King did not make a speech that day. He preached a powerful, powerful sermon. Standing on the other end of the Reflecting Pool, I could hear echoes of his voice but could not make out every word. Still, the singsong cadence of the skilled preacher—familiar and comfortable to my Southern Baptist ears—punctuated with rounds of applause and thousands of "amens" shouted out spontaneously throughout the crowd, left no doubt that King was connecting with his massive audience.

Hanging on each word and phrase and responding whenever possible, the sprawling crowd of hundreds of thousands started to behave like a few hundred worshippers packed into a black Baptist church. After King had been speaking for six to eight minutes to louder and louder waves of noise and reaction, his words rose in a crescendo, as did the applause of the crowd. As I watched through the binoculars and King's voice soared higher and higher and culminated in a series of shouts, he turned away quickly, waving back over his shoulder as he walked from the podium. While I had caught some of the words and even a few phrases in his closing, I had no idea what Martin Luther King Jr. had really said. However, I could feel—almost a half a mile away— the impact of his words, reverberating from the large speakers posted around the Reflecting Pool, creating a louder and louder roar, which swept like a mighty wave from the Lincoln Memorial, rolling up the Mall toward the Washington Monument, where we stood.

The crowd—sitting in lawn chairs carried from home on the edge of the Reflecting Pool or sprawled on blankets spread on the grass—was finally energized and standing. Waves of clapping and shouting continued for ten or fifteen minutes after his speech ended. Through the binoculars, I could see the people on the podium hugging and shaking hands with each other. They knew that they had closed their day on the high note and that—through King—the march had found its message and its messenger. After a few more minutes of dwindling applause, the major players—King, Roy Wilkins, A. Philip Randolph, Bayard Rustin, and the young John Lewis—exited the stage, surrounded by their own black security team. Suddenly, I could see a caravan of police cars with sirens wailing and lights flashing take off as it knifed its way through the crowd, moving away from the Lincoln Memorial. When I wondered out loud what was happening, my detective buddies got on their radios and soon reported that the "colored leaders" were on the way to the White House to meet with President Kennedy.

The crowd was transformed by King's comments. They had come to life, were smiling and laughing, others teary eyed, moved by King's eloquent plea. Most of all, they were proud of the day, proud of what *they* had done. No longer melting away, the crowd now clearly wanted to relish the moment and looked like they were unlikely and unwilling to leave.

They all faced long bus rides home. Some, I am sure, were expected early the next morning to perhaps clean or cook or do yard work at some white person's home, to work on a farm, or to do manual labor at some business. With the speeches and music over and the big names gone, the crowd reluctantly headed back to one of the twenty thousand buses scattered all around downtown Washington. Even my two new friends from Capitol Security picked up on the change in the mood as we got back inside the car. There were no more jokes, snide comments, or racial insinuations . . . we just rode in silence and watched, looking from side to side as the outpouring of proud marchers clogged the streets. Pausing between the endless swarm of black people returning to their buses, our car was constantly stopping and starting. At times, we were surrounded, and my "security detail" seemed a bit uncomfortable, three white guys in a police car. The driver muttered to himself, "Okay, fella, don't get too close. That's right, let us through. We don't want any trouble."

But I was not concerned at all. These "troublemakers" were just like the black folks back in my hometown, students from Albany State, and poor black people like our dear maid, Hattie, trying to make some peaceful changes in their lives. I was not scared, but I *was* embarrassed to be sitting in what must have looked like a cop's car—which it was. Me, Hamilton, just part of the white establishment. Just one more white guy trying to hold them down and "keep them in their place," as many Albany whites would express it.

I was most struck by the change in the demeanor of the crowd over the course of the day. They arrived visibly unsure of their mission and uncertain as to what to expect, nervously looking around. They left focused, happy, and most of all, proud. While it was not clear to me what this march actually meant, I knew that it meant *something*—probably a great deal. And I had watched it all from a police car. I was not proud of myself that day. I was still straddling the fence. Enamored with JFK one day, sitting in a police car monitoring the marchers the next. What did I really feel? Where did I really stand? I was certainly on the "other side," at least in the sense that I felt great loyalty toward Senator Russell and my beloved grandfather Hamp. But that also put me on the same side as George Wallace, Strom Thurmond, J. Edgar Hoover, and *Albany Herald* editor Jimmy Gray—men whose actions and opinions were despicable, and with whom I could never agree.

Sure, I was only a kid, a lowly summer intern who ran an elevator. But there were kids younger than me marching that day. And kids younger than me who were jailed in Albany, beaten in Montgomery and Birmingham, among other places. Almost by default and by virtue of the fact that I worked for Senator Russell, it seemed that I had made my choice. And it was clearly not with the marchers that day.

March on Washington: Postmortem

The mood was very somber in room 205 of the Old Senate Office Building the next morning. My hunch was that it was probably the same in the offices of the other members of the Southern Caucus. The Senate was back in session, and there were the usual tasks and chores to be performed: calls to be made and received, bills to be read and analyzed, votes to be scheduled, committee meetings to prepare for, and always, the endless constituent mail.

While it was business as usual among the senior staff in Senator Russell's office, a few of the younger staff and interns whispered quietly to one another what others were thinking. The much-ballyhooed march had *not* been a disaster for the civil rights movement. It was *not* a collection of deadbeats, Communists, troublemakers, and anarchists but best described by "Communist organizer" Bayard Rustin as a "gentle army" of the black middle class from all over the country, mostly from the South, "who came to their nation's capital to claim the rights promised in the Constitution and its subsequent amendments." There had been no disruption and only a few minor arrests. Washington's chief of police even held a press conference to boast that the overall crime rate in the city of Washington was actually *down* during the twenty-four-hour period of the march.

Strom Thurmond, hearing the chief's claim, retorted, "No wonder crime was down in Washington—every criminal in the city was marching."

It was like reading tea leaves to know what the "company line" was for those of us at the bottom of the pecking order in Senator Russell's office. While we studied the press releases and the speech that Senator Russell made on the floor of the Senate following the march, the senator's real feelings were most likely reflected by Bill Jordan's comment to several of the senior staff (who passed it down to us in conversations in the mail room or over the water cooler): "Not a single vote in the Senate was changed by that march!"

But even the major paper in Senator Russell's home state saw it differently. Gene Patterson, writing in the *Atlanta Constitution*, reported, "The civil rights movement is not likely ever to be the same again after this monumental display of Negro will and cohesion." Not only had the Washington March been peaceful and orderly, but also Martin Luther King Jr. had finally given the movement a national face and a voice. All of the newspapers—even the conservative ones—quoted from King's speech and featured his picture on the front page. Many newspapers also featured front-page stories of President Kennedy and the black leadership at a late-afternoon meeting at the White House, which seemed to give the march and its leadership the credibility and public momentum it had sought.

"It hasn't changed a single damn vote in the Senate," Bill Jordan insisted. "Show me one vote that has changed!"

No one did or could.

In the final analysis, "Cousin Bill" was more right than wrong. While the March on Washington was a great public relations success that heightened public awareness and engendered feelings of great self-confidence among the national and grass-roots leadership of the civil rights movement, its short-term impact was almost nil in terms of the politics and dynamics of the U.S. Senate. Perhaps the most important result—invaluable, although intangible—was that the movement finally had a face, a leader, and a voice. With every day that passed, Martin Luther King began to personify the march and the grievances of black Americans. For those whose job it was to describe the march and its consequences, more and more press attention was paid to King's words, which, the *Washington Post* wrote, "electrified the marchers and defined their goals."

King's remarks reminded me of my high school history class, where we studied Lincoln's Gettysburg Address, a speech so brief as to be considered insignificant by those who actually heard it at the time. Yet, the 278 words that comprised Lincoln's remarks were considered—over time—a perfectly honed and balanced expression of our nation's belief in personal freedom and our responsibilities as citizens in protecting that right.

The principal speaker at the Gettysburg dedication was the great author, clergyman, and noted orator Edward Everett Hale. Lincoln's role just called for remarks from the commander-in-chief. Hale spoke for over two hours but wrote the president after the event, "I should be glad if I could flatter myself that I came as near to the central idea of the occasion in two hours as you did in two minutes."

There was also a story in the *Washington Post*, obviously leaked by some White House aide, that said that after watching King's speech, President Kennedy had commented, "This guy is damn good!"

But the March and King's nonviolent message had no impact on Russell of Georgia or Thurmond of South Carolina or Stennis of Mississippi or Fulbright of Arkansas nor any of the rest of the members of the Southern Caucus, other than to harden their resolve to defeat—or at least stall—the pending civil rights legislation considered so obnoxious by white southerners.

I had read stories that when Richard Russell was a small boy in Winder, Georgia, his favorite past time was playing War between the

States with his siblings in his backyard with wooden guns. Many years later, his childhood friends recalled that young Russell, even at age six or seven, always insisted on being Robert E. Lee in their war games. When the real General Lee realized that the eventual defeat of the South was inevitable, he refused to let his men die in vain; his honor as a Virginian and a soldier would allow no less. Finally, Lee surrendered to General Grant at Appomattox, after his valued Stonewall Jackson had been accidentally killed by his own men at Chancellorsville, and with Lee's troops surrounded on all sides by vastly superior forces. There were no miracles left.

Richard Russell was a modern Lee—a bold legislative general and strategist, fighting a rear-guard action against overwhelming forces that he fully understood he could not defeat. He could fight and stall and delay for months and maybe even years, but even though it was a war he would not concede, it was also a war that Russell of Georgia could not win.

. . .

Chapter Fourteen

UNCLE CLARENCE

My father's family lost everything in the stock market crash of 1929 and the Great Depression, and his father died shortly afterward of a heart attack. Overnight, my daddy went from being the son of one of the wealthiest men in Macon to selling Maxwell House coffee door-to-door to support his family and send his brother and himself to Mercer University.

As a boy, my daddy spent a lot of time with his first cousins who lived nearby in Talbotton, a small farm town in middle Georgia known as the peach capital of the world. My father's seven Talbotton cousins became more like siblings to him. The middle son was named Clarence. By the time I came along, Clarence Jordan had become a mysterious figure in the life of our extended family, rarely present at family reunions or the annual gatherings in Talbotton. Every Thanksgiving and Christmas, we chose up sides and played football on the big pecan tree–speckled lawn before stuffing ourselves with turkey, country yams, and pecan pie. I can remember family members talking quietly among themselves at these functions about "what Clarence was doing," then shaking their heads with shame or disgust.

When I was eight or nine, during one of those rare occasions when we got to see Uncle Clarence, I told him, "We see Uncle Frank and Uncle George and Uncle Robert all the time, but we never see you except at weddings and funerals!"

The big man smiled, hugged me, and then pulled back to look me directly in the eye. "Well, Hamilton," Clarence said, "you are half right

Sections from this chapter originally appeared in Hamilton Jordan's 2000 memoir *No Such Thing as a Bad Day.*

. . . you actually only see me at family funerals, because you have to be invited to weddings." He laughed. "I love your daddy and mamma so much. We have got to get together more." But we didn't, and Clarence continued to be the black sheep of the family. It was a long time before I would understand why.

Later on, when I was in high school, Clarence, his wife, Florence, and their children started visiting us every couple of weeks throughout the summer of 1962. They always came at night, unannounced, piling out of the same old beat-up car, usually carrying pecans or peaches or vegetables in a brown paper bag from their farm. The whole family wore overalls or khaki pants—obviously farming clothes—but as we romped and played in the backyard, the kids seemed pretty normal to me. What didn't seem normal, though, was that as soon as Clarence and Florence left, my parents shook their heads and agreed that it was "just a shame" what Clarence was putting his family through.

As I later came to learn, by this time, Clarence Jordan was a marked man. It was Clarence himself who eventually explained the reason for his frequent visits to my family that summer. Martin Luther King Jr. and the Albany Movement were trying to integrate the public facilities, and over a three- or four-month period, King and the leadership of the civil rights movement were in my hometown—either in jail or in hiding in the houses of supporters. Clarence told us that he regularly saw Martin—as he called him—during this period, and that on the way out of town, he and Florence enjoyed dropping by our house at night to catch up with the Albany Jordans.

As I grew older, I learned both to understand and to appreciate my unusual uncle Clarence. As soon as I had access to a car, I began to visit him (without my parents' knowledge) once or twice a year, starting my senior year in high school.

G. K. Chesterton once said, "The only problem with Christianity is that no one has ever tried it." Chesterton obviously never met my uncle Clarence.

In 1942, while Martin Luther King Jr. was still in the seventh grade, Clarence Jordan founded an interracial commune called Koinonia in rural South Georgia. This was twelve years before the Supreme Court declared "separate but equal" education unconstitutional and more than two decades before blacks could drink from a public water fountain or use a public bathroom. Strict segregation was not only prevalent in the South . . . it was the law.

Clarence Jordan committed himself to living his faith—ironically, the same Baptist faith that rationalized segregation and racism, and the same faith that first tried to silence him, then tried to run him off, and finally tried to destroy him. Clarence lived his life in scorn of the consequences, risking everything: the love of his family and friends and the safety of the lives of his own wife and children. For twenty-five years, Clarence and his family stood alone against the rising tide of the white South's worst violence and bigotry.

Asked by a reporter after one bombing of Koinonia if he was ever scared, Clarence responded, "Was I ever scared? I am always scared, particularly for my wife and children. But being scared is not the question . . . the question we face every day is whether or not we will be obedient to a system and to a group of people who insist that we hate and mistreat our fellow man."

Martin Luther King Jr. called Clarence Jordan "my friend, my mentor, and my inspiration." Recalling their first meeting, King said, "When I first invited him to speak at Dexter Street Baptist Church [in the early 1950s], Clarence told us about his interracial commune in rural South Georgia. It was shocking and inspiring and sounded too good to be true. Here was a son of the Old South, a white Baptist preacher doing what we were just talking about doing. I went to Koinonia later to see it for myself and couldn't wait to leave because I was sure the Klan would show up and kill us both."

Corranzo Morgan, a black farmer, recalled, "I almost fell off my chair when Clarence come over the first time, shook my hand, and invited me and my family for Sunday dinner. I hemmed and hawed and finally said we was busy. I'm thinking, this young white boy must not know that coloreds and whites eating together just isn't done . . . he is going to get hisself kilt. My next thought was that we might get ourselves kilt too . . . living cross the road from him."

"When we first heard about Clarence Jordan and Koinonia," Andrew Young recalled, "we considered it too radical, too dangerous. Martin and I were trying to get folks the right to ride on the bus and to shop where they wanted—huge challenges back then. But here Clarence was—smack dab in the middle of Ku Klux Klan country—going for the whole loaf. Clarence did not spend all his time telling others what to do or making a fuss about it—he just kept living his faith. And Clarence put all the rest of us to shame until we did something about it."

Clarence himself was a bundle of contradictions. He was, in the words of his biographer Dallas Lee, "a gentle man who thundered against injustice, a nonviolent man who stared down the Klan, a genuinely humble man who could walk into the home of a rich man and say, 'Nice piece of plunder you got here.' He was a dirt-farming aristocrat, a good ol' Georgia country boy with a doctor's degree, a teacher with manure on his boots, a scholar in working clothes."

Clarence's faith was not a remote, prissy, sanitized doctrine or ritual but a gritty, folksy, in-your-face way of life, based on respect and love for all of humanity and applied to every decision and every action. The hard moral choices that Clarence forced on a defiant white South were often sugarcoated in his rich sense of humor and sounded a bit less threatening when delivered in his melodious drawl.

The civil rights struggle dominated every aspect of southern life in the 1950s and 1960s. Clarence saved his special scorn for his own Baptist Church. Caught in this moral crossfire, most of the white churches—especially of the Baptist variety—were the major forces for rationalizing segregation and maintaining the status quo.

"Here you are," he lectured a group of Baptist ministers, "sitting smugly on your hands while the greatest moral dilemma since the Civil War is ravaging your communities. What is your response, ye moral pillars of the South?" Clarence mocked, "I'm sorry, but I can't afford to get involved."

"Brother Clarence," one minister protested, "you are being too hard on us . . . every person here is praying for you."

"Save your prayers for each other," Clarence thundered. "You need them more than we do. Your silence in the face of this hate and violence makes you an active accomplice to the cowards who shoot up our homes, beat our children, and bomb our farms."

No one clapped as he sat down.

Talbotton, Georgia

Clarence Jordan was born in 1910 in the central Georgia town of Talbotton, where his family members were prosperous farmers and merchants. There was little in his early years to suggest the remarkable life he would lead. The fires that would erupt later in his life simmered quietly for years as young Clarence began to measure and weigh what people said against what they did. He attended Sunday school at the First Baptist Church and learned to sing the same songs of love and faith sung by Baptist children everywhere. One of his favorites went:

> Red and yellow, black and white,
> They are precious in His sight,
> Jesus loves the little children of the world.

Years later, Clarence would write about the torment this little ditty caused him: "It bothered me greatly . . . even as a child. Were the little black children precious in God's sight just like the little white children? The song said they were. Then why were they always so ragged, so dirty and hungry? Did God have favorite children? I was puzzled and started to think that maybe it wasn't God's doings, but man's. God didn't turn these black children away from our churches—we did. God didn't pay them low wages—we did. God didn't make them live in another section of town in miserable huts and pick rotten oranges and fruit out of the garbage for food—we did. Maybe they were precious in God's sight, but were they in ours? My environment told me that they were not very precious in anybody's sight. A nigger was a nigger and must be kept in his place—the place of servitude and inferiority."

The sprawling Jordan home was just down the street from the courthouse. Clarence recalled that the jail was about one hundred yards from his home and a group of chain gang convicts was often camped in the jailhouse yard. Fascinated by these strange characters, so different from anyone he had ever known, Clarence began purposefully passing through the camp in the afternoons after school, occasionally striking up brief, casual conversations with some of the chain gang members. The acquaintances he developed gave him a glimpse of life that seemed altogether alien to what he was being taught at home and in church:

> I saw men with short chains locked between their feet to keep them from running, men bolted into the agonizing shame of primitive pillories, men beaten with whips or their bodies torn under the stress of the "stretcher"—a small frame structure in which a man could be placed with his feet fastened at the floor and his hand tied to ropes above him that extended to a block and tackle on the outside. I saw that almost all these men were black. This made a tremendous, traumatic impression on me.

Another indelible boyhood memory was of a revival one summer night, when Clarence, from his place in the church choir, looked out into the congregation and saw the warden of the chain gang getting all carried away as he sang "Love Lifted Me." But the next night he was awakened from sleep by the agonizing screams of one of his chain gang friends; the warden had the man on the stretcher.

"I was torn to pieces," recalled Clarence. "I identified totally with that man in the stretcher. His agony was my agony. I really got mad with God. If the warden was an example of God's love, I didn't want anything to do with Him."

Clarence carried the contradictions of his early life with him to the University of Georgia, where he studied agriculture but continued to read his Bible. The summer after graduation, he went to ROTC camp to complete the military training that would allow him to be commissioned as an officer in the U.S. Army. It was while playing soldier atop a galloping horse that Clarence's priorities became abundantly clear. Later, he wrote about it:

The class that day was a mounted drill held on the edge of the woods. I was on horseback and galloping through the woods with my pistol and saber drawn. We were to shoot the cardboard dummies and stick the straw dummies with our sabers. Every time I would shoot one of those dummies, that verse, "But I say unto you, love your enemies," would flash through my mind . . . At that moment, I saw the conflict between the mind of Jesus and the mind of the commanding officer. It was crystal clear that Jesus was going one way and I was going another. Yet, I claimed to be His follower.

When Clarence had completed the obstacle course and cleared the woods, he found his commanding officer, dismounted, and resigned his army commission on the spot. The officer tried to talk Clarence out of such a rash decision. When he got nowhere, he suggested that Clarence should become a chaplain.

"I told him," Clarence said, "that would be the worst thing I could do. I could not encourage someone else to do something that I myself would not do."

His course was set, and he surprised family and friends when he announced that he had decided to become a preacher.

The Southern Baptist Seminary, Louisville, Kentucky

His fellow students at the Southern Baptist Seminary in Louisville were not sure what to make of the tall, high-hipped, slow-talking Georgia boy who quickly earned the nickname "Tall-Bottom." Clarence soon began preaching and working in the poor black neighborhoods of the city—a practice unheard of in those days—and the idealism of theology school crashed headlong into the harsh reality of the urban poor. Clarence became a familiar face in the crowded shanties of "South Town," befriending people and inviting black families to dinner at his modest apartment on campus.

For these activities, needless to say, Clarence was rebuked by his professors. He offered a spirited defense, using the very Bible teachings of those now chastising him to devastate their objections. The flustered head of the seminary finally ended the discussion: "Brother Jordan, you are supposed to minister to these unfortunate people, not entertain them in your home. It just is not done."

Outraged to find the same hypocrisy in theology school that he had found as a little boy at the Baptist church in Talbotton, Clarence set a course from which he would never depart: "I made up my mind then and there that I was going to try to live my faith . . . not act it."

Clarence was inspired to a new vision by Florence Kruger, the tall, blue-eyed daughter of German immigrants who worked as the assistant librarian at the school. Clarence started spending more and more time at the library with Florence; they talked about their beliefs and faith, and soon they announced they were to be married. They conceived a plan to return to the rural South to establish a demonstration project where they could live their faith and combine their religious beliefs with their practical knowledge of agriculture in order to help the rural poor, black and white.

Koinonia—the Early Years

In July 1942, Clarence and Florence Jordan opened their demonstration project in rural South Georgia near Americus, down the road from Plains. They called it Koinonia, the Greek word for "community."

Clarence had a strategy for realizing his dream. He wrote one of his friends from theology school:

At first, we'll set up simply as farmers, trying to win the confidence of the people as good citizens and good neighbors. Once we feel that we are part of the community, we will try to bring in some of the principles that we believe in. In this way it will be growth from within instead of a system imposed from without. We'll hold all things in common, distribute to people according to their need, and every worker will be given an equal voice in governing our community.

Over sixty years later, it is difficult for me to comprehend the courage of white people in rural Georgia establishing an interracial commune flying under a Christian banner. Indeed, Clarence's vision was so radical for the times that it was not initially understood nor taken seriously by either the local whites or blacks. The white churches found the young man fresh out of the seminary a witty and entertaining preacher. Later, Clarence would say, "They must notta listened to what I was saying."

But the tolerant atmosphere changed when the good folks of Americus began to see blacks and whites eating, living, and working together at Koinonia. It was doubly threatening that Clarence was one of their own—a Georgia boy, a Baptist, and a farmer. Twenty years later, when those "outside agitators" were swarming into the South in support of King's activities, a familiar refrain of the white southerner was, "You just don't understand the South." They could never say that about Clarence.

Churches led the attack when they realized that "race-mixing" was part of the Koinonia agenda. The local Baptist church voted Clarence and the Koinonians out for "violating the social customs of our community." Clarence feigned surprise. "I don't understand your action in throwing us out. If we are sinners as you suggest, we are in bad need of being at church and getting straightened out. If we are the saints, you are in bad need of our fellowship," he said.

The Difficult Years, 1955–1965

When the Supreme Court ruled in 1954 that the "separate but equal" doctrine was unconstitutional as applied to public education, the South prepared to refight the Civil War. Yet here in the heart of Dixie was Koinonia, which embodied the worst fears of the white South. The people of Sumter County resolved either to drive them out or to snuff them out.

It all started as a series of mean-spirited "pranks"—threatening phone calls in the middle of the night, signs torn down at the roadside stand on Highway 19 to Atlanta where Koinonia sold its eggs and farm products to passers-by, and sugar poured into the gas tanks of cars and trucks parked at the farm. Initially, the Koinonians tolerated these minor annoyances with little complaint; then, the harsh jokes escalated into a stream of violence.

In July 1956, a bomb was thrown into the roadside stand in the middle of the night, causing significant damage. No one was ever charged or even questioned about the bombing. Koinonia responded by running ads in the local paper, stating clearly that they were not there to harm anyone and asking the same of their neighbors. The plea not only fell on deaf ears but earned the official condemnation of the Sumter County district attorney: "Maybe what we need right now," the elected official said, "is for the right kind of the Klan to start up again and to use the buggy whip on some of these race mixers . . . I had rather see my little boy dead than sit beside a nigra in the public schools."

With this official sanction, the violence escalated and became more focused on Clarence and his family. His son Jim, subjected to constant abuse at the local high school, was shipped off to finish high school among friends in North Dakota. Still, in the face of mounting violence, Clarence always argued against abandoning their project, saying that if they left, it would only encourage the forces of hate and evil. As Florence expressed it at one meeting, "There was never any feeling in Clarence's mind or my own that we should leave. We would not be the first Christians to die for their beliefs, and we certainly would not be the last."

One night while Florence and Clarence were driving from Americus to Koinonia, a pickup truck of good old boys started to pass them, slowed down long enough to yell insults at them, then darted ahead. When Clarence rounded the curve, the same pickup truck was blocking the road, and three men were standing in the middle with shotguns. Clarence screeched to a halt and later claimed to have set a "world record for a 180-degree turn on a dirt road. I recalled that the Scripture said, 'If a man strikes you on your right cheek, turn to him both heels.' They may have shot at us, but I didn't hear it if they did because I was traveling faster than the speed of sound."

Reports of violence against them were routinely filed with the police and routinely dismissed. In January, their roadside store was bombed again—this time completely destroyed, with a loss of more than $7,000 worth of goods.

The violence moved closer to home. In the middle of the night on January 27, 1957, the peace of Koinonia was interrupted by screams as a machine gun strafed several houses, miraculously missing the inhabitants. Several days later, two cars rode by the farm in the early evening, firing shotguns at the lighted playground where the children were playing volleyball. As the children ran for cover, Clarence erupted with anger and ran toward the cars, shaking his fist and yelling, "Come back here and face me, you cowards! Come back!"

As the intensity of the violence directed at Koinonia increased, Clarence searched for ways to protect his followers. In 1957, he wrote to President Eisenhower:

> Dear Mr. President,
> A peaceful community of sixty men, women, and children is facing
> annihilation unless someone in authority does something about it be-
> fore it is too late. Groups of ten to twelve cars are harassing us every
> night. We have been bombed, burned out, and shot at. Our children
> are beaten going to and from school. Until the Supreme Court de-
> cision and the rise of the White Citizens' Council, we were not mo-
> lested. Since then, our life has become difficult and our existence pre-
> carious. We have been told that the end is near, but we shall not run,
> for this is America. Should freedom perish from our land, we would
> prefer to be dead. Someone in authority must do something before it
> is too late!

President Eisenhower did. He passed Clarence's letter on to J. Edgar Hoover, who promptly initiated a federal investigation of Koinonia as "known race mixers and probable Communists." Hoover also passed the letter on to the Georgia attorney general and encouraged the Georgia authorities to begin their own probe. Emboldened by the federal and state actions—ironically instigated by Clarence's plea for help to the president—the Sumter County Grand Jury launched its own investigation with the goal of ridding itself of Clarence Jordan and Koinonia once and for all. Clarence was called to testify and told a reporter when leaving the courthouse, "I tried to explain to the good folks on the grand jury the difference between Karl Marx and Jesus Christ . . . ended up they didn't know very much about either one of 'em."

The grand jury issued a public report that held the white community blameless and accused Koinonia of "bombing itself" and creating "incidents" for the purpose of drawing attention and "stirring racial passions." When Clarence read the report, he said that the white community had sanctioned the past crimes committed against them and had given a "hunting license" to anyone who wanted to do them harm.

Boycott

Having tried logic and violence and failed, the white community turned to coercion and imposed a highly effective boycott on Koinonia. It was simple—any people caught selling anything to Koinonia would themselves be boycotted. The boycott applied to everything—gas, fertilizer, food, and medicines—and soon the Koinonians were traveling seventy-five to a hundred miles to get outside of the area of the boycott to make anonymous purchases in cash. When the Birdsey Feed Store in Americus (owned by a Macon man who knew the Talbotton Jordans) refused to honor the boycott and continued to sell to Koinonia, his store was completely destroyed by a bomb. The good people of Americus meant business.

During the boycott, a prominent Americus banker wrote Clarence's father, who was on his deathbed, to tell him "your integrationist son is tearing our Christian community apart." The sick old man sent for his son and chastised him for "bringing shame on our good Christian name." For once, Clarence bit his tongue and did not argue. Instead, he marched into the banker's office unannounced, jerked the surprised man up by his necktie, and promised him, "The next time you bother my sick daddy, I am going to forget about Jesus Christ for about fifteen minutes and beat the hell out of you."

1965–1969 . . . Hard Times

By the late 1960s, Koinonia was running out of steam. The hard work of the civil rights struggle had moved to the ballot box and the courtroom. While people came and went, the actual number of devoted Koinonians dwindled sharply. Some left because of the violence; others left simply because it was a hard and demanding existence. Clarence began to spend more and more of his time preaching and writing, translating the Bible into a modern version cast in contemporary times. He called it *The Cotton Patch Gospel*, a version of the Bible that Harry Chapin turned into a successful off-Broadway musical in the early 1980s.

Unlike Clarence, I kept my own doubts about "the system" to myself, but we still managed to cultivate a friendship. The last time I saw Clarence, I had just returned from Vietnam and was going to work for his neighbor, Jimmy Carter, who lived just a few miles down the road and was planning to run for governor of Georgia. I wondered what Clarence thought of him.

"He is a nice fella, Hamilton, but he is just a politician."

He was in a reflective mood that day as we sat in his "writing shack," the cozy ten-by-twelve-foot structure where Clarence read, wrote, and studied. I had not seen him in two years, so there was some catching up to do. He talked with a touch of sadness about the past, the defection of so many of their people from Koinonia, and the hatred that persisted. I was surprised to find him so low.

"Haven't you accomplished a lot here?" I asked.

"That is not for me to say. I hope that we have made a good try at living according to the Lord's teachings."

Then he continued: "We have made progress, but not much." And holding up his large, rough hands, he put his thumb and forefinger almost together. "Every inch, every centimeter has been so hard . . . and at such a great price. But we have survived and persevered. We have survived," he repeated. "A tiny light in a vast sea of hate."

He looked out the window of the little shack as if counting the years and remembering all the people who had come and gone, all the violence directed against them. His eyes glistened. He continued, softly, "We have accomplished so much less than we had hoped for when we bought this old run-down piece of land. I underestimated the raw hatred of these people for their fellow human beings . . . the lengths to which they would go to justify their own corrupt system . . . the good people who lacked the moral courage to speak out. My greatest disappointment was the hypocrisy of the church . . . these so-called preachers who should have been pillars of strength and examples, moving people toward understanding and reconciliation. Instead, they were moral cripples whose silence aided and abetted those who hate us and try to destroy us."

Clarence told me that he would never leave Koinonia but that their struggle for economic justice must move to the growing cities, where the urban poor had no jobs, no houses, and no hope. He called his new vision "Dream for Humanity," which was focused on the reality that people without a home were not a family, could not live in dignity, and did not have self-respect. "I think the Lord is pushing me to be practical in my old age," he chuckled, "and become a house builder in the city instead of a farmer."

Six months later, Clarence suffered a massive heart attack while working in his writing shack. His son Lenny gave him mouth-to-mouth resuscitation but was unable to revive the man. Panicked calls went out to the emergency room and several doctors, but they knew that no doctor would risk coming to Koinonia, particularly not to save Clarence's life. Clarence Jordan was dead, of "natural causes," at age fifty-nine.

The "good people of Americus" tried to humiliate Clarence in death as they had been unable to do in life. The coroner refused to come to Koinonia to issue a death certificate and insisted that the body be brought to him. Millard Fuller, one of Clarence's most devoted disciples, loaded Clarence's limp, lifeless body into the back of a broken-down station wagon and drove him to the hospital, where he had to wait before bringing Clarence in. The coroner insisted on doing an autopsy. Millard called Florence at the farm for approval; she assented, and in a few hours Fuller was ready to carry Clarence home.

"They may have cut out his heart," observed Clarence's older brother, Frank, when he heard about the autopsy, "but they couldn't get his soul."

Remembering Clarence's opinion of funerals ("a waste of money on an empty shell . . . you can send a kid to college for a year on what some people spend celebrating their dead selves"), Millard Fuller put a few coins, a pocketknife, and a Timex watch—representing all of Clarence's worldly possessions—in a paper bag. On the way back to Koinonia, he found a used shipping crate and strapped it to the top of the car. The next morning, following a simple service attended by about a hundred friends, Clarence, with his few possessions, was buried in his work clothes in the pine box in an unmarked grave.

I was in Savannah organizing for Jimmy Carter's campaign for governor when my mother called to tell me Clarence had died. I immediately asked about the funeral arrangements, but I was already too late.

I felt sad not to be able to say good-bye to this great man I had barely known but who had brushed against my own life and would continue to do so in my memory. I smiled when I thought about Clarence's sudden exit—he left this earth just as he had lived: on his own terms as defined by his God. No one would be more disappointed than Clarence that the hard challenges to his life and faith would still be so highly relevant decades later. It would bring tears to the good man's eyes to realize that the grandchildren of the white southerners who bombed Koinonia, shot up his home, and beat his children still occasionally burn black churches in the South.

On the other hand, it would bring a smile to his face to know that one of his followers—Millard Fuller—took Clarence's vision and transformed it into Habitat for Humanity. Clarence would also find it a great and pleasant irony that his farmer-politician neighbor down the road, Jimmy Carter ("just a politician"), was one of its main supporters.

Maybe this good man, this hero of mine who demanded so much of himself and others, would take some small satisfaction from all of the good that had come from the example—he would call it "witness"—of his own life. But I doubt it. Clarence was never satisfied with anything, particularly himself and his own life. And there remains so much to be done.

Chapter Fifteen

■ ■ ■

THE MAN FROM PLAINS

I didn't really want to go to the luncheon to meet the no-name politician who was running for governor of Georgia, but at least it got me out of the worst job I ever had: spraying mosquitoes as part of a federal eradication program. Hugh Gaston, a local architect and a friend of my parents, was really just looking for warm bodies to fill up chairs at a last-minute luncheon he had arranged at the Elks' Club to meet Senator Jimmy Carter. Carter had just jumped into the already crowded Democratic primary for governor and was given zero chance by the pundits.

The place was about one-third full as the boyish-looking state senator with a big smile on his face stood to speak. His speech was halting, his voice so soft that I had to strain to hear him at all. He rambled on and on for about ten minutes. It was clear to me that he was poorly prepared for a major race. For several long and awkward moments after Carter stopped speaking, there was absolute silence in the large room until Hugh Gaston stepped up beside Senator Carter at the podium and started to clap. It was followed by polite, but modest, applause. "This guy has zero chance," I thought to myself, and my main feeling after his miserable performance was one of embarrassment for Hugh as our host who had brought this group of people together!

But when Senator Carter started taking questions from the floor, answering them directly and thoughtfully for nearly an hour in a much stronger voice, I realized that this was a man of considerable intelligence and enormous experience in state government. He simply had not known how to present himself in his "prepared" remarks.

The more I listened to him, the more intrigued I became with his candidacy. This was the new voice for Georgia that I had been looking for—someone who could bridge the enormous gulf that existed between rural and urban Georgia on so many issues, particularly the issue of race. When I got home, I wrote Senator Carter a long letter. I told him I had worked in the local campaign of Carl Sanders when he successfully ran for governor, exaggerating my own involvement, and offered to help him in Albany. Several days later—on the Fourth of July—the phone rang at 6:15 in the morning. My father scolded the caller before he said, "Hamilton, it's for you."

It was Jimmy Carter offering me a job in his campaign. Barely awake, I mumbled that I was honored but that I already had a full-time job spraying mosquitoes in a federal program. Carter laughed and said that he was going to have a tough time getting elected if people like me who supported him couldn't choose between mosquitoes and him. We talked for about five minutes, and I found his confidence and total commitment both impressive and infectious. Several hours later I was on a bus to Atlanta, entertaining visions of high-level strategy sessions and crucial campaign decisions. One of his cousins met me at the bus station and less than an hour after arriving in Atlanta, I found myself driving candidate Carter down Peachtree Street in a big convertible in a Fourth of July parade. No one in the crowd paid much attention to our candidate or our car, decorated at the last minute with homemade signs because printed materials for Carter's governor's race had not even been ordered. By the end of that first day, I was wondering if I should have stuck with the mosquitoes.

But as Jimmy Carter and his family began to crisscross the state, working as hard as a family could work, and spreading his message of a new Georgia, we could feel the momentum and support building and knew that we might win. In a matter of eight weeks, he went from being considered almost a joke in a ten-candidate field to one of the top three candidates.

Jimmy Carter was one of two candidates in the runoff until four or five in the wee hours of the night when the rural vote came in; he lost by only several thousand votes. It was tough to lose after having come so far and gotten so close; it was doubly difficult to lose the runoff spot to Lester Maddox, the segregationist clown from Atlanta whose sole claim to fame and political high office was that he had used an ax handle to chase young blacks from his restaurant. Maddox went on to win the runoff and become governor of Georgia. Once Carter saw that he was going to lose, he loaded his family into their car and drove off in the middle of the night without thanking his supporters or even saying good-bye. It was obvious to me that he had never failed before and simply did not know how to publicly deal with his defeat.

A couple of weeks later, Jimmy Carter called me at home and apologized for leaving that sad election night without properly thanking me for my help. I told him that it had been an honor to work for him and that he had run a good campaign.

"I'm tired of people saying that I ran a good campaign," he complained. "It was not good enough because I lost. I never intend to lose another election."

When members of my family and several friends from the campaign received hand-addressed Christmas cards from Jimmy and Rosalynn Carter later that year, I knew the defeat had only stimulated him to greater efforts.

After graduating from the University of Georgia and a stint doing refugee relocation in Vietnam for a voluntary organization, I went to Plains. I wasn't surprised to learn that Jimmy Carter was already planning another race for governor—this time against Carl Sanders, the very popular former governor who was considered a shoo-in. I argued that Carter should run for lieutenant governor and lay the groundwork for a race for governor in 1974.

Carter smiled, shook his head, and said that he wasn't interested in running for lieutenant governor. "I am going to run for governor if I don't get but two votes—mine and Rosalynn's.

I found his confidence contagious and said I would help him. "You'll get at least three votes."

AFTERWORD FROM THE EDITOR

"Some things go. Pass on. Some things just stay. I used to
think it was my rememory. You know. Some things you forget.
Other things you never do. But it's not. Places, places are still
there. If a house burns down, it's gone, but the place—the
picture of it—stays, and not just in my rememory, but out
there, in the world. What I remember is a picture floating
around out there outside my head. I mean, even if I don't
think it, even if I die, the picture of what I did, or knew, or
saw is still out there. Right in the place where it happened."
TONI MORRISON, *Beloved*

William Hamilton McWhorter Jordan Sr. died in his Atlanta home on
May 20, 2008, in the company of his wife, three children, extended
family, and close friends. His cause of death was peritoneal mesothelioma, his sixth and final cancer. He was sixty-three years old.

While my dad saw the arrival on the national scene of a young man
from Chicago, he was not able to witness when that man became the
first African American president of the United States. I have no doubt
that he would have been very, very moved by this moment in history.

I cannot presume to know how my dad planned to finish this book,
and I won't. What I can do is draw some conclusions based on what
we know of him and what he left for us in this text.

Hamilton intended to delve into those initial years working with
Jimmy Carter. Upon further review of this text, a thought occurred to my
brothers and me: that in the formulation of his ideals and his life goals,
Hamilton may have thought upon Carter as an ultimate hero. Carter
seemed to represent a bridge between the two strains of role models
in Hamilton's life, with Clarence Jordan on one side, and Hamp and
Richard Russell on the other. As we can see throughout his growth in
the book from boy to man, Hamilton's conflict about politics and the

civil rights movement grows and festers; particularly after the March on Washington, he seems disheartened and defeated when thinking back on his summer working for a man as powerful and important as Richard Russell. How can such a wonderful and respected politician be firmly against something that felt so real and so right?

Jimmy Carter enters Hamilton's life and shows him that he can work for progress and social justice while still maintaining a healthy pride in his home state and the South. Clarence may have said that Carter was "just a politician," but his cynicism isn't surprising when we consider the roster of southern politicians at that time: Eugene Talmadge, George Wallace, Lester Maddox. It wasn't until after Clarence died that Carter was elected governor; Clarence never had the opportunity to see Carter demonstrate to the people of Georgia (and later America) that politics and government in the South don't have to align with oppression, inequality, and disenfranchisement. While Carter was not perfect, he was a real step forward, and his entry into Hamilton's life provided what seems like a beautiful resolution to some of the dissonance Hamilton might have been feeling between his love for family and interest in politics versus his disappointment in his family and the South for being on the wrong side of the fence on the race issue.

A question remains unanswered: if it was indeed true that Hamp did not run for governor because of his Jewish wife. Hamilton's parents both died long before he conceived of writing this book (his father in 1978, and his mother in 1988, three months after I was born), but one member of that generation, his uncle Hamilton McWhorter, outlived my father. When my dad was working on this book and struggling with this particular issue, from my perspective, it seemed surprising that he refused to speak with his uncle about this very significant and shadowy part of their history. My dad joked that it would have killed Uncle Hamilton to bring it up, and that was that. We didn't press anymore.

When my older brother Hamilton Jr. was working on this book a few years ago, he intended to go to Uncle Hamilton's nursing home and ask him about his mother and her religion. He went a couple of times and got close—but he never asked. It didn't feel right. And I understand why. We couldn't comprehend our father's hesitance in approaching what should be such a comfortable subject until the responsibility lay directly in our hands. This was another lesson of our father's: respect. Our selfish desire to confirm what we basically already knew was quashed by our love of Uncle Hamilton and respect for his wishes. He did not wish to talk of it. We didn't pursue it. He died on October 18, 2011, at the age of ninety-eight.

Our father's last living lesson to us was, ironically, in dying; he did a damn good job of it. In late May 2008, he announced that it was time, and it was. We sat with him, in groups and individually, during those final days. He'd drift in and out of consciousness; I never knew when he closed his eyes if he had died, and I told him that. "Dad, I don't even know if you're dead or not," I said softly. He smiled and held his middle finger up to me. Once, he had been sleeping for a while when he suddenly sat up with a surprising energy. Cautious of any and every inconsistency, I asked, "Are you okay? What's wrong?" Straight-faced, he said, "I have to pee . . . or die." I told him that either way would relieve the feeling. We laughed at our poignancy, and he fell back to sleep.

The last coherent conversation I had with him was when we were deciding what would be the best way to spend his last few earthly moments. I suggested a hooker. He suggested methamphetamines. Ultimately, we decided on a glass of water. When I crawled into bed that night, I fell asleep right away.

Planes and cars brought waves of family the next morning and afternoon, but the most important flight was my brother's, a last-minute flight from Germany. My dad would wake and say, "Where's my boy?"

"He's coming, Dad. He's on a plane from Germany. He'll be here soon." He held on until Hamilton Jr. got home. It had been a beautiful, bright day outside, but then it began to storm. My mom, a woman aligned with the weather, walked silently into my dad's home office attached to our kitchen and laid herself down on the carpet. I could see her and saw what she knew. She willed him to go, mouthed: "Go. Please go."

The storm passed quickly, and my dad died. His death was simple and understated. It did not ask very much of us except to just be there and love him and one another.

My brothers and I had the distinct honor of eulogizing my father at his funeral, and we were followed by words from President Carter. Knowing what profound respect and admiration Hamilton had for President Carter, we found his eulogy was a perfect end to my dad's narrative. This incredible man who put his faith in my father from the beginning and shaped his life's path was there to put him to rest. It was stunning.

When Dad was dying, he told us of his ashes, "I want to go to the beach." A few months after he died, at Thanksgiving, we took Dad in a wooden box to the Outer Banks in North Carolina. On a very cold November day, we gathered on the beach. My brothers looked old to me. "They're men now," I remember thinking. They looked like him.

The family stood on the beach, arms linked, wrapped in big blankets that the wind whipped against our bare ankles and feet. We cried and hugged and laughed in recognition of the joy of being a family. Then, it was Mom, Hamilton, Alex, and I facing the ocean. Four ash-filled parcels, three children, two bonfires (on the beach, in the sky), one widow. We walked toward the dimming sun and into the cold saltwater. We were holding each other and holding our share. We sang and we cried and we waded out and out. Holding our own bodies, holding our ribs, we tossed our ash-filled parcels, and they did not go far enough. They floated, unfolding on the furrowed pelt of sea.

One final note: as my older brother Hamilton Jr. so succinctly stated in his eulogy of Hamilton Sr., our dad never overlooked a platform to discuss cancer awareness. I would be remiss to neglect this opportunity. Statistics change daily and can sometimes feel out of reach or impersonal, and so I've taken a different approach. The following is a list of some people mentioned in this book who later died of cancer.

July 23, 1885—Ulysses S. Grant, the eighteenth president of the United States, died of throat cancer at the age of sixty-three.

September 7, 1954—Glenn "Pop" Warner, American football player and coach, died of throat cancer at the age of eighty-three.

March 20, 1963—Helen "Mur" Gottheimer McWhorter, the author's grandmother, died of lung cancer at the age of seventy-nine.

August 2, 1963—Hamilton McWhorter, the author's grandfather, died of cancer at the age of eighty-five.

October 20, 1966—Senator Harry Byrd Sr., United States senator from Virginia from 1933 to 1965, died of brain cancer at the age of seventy-nine.

September 7, 1969—Everett Dirksen, United States senator from Illinois from 1951 to 1969, died of complications from adenocarcinoma at the age of seventy-three.

December 26, 1974—Jack Benny, comedian, died of pancreatic cancer at the age of eighty.

December 26, 1976—Philip Hart, United States senator from Michigan from 1959 to 1976, died of melanoma at the age of sixty-four.

January 13, 1978—Hubert Humphrey, United States senator from Minnesota and vice president to Lyndon B. Johnson, died of bladder cancer at the age of sixty-six.

February 1, 1978—Richard Lawton Jordan, the author's father, died of prostate cancer at the age of sixty-nine.

May 31, 1983—Milton Young, U.S. senator from North Dakota, died of cancer at the age of eighty-five.

November 22, 1988—Janet Ertel Bleyer, member of the Chordettes, died of cancer at the age of seventy-six.

December 30, 1988—Adelaide McWhorter Jordan, the author's mother, died of adenocarcinoma at the age of seventy-eight.

September 28, 1990—Larry O'Brien, U.S. Postmaster General and head of Congressional Relations in the Kennedy White House, died of complications from cancer at the age of seventy-three.

March 15, 2000—Albert Bruce Jones Jr., the author's cousin, died of cancer at the age of seventy-three.

May 19, 2003—Jinny Osborn, a member of the Chordettes, died of cancer at the age of seventy-six.

June 25, 2003—Lester Maddox, governor of Georgia from 1967 to 1971, died of complications from prostate cancer and pneumonia at the age of eighty-seven.

May 7, 2004—Rudi Maugeri, member of the Crew-Cuts, died of pancreatic cancer at the age of seventy-three.

April 23, 2006—Phil Walden, promoter for the Hot Nuts and co-founder of Capricorn Records, died of cancer at the age of sixty-six.

May 20, 2008—Hamilton Jordan, the author of the book, died of mesothelioma at the age of sixty-three.

April 5, 2009—Nancy Overton, member of the Chordettes, died of esophageal cancer at the age of eighty-three.

August 25, 2009—Ted Kennedy, United States senator from Massachusetts from 1962 to 2009, died of brain cancer at the age of seventy-seven.

September 16, 2009—Mary Travers, member of Peter, Paul, and Mary, died of leukemia at the age of seventy-two.

January 12, 2013—Gene Patterson, columnist at the *Atlanta Journal-Constitution* and an early supporter of civil rights, died of complications from cancer at the age of eighty-nine.